A NEW DICTIONARY OF KENT DIALECT

THIS BOOK IS DEDICATED

to

MY COUNTRY GRAND-PARENTS

George William Major   m.   Eliza Plum

(muddie/farm labourer)   (Rainham)

(Rainham)

and

Joseph Edwin Norton   m.   Alice Sarah Windle

(ploughboy/footman/   (Shalmsford Street, Chartham/
general workman)   Petham)

(Great Chart/Bethersden)

also

MY FATHER

Percy Edward Major

"The best of people"

A NEW DICTIONARY OF KENT DIALECT

Alan Major

An augmented and expanded edition of "A Dictionary of the Kentish Dialect" by W.D. Parish and W.F. Shaw published in 1888.

Illustrated by Alan Major

MERESBOROUGH BOOKS
1981

Meresborough Books specialize in the publication of books on Kent local history. Twelve books are currently in print and a further eight titles are scheduled for spring and summer 1981. In addition Meresborough Books publish a monthly journal on all aspects of Kent history 'Bygone Kent'. Full details from your local bookshop or direct from Meresborough Books, 7 Station Road, Rainham, Kent. ME8 7RS.

A DICTIONARY OF THE SUSSEX DIALECT
is published, in a uniform edition with this book, by Gardners of Bexhill Ltd., Providence Way, Eastwood Road, Bexhill on Sea, Sussex. Also available through Meresborough Books.

Printed and bound by Mackays of Chatham Ltd.

CONTENTS

PUBLISHER'S NOTE

While this Dictionary was in the proofing stage a further list of 140 words was sent in by Mr Ray Baldock of Lamberhurst. These have been included in the main body of the Dictionary.

Doubtless many readers will be able to add additional words from their own areas. Please send them to me for forwarding to the author so that they can be included in any reprint or revised edition.

In the first instance, however, some will be printed as pull out supplements in our monthly local history journal "Bygone Kent".

Hamish Mackay Miller
Meresborough Books
7 Station Road, Rainham, Kent. ME8 7RS

BIBLIOGRAPHY

My augmented edition of A Dictionary of Kentish Dialect has been based on the four major sources listed below, with addition of my own collection plus words received from various people interested in the project, as I have acknowledged.

"An Alphabet of Kenticisms" compiled by Rev. Samuel Pegge, 1735-6, published in Archaeologia Cantiana, Volume IX, 1874.

"A Dictionary of the Kentish Dialect", by Rev. W.D. Parish & Rev. W.F. Shaw (Farncombe & Co., Lewes) 1888.

"A Provincial Glossary", by Francis Grose. A Glossary of Kent Dialect Words In Common Use during the Year, 1811. Published that year by Edward Jeffery, Pall Mall, London.

"The Dialect of Kent", by Frederick Sanders (A limited private edition of six copies published by the author, 1950-1965, Chatham).

Parish and Shaw listed seven books from which they frequently took quotations, repeated in this edition.

Lambarde, William. A Perambulation of Kent, 1596.

Lewis, Rev. J. History and Antiquities, as well Ecclesiastical as Civil, of the Isle of Tenet, in Kent, 1736.

Sandwich Book of Orphans, 1586 and 1685. Published in Archaeologia Cantiana, Vol. XVI.

MS. Accounts of St. John's Hospital, Canterbury, 1511 to 1647. Communicated by Mr J.M. Cowper.

M.S. Accounts for the Churchwardens of S. Dunstan's, Canterbury, 1484 to 1580. Archaeologia Cantiana, Vol. XVI.

Overseers' Accounts, Holy Cross, Canterbury, 1642. Taken from "Our Parish Books", Vol. I and II, by Mr J.M. Cowper.

The Bargrave Diary and Various M.S. Accounts of the Boteler Family have been kindly placed at our disposal by the Misses Boteler, of Brook Street, Eastry.

AUTHOR'S PREFACE

In recent years various associations and societies have been formed to save, in some instances, the last examples of our rural past and its daily life still surviving, or to preserve areas of countryside of outstanding beauty, containing rare flora and fauna, from being destroyed, or to restore and save historic churches and other buildings from ruin. With a similar aim in mind it has been my intention in this book to complete as far as possible a work on the Kentish Dialect.

Parish & Shaw's "Dictionary" was largely composed of Kent dialect words from the coastal areas and its ports and East Kent and the Kent-Sussex border, plus Pegge's collection from the Godmersham-Canterbury area. By adding in my own collection of words from Kent, with Sanders' valuable collection from the Medway Towns and the Weald of Kent, it is hoped this book will prove to be the most comprehensive so far on the subject of Kentish dialect. It has also been my intention to emphasise those words which to my knowledge are still in use.

At this late stage, with Kentish dialect *as a language* dead, this has been a tremendously difficult but, I hope, worthwhile task. The speech in Kent today is a mixture from other parts of Britain and overseas, through an influx of settlers past and present and the influence of literature, radio, films and television broadening people's word range. This added immensely to the job of disentangling what is true dialect and what are local names, slang, peculiar and individual pronunciations, poor speech, Romany language and dialect from other counties that was also used in Kent or have been brought here by residents from those places.

Every effort has been made to trace and check the origins and worthiness of words included as Kentish dialect, but in some examples it proved impossible, except by relying on their similarity to other known examples in past use or the ancestry and knowledge of the person who either used or remembered the words.

Should some of the examples be open to conjecture or the dialect words from another county or non-dialect be included I ask for the tolerance of the reader in considering this and that "all errors and mistakings as shall fall out to be found, the Learned Modest Reader will be pleased to correct with their pen".

As there are few comprehensive accounts on the Kentish dialect published and the 1888 Dictionary of the Kentish Dialect is difficult to obtain, I hope that my augmented edition will fill a need by presenting the subject in a convenient form to whet the interest of not only language students but also all other people who have enjoyment in anything concerning our rural past. It would be even more gratifying if such an interest was stimulated into the formation of a Kent Dialect Society, as exists in several other counties and regions, to record on tape the actual words when being spoken by those who remain who can do this, a more complete way of preserving such words. Otherwise future generations will never know the sound of the spoken words of the Kentish dialect.

I shall always be pleased to hear of dialect words not included in the present book, and of meanings different from those recorded by me.

Alan Major

ACKNOWLEDGMENTS

No work such as this is possible without the generous and unstinted assistance of other people and to each I acknowledge my grateful thanks.

This applies especially to Messrs Farncombe & Co., Lewes, Sussex, publishers of the original "Dictionary of the Kentish Dialect" by Parish & Shaw in 1888, for permission to use this as a basis for my own book, and to Mr Frederick Sanders, author of "The Dialect of Kent", for permission to quote freely from his book. I also record my thanks to the Editor of the "Kent Messenger", Maidstone, for allowing me to re-publish in my book examples of dialect previously used in my "Dialect Corner" published in that newspaper.

I am indebted to Mr R.F. Farrar, Hon. Curator of Wye College Agricultural Museum, Kent, for guidance concerning agricultural implements; Mr S.T. Dibnah, Chief Librarian and Curator, Kirklees Metropolitan Council, Huddersfield, Yorkshire, for information regarding the life of Rev. W.F. Shaw; the Reference Librarian, Chatham Public Library, Kent, for the loan of a copy of Sanders' "The Dialect of Kent"; Mr D.S. Cousins, Reference Librarian, the Reference Library, Canterbury Public Library, Kent, for obtaining and the loan of "Archeologia Cantiana, Vol. 9, containing Pegge's "Alphabet of Kenticisms" and for other helpful assistance; and to Miss Anne Oakley, Archivist, Canterbury Cathedral Library, for assistance and information concerning the early life of Rev. W.F. Shaw.

My work on this Dictionary has also included receiving advice from a number of people and I have been sent numerous examples of the Kentish dialect words and memories of their being used by other correspondents and to the following I tender my thanks: Ralph Whitlock; Hon. Mrs Maurice Lubbock; Rev. Canon S.G. Brade-Birks, F.S.A.; Joan Coxhead; M.H. Mansell; M. Dilworth; S. Bolton; M. Marchant; E. Startup; M. Horton; J. Gurr; B.J. Akers; E. Williams; T.A.M. Jack; D. Marsh; John W. Bridge, F.S.A.; T.C. Stanbridge; L.J. Osborn; S.M. Pearce; J. Baker; C. Hook; C.P. Kingsland; H.E. Ward; R. Ely; S. Mercer; L.L. Hoare, D.S.O.; M. Beeton Pull; M. Saunders; N. Lurcock; M. Judges; Rev. F.J. Cooper; J. Bones, J.P.; C.W. Lindsay-Blee; V.H.D. Nutting; R. Baldock; Muriel V. Searle, B. Padbury, J. Rigden; Mrs H. Thomas; also to the late Wallace Arter; the late Robert H. Goodsall, F.S.A.; the late A.W. Coultrip; and the late A.E. Camburn.

If I have unwittingly omitted giving acknowledgment where due I would ask to be informed so the omission can be corrected in following editions.

Lastly, but by no means least, I would like to thank Hamish Mackay-Miller, of Meresborough Books, for his enthusiasm and courage in publishing this Dictionary.

Alan Major

A Biographical Sketch of
WILLIAM DOUGLAS PARISH

The Revd William Douglas Parish, M.A., was born on 16th December, 1833. He was the son of Sir Woodbine Parish, F.R.S., the diplomatist and naturalist who did much to establish British relations with the South American republics; he also discovered the fossils of the Megetherium, Mylodon and Glyptodon, and the Treaty of Peace signed at Paris, 20th November, 1815, on the conclusion of the Napoleonic War, was in his handwriting.

William was educated at Charterhouse and Trinity College, Oxford. He was ordained in 1859 and after four years as a curate at Firle, was preferred to the vicarage of Selmeston with Alciston.

At that time the names of these places were pronounced Simpson and Ahson, and it was as Vicar of Simpson that he was always known. In 1866 he superintended the rebuilding of Selmeston church, having each stone marked and reset in its place. As curate he was an inspector of schools and his own school at Selmeston was considered a model for the county.

In 1877 Bishop Durnford appointed him Chancellor of the Cathedral of Chichester. In 1886 he was elected a member of the Council of the Sussex Archaeological Society, and in 1895 became the first chairman of that body, a function for which he showed the necessity and which he exercised until his death.

In literature Parish is most generally known as the author of A Dictionary of the Sussex Dialect, but his other publications covered a wide field. His educational works range from poetry for elementary classes to a manual of instruction on the electric telegraph. With W.F. Shaw, vicar of Eastry, he published a dictionary of the Kentish dialect; but his most important work was editing the Sussex Doomsday for the Archaeological Society. In that work a facsimile of the original record is printed, with a literal extension of the Latin text and an English translation in parallel, together with a list of tenants, historical notes and an explanation of the terms.

He died on 23rd September, 1904, and is buried in his own churchyard among the people he loved and whose speech he knew so well.

A Biographical Sketch of
WILLIAM FRANCIS SHAW

The Revd William Francis Shaw, M.A., was born on 4th March, 1839, at Bath, the son of a schoolmaster there, William Flamank Shaw. He was at first educated at home by his father and then admitted at Caius College, Cambridge, on 15th February, 1858. In 1862 he gained his B.A. and was ordained deacon at Chester that same year, becoming a priest in 1863. From 1862 to 1865 he was curate of Acton, Cheshire, gaining his M.A. also in 1865, and in the latter year he became curate of St John's, Thanet, Kent. In 1866 until 1867 he was curate of Bidden-den, Kent. In 1867 he was preferred to the vicarage of Eastry, Kent where he remained as vicar until 1890. He gained his B.D. in 1885, D.D. in 1899, becom-ing an F.S.A. in 1894. He married Gertrude Ann, the second daughter of Rev. Canon J. Bateman and grand-daughter of Rt Rev. D. Wilson, Bishop of Calcutta. In 1890 he moved to become Vicar of St Andrew's church, Huddersfield, York-shire, and during 1895-96 also served as Mayor's chaplain. He resigned from St Andrew's in 1903, this being reported in both the Huddersfield Weekly Examiner and Huddersfield Weekly Chronicle, for 18th October, 1902. From 1903 until his death he was a Licensed Preacher for the Diocese of Wakefield.

His literary output, particularly on ecclesiastical subjects, was enormous. In 1870 his "Memorials of the Royal Ville and Parish of Eastry in the County of Kent" was published. It is interesting to note that in the list of subscribers to "Memorials of Eastry" is his father, William Flamank Shaw, Bodmin, Cornwall, Rev. William S. Shaw, M.A., Beechen Cliff Villa, Bath, and Rev. John Shaw, M.A., St Margaret's, Westminster, the latter two evidently also being members of his family.

This book was followed by: "Bible Class Notes on the Holy Gospel Accord-ing to St Matthew, parts i-vii, 1877; "Sermon Sketches", 1879; "Foreshadowings of Christ", 2nd ed. 1884; "The Mourner's Manual", 1882; "The Preacher's Promptuary of Anecdote", 1884; "A Manual for Communicants' Classes", 1884; "A Manual for Confirmation Classes", 1887; "A Manual of Guild Addresses", 1889; "A Manual for Catechising", 1890; "Sermon Sketches for the Christian Year", 1896; "Chapters on Symbolism", 1897; "Legal Historic Usages", 1899; "The Use of the Early Christians in reference to the Preparation for and Recep-tion of the Holy Communion", 1899; "Commentary on St Matthew", 1901. among others. The volume for which he is best remembered in Kent no doubt is his joint editorship, with Rev. W.D. Parish, of "The Dictionary of the Kentish Dialect" published in 1888.

He died at Huddersfield on 21st November, 1904. The local weekly news-papers for 26th November stated: "The late Dr Shaw from his youth lived a most strenuous life and his many and varied talents are reflected in his several impor-tant publications".

INTRODUCTION
TO THE
AUGMENTED EDITION

After I began the task of augmenting and expanding the Dictionary of Kentish Dialect compiled by Parish & Shaw incorporating Dr Samuel Pegge's Alphabet of Kenticisms into it, with dialect from other sources, it soon became evident how heavily Parish and Shaw had leaned on Pegge's compilation as a basis for their own Dictionary. Virtually all of Pegge's words are in the Parish and Shaw Dictionary, the entries being as Pegge wrote them or with a few alterations to update them to Victorian speech and understanding. This is not difficult to understand. The Rev. Professor Walter W. Skeat, who published Pegge's manuscript in 1876, was a friend of Rev. Parish and Rev. Shaw and all had the same interest, the Kentish dialect. Skeat suggested to Parish and Shaw they produce a "more complete glossary" of the Kentish dialect and no doubt he placed Pegge's manuscript, which he owned, at their disposal for the purpose.

This, however, is not a matter of discredit to Parish and Shaw. In fact a debt is owed to them. By their work in recording and incorporating the words they knew of the dialect, with Pegge's, they saved such words from being forgotten. Now whenever Kentish dialect is discussed or researched into Parish and Shaw and their Dictionary immediately come to mind and we have to acknowledge that they successfully made the subject of Kentish dialect of interest and available to a much wider public.

When they were compiling their Dictionary, prior to its publication in 1888, Parish and Shaw had the great advantage they were able to hear first hand the dialect words being spoken by those who used them in their daily speech as such people's only way of communicating to others who equally knew these words and used dialect in reply. These folk now lie interred in the county's churchyards and the Kentish dialect as a language with them. Today what survives is the dialect word occasionally used in conversation, perhaps passed on from parent to child. Elderly people remember words used by their parents or from their own early life and these have been a valuable source for my own collection. Talking to such people who heard and remember Kentish dialect being used, but were unfortunately not taught it themselves, it is realised what a loss this is. When the generations born in the 1890s and 1900s have also passed away the last real links with Kentish dialect will have gone, too. The position already with the majority of words is that it is only possible to visualize in the mind how they were used. No doubt also that many words have been lost forever or lie undetected, hidden in place names, farm words, etc.

It may come as a surprise that Kent did not ever have a very large number of purely dialect words, as are found in dialects that still strongly survive, as in Yorkshire, Lancashire and the West Country. The Kentish dialect consisted more in phrasal usages and in pronunciations deviating from those of Standard English. These were descended from a variety of sources, chiefly Anglo-Saxon but also Middle English, Old German, Dutch, perhaps Scandinavian. Considering the geographical position of Kent and its proximity to France it is also surprising that few French words were adapted and used in the Kentish dialect vocabulary. At the time of Caxton's introduction of printing into England Kentish dialect was one of the dialects, with imported "foreign" words, from which Standard English was gradually developed and a number of Kentish dialect words are now in national usage.

When discussing dialect it is safest to say it is a speech common to a certain area, but that no county boundary can prevent a use of the same words on each side of that boundary. The Kentish dialect can be divided into several areas and one of these is on the Kent-Sussex border and in the area on each side of it where there are dialect words common to both counties.

Some authorities have stated that there was virtually little difference between the dialect of East Sussex and West Kent, though each have their own characteristics. The Sussex dialect pronunciation was generally broad and rather drawling, whereas the Kentish pronunciation was considered more coarse or sharper, or a kind of nasal sing-song, some would say uncouth, so that the same words used in each county were in fact mutually unrecognisable and became strangely altered.

Another of the areas of Kentish dialect was that close to London and greatly under the influence of that city. This area was spread along the North Kent coast to Woolwich, Dartford, Gravesend and the Medway Towns of Rochester and Chatham. It dates from the time of the expansion of the boatyards and shipyards along this coastline and the influx of labourers and craftsmen from London to work in them. These brought their own Cockney "lingo" with them. In the Medway Towns this was so incorporated that the local speech became known as "Chathamese" and much of what Dickens heard and used in his books most likely was this purely local language.

The other areas, where the pure dialect of Kent survived longest, were East Kent, particularly the Weald, the Dover, Deal and Folkestone ports (these for fishermen's words), and the Romney Marsh.

The main peculiarities of Kentish dialect pronunciation were detailed by Parish and Shaw in their Dictionary, which I quote in the Original Introduction, but there are also a number of exceptions to this that defy reducing them down to such a well-defined system. The pronunciation of a word could vary slightly from one village to another. It was also not uncommon for people or a person to "invent" a variation of their own. Should a word present constant difficulty in pronunciation to express themselves they would either alter the word to something they could say or invent a new one in its place. It is likely this was the source for some of the curious words and now unable to be disputed. Other villagers heard and used the words and so they became established and may have spread elsewhere. This situation added to the difficulty of a stranger, or even a person from another part of the county, from understanding what was being said.

Although it is possible to spell the dialect words it is impossible satisfactorily to reproduce their accent by printing them, or their intonation and the homely "burr" that was so characteristic of them. A few examples of this give a clue to the speech. "Ye", "ee" and "yew" were alternatives of you, singular. "W" at the beginning of a word was usually suppressed, John Wood being John 'ood. The H was also often silent, hog was 'og, huvver was 'uvver, hood was 'ood. Another prominent characteristic of the Kentish dialect was the use of d for th. "Dis'n 's better'n dat"; "Dere's de man". A parody explains "By dis, dat, den, yew can tell de Kentish men". D on the end of a word was also rarely sounded; pond was pon', but the weight was put on the n to prolong the utterance of the word. V was turned into w, Wan for Van, wery for very.

Where other counties said I be, as it was in Kent, the Kentish people also used I're and I are. "Well, I are sorry". Mr was either Muster or Mus, maybe was mebbe, was was wus, road was ro·ad or roo·ad, ashore was ashoore, wagon was waggin, oats was wuts, soot was sut, to rhyme with but, trough for feeding pigs was pronounced as trow to rhyme with how, solder was sod·ur, split was splut, shut the door was shet de do·er, coal was coo·ul, four was fower, gate was ge·ate, going was either gooin' or gween. If two men met they could use both: "Where be yew goin'?". To which the other would reply "I're gween to de foorge to git de 'oss shod".

Place names in Kent, the pronunciation of which still confuses visitors and commuter-settlers today, also had their own especial pronunciations then among the native-born inhabitants: Maidstone was Metstun; Bearsted was Bursted; Trottiscliffe was, and is, Trossley, Headcorn was Edcorn; Ulcombe was Oocum, Aylesford was Elcefoord.

Mr Charles Kingsland of Guildford kindly forwarded me the following two examples of the speech and conversation heard in Kent some seventy years ago. An old man was walking along a road with a large bottle protruding from a pocket. When this was commented on to him the old man replied "I're takin' a bottle of cider to Mus (Mr) Smiff (Smith). Mus Smiff ee's got de bronkittis turrble bad and cider dat cuts de phlegm ye know. Arr; dat does cut de phlegm ye know".

The second example concerns a parson who ran a night school to try and educate some of his congregation. "Time when I was a boy and lived up Eg'ton (Egerton) way. Paason 'ee kep' a night school. Der wus a terrble dull feller come to dis ere school. 'is name was Joans (Jones). Paason 'ee sed one night to Joans 'Can you spell wasp, Jones?' Joans 'ee scratched 'is 'ead and presently sez 'Do yur mean wot we call wopse, sur?' 'Yes, Jones' said the parson. 'What you call wopse'. Joans 'ee leered about fer a bit and den 'ee up and blurts, 'We, O, Epse — Wopse, sur'."

The decline in pure dialect speech began with universal education, the Board School and its successor, the Council School, when the teaching of the King's Standard English ousted the usage of the more rustic words. The benefits of a standardized school education in fact replaced the homely dialects with their sources wrapped in the ancient county history. The dialect had been kept pure by the fact that people lived and spent practically all their lives in the same village or at least inside their county, with probably visits to certain towns on market days as a highlight of their lives. When transport facilities improved the use of these by previously isolated rural communities meant they could travel further afield, visit towns and cities at a greater distance more frequently and were in turn visited by people from other areas. This influenced speech.

In more recent times the invention of the radio has brought into people's homes BBC English, thought to be the correct way to talk. A further influence against using dialect was the social snobbery that classed a man as an illiterate, unintelligent bumpkin if he had a provincial "twang" or rural accent to his speech, whereas a man who spoke Standard English in an affected, ostentatious way, usually quite wrongly was thought to have a better education and be more suitable for certain jobs. Fortunately this attitude has largely been swept away although there is the remains of a class barrier against some of the more northern and Midlands speech. The popularity of American films, followed by gramophone records, with their content of slang and Americanisms, further widened the population's range of words, influencing their vocabulary.

Fortunately dialect still survives in those counties which are geographically remote from the industrial centres or those areas of Britain which people migrate to in order to obtain better living and working conditions. In these remote counties there has been a much lower influx of "outsiders" to settle to work or retire. In other counties their dialect survives where there is a strong "county" tradition as a characteristic of its true-born inhabitants and who have cared enough to save their own dialect.

But in recent years there has also been a somewhat nostalgic renewal of interest in rural subjects, which includes the speech and songs. Even pop songs sung in a dialect style, such as "The Singing Postman" from Suffolk singing "Hev you got a light, boy?" and Adge Cutler and the Wurzels from Somerset with "Hark at 'ee, Jacko" found popularity with a section of the public who would probably not otherwise have been interested in this subject.

It is a matter of regret that efforts were not made in the 1920s and 1930s, when it should have been realised that our county dialect was fast disappearing due to the influences described, at least to record on gramophone records the voices of those who could still speak such words fluently. Now we have only the printed word, imperfect as such a medium is, to preserve the formerly common and distinctive Kentish dialect.

Alan Major

PARISH AND SHAW'S INTRODUCTION

The Kentish Dialect finds its expression in pecularities of phrase and pronunciation rather than in any great number of distinctly dialectical words. In many
respects it closely resembles the dialect of Sussex, though it retains a distinctive
character, and includes a considerable number of words which are unknown in
the neighbouring County.

The Kentish pronunciation is so much more coarse and broad than that of
Sussex, that many words which are common to both dialects can scarcely be
recognised a few miles away from the border; and many words of ordinary use
become strangely altered. As an instance, the word "elbow" may be taken, which
first has the termination altered by the substitution of "ber" (ber) for "bow"
(boa) and becomes "elber" (el·ber). The e is next altered to a, and in Sussex the
word would be generally pronounced "alber" (al·ber), in which form it is still
recognisable; but the Kentish man alters the "al" into "ar" (aa), and knocking
out the medial consonant altogether, pronounces the word "arber" (aa·ber), and
thus actually retains only one letter out of the original five. The chief peculiarities of pronunciation are these:—

Such words as "barrow" and "carry" become "bar" and "car" (baa, kaa).

a (a) before double d is pronounced aa; as "laader" (laa·der) for ladder.

a (a) before double l becomes o; as "foller" (fol·er) for fallow.

a (ai) before t is lengthened into ëa; as "pleät" (plee·h't) for plate.

Double e, or the equivalent of it, becomes i; as "ship in the fil" (ship in dhu'
  fil) for "sheep in the field".

Then, by way of compensation, i is occasionally pronounced like double e;
  as "The meece got into the heeve" (Dhu' mee·s got in·tu' dhu' hee·v) for
  "The mice got into the hive".

i appears as e in such words as "pet" (pet) for pit.

o before n is broadened into two syllables by the addition of an obscure
  vowel; as "Doänt ye see the old poäny be all skin and boäns" (doa·h'nt ye
  see dhu' oald poa·h'ny bee aul skin un boa·h'ns).

ou is lengthened by prefixing a (a); the resulting sound being (aew). "The
  haöunds were raöund our haöuse yesterday". (Dhu' haewnds wer
  raewnd our haews yest·erdai).

The voiced th (dh) is invariably pronounced d; so "that", "this", "then".
  "though" became "dat", "dis", "den", "dough" (dat, dis, den, doa).

In such words as "fodder" (A.S. fódor), where the old d comes between two
  vowels, the dialect has th (dh), as (fodh·er).

The final letters are transposed in "wasp", "hasp", and many words of similar
  termination. Hence these become (wops, haps).

w and v change places invariably when they are initial; as "wery vell" for
  "very well".

Pecularities of construction appear in the case of a large class of words, whereof "upgrown", "outstand", "no-ought", "over-run" and others may be taken as
types.

Almost every East Kent man has one or two special words of his own, which he has himself invented, and these become very puzzling to those who do not know the secret of their origin; and as he dislikes the intrusion of any words beyond the range of his own vocabulary, he is apt to show his resentment by taking so little trouble to pronounce them correctly, that they generally become distorted beyond all recognition. "Broad titus", for instance, would not easily be understood to mean bronchitis.

The East Kent man is, moreover, not fond of strangers, he calls any new-comers into the village "furriners", and pronounces their names as he pleases. These peculiarities of speech and temper all tend to add to the difficulty of understanding the language in which the Kentish people express themselves.

The true dialect of Kent is now found only in the Eastern portion of the County, and especially in the Weald. It has been affected by many influences, most of all, of course, by its geographical position, though it seems strange that so few French words have found their way across the narrow streak of sea which separates it from France.

The purity of the dialect diminishes in proportion to the proximity to London of the district in which it is spoken. It may be said that the dialectal sewage of the Metropolis finds its way down the river and is deposited on the southern bank of the Thames, as far as the limits of Gravesend-Reach, whence it seems to overflow and saturate the neighbouring district. The language in which Samuel Weller, Senior and Junior, express themselves in the pages of the Pickwick Papers, affords an excellent specimen of what the Kentish dialect is, when it is brought under the full influence of this saturation.

Our collection of Kentish words and provincialisms has been gathered from various sources. Much has already been done to rescue from oblivion the peculiarities of the dialect. As long ago as 1736 Lewis published a glossary of local words in the second edition of his History of the Isle of Tenet; this was reprinted by Prof. Skeat for the English Dialect Society as "Glossary B. II", in 1874. Dr Pegge's attention was drawn to the subject at the same time and he compiled a glossary entitled "Kenticisms", which remained in manuscript till it was communicated, in 1876, by Prof. Skeat, to the English Dialect Society and to the IX. Vol. of the Archaeologia Cantiana. The MS. was purchased by him at Sir F. Madden's sale, and will be presented to the English Dialect Society.

A large number of Kentish words were found in the pages of Holloway's General Dictionary of Provincialisms (1839) and also in Halliwell's Dictionary of Archaic and Provincial Words (1872) and when Professor Skeat suggested to us a more complete glossary of the dialect, we found that these publications had aroused such a considerable interest in the collection of Kentish words, that several collectors were at work in different parts of the County, all of whom most kindly placed their lists of words at our disposal. (One peculiarly interesting collection was given to the Society many years ago by Mr G. Bedo.) The learned Professor has never for a moment abated his interest in our work, and has been always ready with a helping hand. Meanwhile the great local professor of the Kentish language, Mr H. Knatchbull-Hugessen, M.P., has given us the full benefit of his thorough knowledge of the subject.

In order to exhibit the modern dialect more clearly, references to the specimens of Kentish in the Early and Middle English Periods have been avoided. It may, however, be well to observe here that the peculiarities of the phonology of the old dialect are well shown in some of these. The most important are the following:

1. The inscription in the Codex Aureus, printed in Sweet's Oldest English Texts, page 174, and reprinted (very accessibly) in Sweet's Anglo-Saxon Reader, Part II, p. 98. This inscription is of the Ninth Century.

2. Some Glosses in a copy of Beda (MS. Cotton, Tib.c. 2), apparently in Kentish. Printed in Sweet's Oldest English Texts, p. 179. Of the end of the Ninth Century.

3. Some of the Charters printed in Sweet's Oldest English Texts, pp. 425-460. See, in particular, a Charter of Hlothere, No. 4; of Wihtred, No. 5; of Aethelberht, Nos. 6 and 7; of Eardwulf, No. 8; and the Charters numbered 33-44, inclusive. Of these, Nos. 4, 5, 6, 7, 8 and 34-42, inclusive, are reprinted in Sweet's Anglo-Saxon Reader, Part II, pp. 174-194.

4. Kentish Glosses of the Ninth Century, first printed by Prof. Zupitza in Haupt's Zeitschrift, and reprinted in Sweet's Anglo-Saxon Reader, Part II, pp. 152-175.

5. Five Sermons in the Kentish Dialect of the Thirteenth Century, printed in Morris's Old English Miscellany, pp. 26-36. Two of these are reprinted in Morris's Specimens of English, Part I, pp. 141-145. The grammatical forms found in these Sermons are discussed in the Preface to the Old English Miscellany, pp. xiii-xvi.

6. The poems of William, of Shoreham (not far from Sevenoaks), written in the former half of the Fourteenth Century, edited for the Percy Society by T. Wright, London, 1849. An extract is given in Specimens of English, ed. Morris and Skeat, Part II, pp. 63-68.

7. The Ayenbite of Inwyt, or Remorse of Conscience, finished A.D. 1340, by Dan Michel, of Northgate, edited by Morris for the Early English Text Society in 1866. An extract is given in Specimens of English, ed. Morris and Skeat, Part II, pp. 98-106.

It may be added that the Psalter, known as the Vaspasian Psalter, printed in Sweet's Oldest English Texts, is now ascertained to be Mercian. It was first printed by Stevenson for the Surtees Society in 1843-4, under the impression that it was "Northumbrian" a statement which will not bear even a hasty test. Mr Sweet at first claimed it as "Kentish" (Trans. of the Phil. Soc. 1877, Part III, p. 555), but a closer investigation proves it to be Mercian, as Mr Sweet has himself shown.

It may be mentioned that the collection of words presented in this Dictionary has been in the process of formation for no less than fourteen years, and in the course of that time we found many instances of folk lore and proverbial expressions, which have been retained in expectation that they may form the nucleus of a separate work to be published hereafter.

REV. WALTER W. SKEAT'S INTRODUCTION*
TO DR PEGGE'S MS. ALPHABET OF KENTICISMS, AND COLLECTION OF PROVERBIAL SAYINGS USED IN KENT

"The following Glossary, compiled by the Rev. Samuel Pegge during his residence at Godmersham, was written in 1735-6. It forms part of a MS book, which now contains the following tracts, all in the handwriting of Dr Pegge himself, and all bound together; viz., (1) An Alphabet of Kenticisms; (2) Proverbs relating to Kent; (3) A First Collection of Derbicisms; (4) A Second Collection of Derbicisms, preceded by a title-page, which properly belongs to the Kenticisms; (5) A Third Collection of Derbicisms; (6) A General Collection of Proverbs and Proverbial Phrases; and (7) A Collection of Oaths, as variously vulgarised and corrupted. The present tract comprises only the *first* and *second* sections of this manuscript. The MS. came into the possession of Mr John Gough Nichols, from whom it was purchased by Sir Frederic Madden, June 6th, 1832. At the sale of Sir F. Madden's library in August, 1873, it was purchased for the English Dialect Society by myself. I have since transcribed the two sections of the MS. here printed and re-arranged them so as to prepare them suitably for the press. In doing this, my chief endeavour has been to adhere as faithfully as possible to the autograph original, preserving nearly all Dr Pegge's peculiarities of spelling and diction. This method of careful reproduction, in all cases advisable, is especially so in the present instance, as the author evidently took much pains with his work and was fairly qualified for the task. The only alterations made have been the following. First, the words have been thrown into a perfect alphabetical order, as they are not altogether so in the MS. Secondly, when words have been entered more than once, with slightly differing explanations, these explanations have been collated, and the general result given. Thirdly when a large number of references to works illustrating such or such a word have been given, I have omitted a few of the references, as being hardly required or not easily traced. And lastly, I have occasionally omitted some of Dr Pegge's etymologies, but only where they were palpably wrong. These alterations and omissions are, on the whole, but very few. I have also added some remarks of my own, which are inserted between square brackets.

In editing the Proverbs, which were not arranged in any particular order, I have re-arranged them. In a few cases, I have slightly abridged the explanations, where they seemed to be of unnecessary length. Here, also, I have added some remarks of my own, marked, as before, by being inserted between square brackets.

Sir F. Madden has noted that the Rev. Samuel Pegge was born at Chesterfield, Co. Derby, November 5th, 1704; admitted fellow of St John's College, Cambridge, 1729; Vicar of Godmersham, Kent, 1731; Rector of Whittington, Derbyshire, 1751; Rector of Brindle, Lancashire, 1751; made F.S.A. in 1751 and LL.D. in 1791; died February 14th, 1796. He was the author of several works, for a list

*Reprinted in part from Archaeologia Cantiana Vol. IX.

of which see Bohn's "Lowndes' Bibliographer's Manual". Amongst his unprinted works, there are three in the Gough collection, in the Bodleian Library; see Gough's Catalogue, page 188, which mentions — "6. Collections for a History of Wye; folio MS. 7. Statutes of the College at Wye; folio MS. 8. An Alphabetical Catalogue of Kentish Authors and Worthies; folio MS." He refers, in the work here printed, to the two former of these.

He married Ann, only daughter of Benjamin Clarke, Esq., of Stanley near Wakefield, Co. York, who died in July, 1746. His son, Samuel Pegge, Esq., born in 1731, was a barrister, a groom of the privy chamber, and F.S.A. He married Martha, daughter of the Rev. H. Bourne, who died June 28th, 1767; the date of of his own death being May 22nd, 1800. This Samuel Pegge the younger was also an author, and is best known, perhaps, for his "Anecdotes of the English Language" and his "Supplement to Grose's Glossary". He had a son, who was afterwards Sir Christopher Pegge.

It may be added that Dr Brett, to whom Dr Pegge's Introductory Letter is addressed, was born in 1667 and died on March 5th, 1743. He was the author of A Dissertation on the Ancient Versions of the Bible, the second edition of which appeared after his death, in 1760; and other works, for which see Bohn's "Lowndes' Bibliographer's Manual".

DR SAMUEL PEGGE'S INTRODUCTORY LETTER*
TO THE REV. AND LEARNED THOS. BRETT, LL.D.
OF SPRING GROVE, IN THE COUNTY OF KENT

As the dialects of this kingdom vary so extremely, those who are born in one county, and go to reside in another, are naturally struck with the difference of idiom. This was the case of Mr John Lewis (Rev. John Lewis, born in 1675; the author of a "History and Antiquities of the Isle of Tenet", i.e. Thanet; the short glossary in which is often cited by Dr Pegge), who was born in the city of Bristol, but afterwards lived chiefly in Kent; as likewise with myself, who was born and educated at Chesterfield in Derbyshire.

Having been born and educated in a different part of the kingdom, upon my coming to reside in the county of Kent, I became more sensible, as may easily be supposed, of some idiotisms and pecularities in the language and pronunciation of the inhabitants and natives thereof, than otherwise I should have been. Some small portion of natural curiosity quickly prompted me to note down such instances of variation from the common English speech, as from time to time might fall in my way, and having gathered together an handfull of those Kenticisms, imperfect, and, as I doubt not, inaccurate, I have ventured to send it to you; intending thereby what you will call a very odd mixture, a little gratitude and a little self-interest; for, as I wou'd willingly have you regard it as a testimony of that respect and veneration I have for your person and learning, I wou'd likewise hope, from the closeness of that friendship subsisting betwixt us, and your undoubted skill in these matters, to obtain from you such improvements and corrections as your multifarious reading, in the perusal, must unavoidably suggest.

It must be confesst that a person of a less retired life and more conversant in business than I have been, might have amasst together a much greater number of obsolete particular expressions. For I ought to know, from amongst the mechanics, the several sorts of artists, and the lower parts of life, the string might have been doubl'd. I have gone as far as my model would permit, and you will please to observe, that I have therein inserted what glossems I found ascribed to the dialect of the Kentish men, in Mr Ray's "Catalogue of South and East Country Words", printed at London, 1675; together with those Mr Lewis has exhibited in his "History of the Isle of Thanet".

But withal, I wou'd remind you, and indeed it is altogether a necessary I shou'd, that I have put down several words and phrases as *Kentish*, which yet, strictly speaking, are not proper to that county exclusive of all others, but are common to it, and one, two, or perhaps more of the neighbouring provinces; but, being most frequently and even daily used in this parts, and at the same time having not obtained a general universal currency throughout the realm, I thought they might reasonably claim a place in this collection. But yet I doubt Mr Ray has sometimes led me to specifying words of too general acceptation. I

*This letter is reprinted from Archaeologia Cantiana Vol. IX with the Rev. Walter Skeat's comments in brackets.

have endeavoured to give the original of most of these words from authors, and sometimes I have guesst at an etymology myself; but with what success, is always submitted to better judgement. Several I have been obliged to pass by, without taking any notice of their derivation, out of real ignorance, owing to want of learning or a natural innate dexterity as to these things; and others I chose to let slip, because, being either monstrous corruptions or low cant phrases, it was impossible, or at least not worth while, to go to the bottom of them.

And whereas some few idioms and observations did not so easily fall into an alphabet, I take the liberty to subjoyn them here.

1. "I don't dare", for "I dare not".

2. They are apt to accumulate negatives, without any design of altering the negation into an affirmative; as when they say — "No more I won't", "No more I don't". This form rather denys stronger, and with something of an emphasis; note the proverb — "The vale of Holmesdale, Never wonne, *nor never* shall"; — "he gyveth *never no* man warning"; Dialogue printed by Wynkin, etc. 'Tis a pure Saxonism; see Hickes's Thesaurus, Gram. A. Sax.

3. The common sort are inclined to put *w* for *v; as weal* for *veal; wiper* for *viper; wery,* for *very;* as "wipers are wery brief (i.e. common) in such a place"; in one instance they put *v* for *w; as skivers* for *skewers.*

4. Nothing is more frequent than to put *a* for *o; as maw* for *mow; rad* for *rod; an* for *on,* as, "put your hat *an*"; *crap* for *crop; Jan* for *John; dan't* for *don't.*

5. *D* they use for *th; wid* for *with;* as, "I'll go *wid* you"; *rade* for *rathe; Hyde* for *Hythe; widout* for *without* (Note also *wiff,* for withe or withy).

6. *U* they put for *i; wull* for *will,* as sign of the future tense; *dud* for *did;* and hither I thought best to refer *mought* for *might.*

7. *O* they sometimes pronounce very long; as *cŏst* (koast) for *cost* (A cost of lamb, i.e. the fore-quarter); *fŏrk* (foark) for *fork;* and at times they shorten it, as in *throt* (throt) for *throat, chock* (chok) for *choke; loth* (loth) for *loath.*

8. *H* they seldom joyn with other letters in pronunciation, but keep it separate and distinct. Mepham is Mep-ham; Adisham, Adis-ham; so Godmers-ham, Hot-hfield (He must mean hot-feeld, as distinct from hoth-feeld); Bets-hanger, Pet-ham, Gres-ham, Cas-halton (Carshalton is in Surrey; it is commonly pronounced kus-haut·un, but also kais-haut·un where the kais is quite distinct), etc. In all these instances, except Hoth-field, they are certainly right, as in a multitude of others; for *ham* being one of the constituents of these compound names, it is preserved hereby distinct and entire.

9. *O* is *oo,* in *go* (goo) and so Caxton writes it in Maittaire, Annal. Typogr., vol. i. *I* is *oo* in *wood you* (wuod eu) for *with you;* and, contracting, "I'll goo'd you" (eil goo'ud eu) for "I will go with you". It is also *a* open; "*sowing* corn" is *sawing* (sau·ing). See above, no. 4.

10. *D* after *l* they sometimes drop; as *chile* (cheil) for *child; hel* (hel) for *held.*

11. Where *sp* occurs, they utter the *p* before the *s,* to facilitate pronunciation; as *waps* (wops) for *wasp* (Dr Pegge writes *whaps, whasp;* which is very singular); *aps* (aps) for *asp* (i.e. an aspen-tree); *haps* (haps) for *hasp.* So in the Old Parish Book of Wye, 5 Edward VI; "for a *hapsor* to the churche-gette, 2d." So Mr Ray — "In Sussex, for *hasp, clasp, wasp,* they pronounce *hapse, clapse, wapse*", etc. But in Somers. (Dr Pegge continually refers to "Somersetshire" words, which he invariably cites from the "Gentlemen's Magazine", vol. xvi, A.D. 1746, where may be found a Glossary to the Exmoor Courtship and Exmoor Scolding. These words are really, therefore, Exmoor words) a *wasp* is a *wop;* Gent. Maga., xvi, and I observe that in Kent they speak *a* very like *o.*

12. Words terminating in *st* have the addition of a syllable in their plurals, *is* being added in lieu of *s* only. For *birds-nests* they say *birdnestis,* etc. I suppose

this has been a general way formerly, for Skelton, Poet Laureat to Henr. VII., has it; see him cited in Aubrey's "Antiq. of Surrey, vol. ii. The nom. acc. and voc. pl. of the 1st declension (or rather, 2nd declension, 2nd class) of the Saxon is a syllable, — *as;* and the genitive sing *-es.* In Wiclife's N.T. you have *dedis of apostlis,* the translation of *actus apostolorum;* and indeed, in our elder English there are a world of plurals in *-ys* or *-is,* as in the Old Parish Book of Wye, etc. In Derbyshire we should say, "he *fasses* all Lent, though it *lasses* forty days"; which shews how natural it is, to assist the pronunciation by lengthening words ending in *-st* a syllable (This is a mistake; *fasses* is from O.E. *fastys* and does not exhibit an additional syllable, but the substitution of *ss* for *st).* For the same reason in that country they say *bird-nesses;* but *beasts* in Derb. they call *bease* (bees). See in the Glossary "raddis-chimney". (Dr Pegge adds "minnis" as an example; but his explanation, that it is the plural of *mean* is certainly wrong). So *jays,* the birds so called, they pronounce *jay-es* (jai·ez) Cf. *steryis,* steers; Will of Jno. Fermor, alias Godfrey, of Lydd, in Kent, 1510; *costys,* costs; Plot's Staffordsh.,: *forrestys,* forests. (A remarkable example is *faries-es* for *fairies;* See Farisies in the Glossary.)

13. In some cases they'll put a short quick *i,* for a long one; as, "to *driv* a waggon", for to *drive* it; or for *ee,* as *ship* for *sheep);* or for *ea,* as *rip* for *reap* (Add *wik* for *week; fild* for *field* pronounced (fil).

14. *E* for *i;* as *Petstreet* for *Pitstreet,* a place in Crundale Parish; *knet* for *knit; Petham* for *Pitham.* And so the long *e;* as *meece* (mees) for *mice; leece* (less) for *lice (yeld* for *yield).*

15. *I* for *e;* as *hin* for *hen.*

16. *O* is *a;* as *crass* (kras) for *cross* (He must mean *cross* as a sb.; for the adj. cross is pronounced (kurs); see Curs in the Glossary). So Somers. *clathing* for *clothing.*

17. *L* for *r; skivels* (skiv·lz) for *skivers,* i.e. *skewers.*

18. *To* as the sign of the infin. they very currently leave out; as "I *begin cut* wheat tomorrow" and "when do you *begin plough?"*

19. "He will be two men", he will be very angry; i.e. as much different from himself at other times, as if was quite another man; a very significant fine expression. So "you will make us two", i.e. you will make us differ (Dr Pegge notes some other things in his Glossary, which may be enumerated here, viz., *hort* for *hurt, mont* (munt) for *month; ketch* (kech) for *catch; keaf* (kee·h'f) for *calf; kew* (kew) for *cow.* Also *rudy, scarcy,* (rood·i, skairs·i), dissyllables, for *rude, scarce,* and *jealousy* for *jealous.* Under the word *hair* he observes that Kentish men sometimes insert an article, as "a good hair" for "good hair" and "a bread and butter" for "bread and butter". He notes, too, the use of "it should seem" instead of "it seems" and the curious use of *to* without an infinitive, as in "I'm going to it" for "I am going to *do* it".).

The Kentish men are said in Caesar's Commentaries, de Bello Gallico, lib. v. c. x., to excell all the other inhabitants in civility and politeness; for so I understand those words — "ex his omnibus, longe sunt humanissimi qui Cantium incolunt". The cause of this was their maritime situation, their proximity to Gaul, and the constant intercourse held therewith, which by degrees softened their manners, civilising their natural ferity, which yet prevailed in the more inland parts. This reason is hinted by Caesar, who goes on (by way of assigning the reason) — "quae regio est maritima omnis; neque multum a Gallica differunt consuetudine". The sense of the word "humanus" in the former place, that it relates not so much to the temper as the manners of the Kentish men, appears from what follows, where the author proceeds to inform us, on the other hand, what kind of people, how rude and rustic, the mediterranean Britons were — "Interiores plerique frumenta non serunt, sed lacte et carne uiuunt, pellibusque sunt uestiti", from whence I conclude that the Kentish men both sowed corn and were better clad. I should imagine that another part of their greater politeness in respect of remoter and interior Britain, must be in their language; which, though it was the original British, yet probably had many Gaulish words intermixed with it (This is guesswork yet probable. At any rate, the Kentish dialect of Old English abounded with French words, though it was, at the same time, remarkably tenacious of native grammatical forms. See the "Ayenbite of Inwyt") and was much softened in pronunciation by conversing with the people of that nation.

Thus the Kentish would have many particularities in their speech different from the other islanders from the most ancient time, even as other maritime inhabitants had who were colonies of the Belgae; v. Caesar, ibid. Thus they had particular words in Domesday Book, as *Solinum*, etc. The code of the Gavelkind Law, which rises as high as Edward I, speaks of the Kentish language; so Kennet "Paroch. Antiq."; and Caxton, in Ames (Kentish writers fall into particular expressions; as Mr John Johnson, Dr Robert Plot, Sir G. Wheeler and Rev. John Lewis).

The pronunciation also is peculiar; thus "tediouslȳ", or "tediouslȳ indeed"; (with a strong accent laid upon the last syllable).

To make an end, Proverbs and old Saws are so nearly allay'd to this subject, that I cou'd not well do otherwise than annex such as I found were vernacular, or in any other respect might concern this county. These were first collected by Dr Thos. Fuller, in the "English Worthies", printed at London, fol. 1662, and were afterwards transcribed into Mr Ray's "Collection", printed likewise at London, in 1670. I have here added a few to the list and withall have entered a remark or two upon their explications.

So many great names have employed themselves in Glossography and some of them in a very confin'd, local, and what ignorant people may call low way, that I need not apologise for laying out a few hours in such an innocent, entertaining, and, what the judicious will allow, usefull part of knowledge; were it necessary, I cou'd rehearse a long list of unexceptionable men, both antients and moderns. But you, who take your seat with the most learned, must be so thoroughly convinct of the use and advantage of such lexicons as these, that it wou'd be impertinence to trouble you with them, and even injurious to your character as a scholar, not to presume upon a favourable reception from you to an enterprise of this sort.

Sir, your most obedient humble servant.

Sam Pegge

Godmersham, April 11, 1735 (This date does not exactly mark the time of the final completion of the Glossary. A few additions were evidently made later, probably on the appearance of the second edition of Lewis's "History of the Isle of Thanet", in 1736).

The Rev. Skeat then adds the following after Pegge's Introductory Letter: (By the kindness of Mr Ellis I am enabled to add the following note on the *present* pronunciation of Kentish words.

Mr Herbert Knatchbull-Hugessen, of Provender near Faversham, Kent, whose mother was born at Godmersham and who is very familiar with the language and pronunciation of Kentish peasantry at the present day, made remarks to the following effect to Mr Alexander J. Ellis on the above pronunciations (those of Pegge).

3. This use of *w* for *v* is still common, but there is no converse use of *v* for *w*.

5. The substitution of *d* for *th* is almost confined to the words, *the, this, these, that, those, there, their, them;* it is not regularly used in *with*.

6. The use of *wull, dud,* for *will, did,* is not now known.

7. *Coast* and *fork* are now (kau·st) and (foork) or (fuo·h'k); (throt, chok) are not known, but (loth) is.

9. (Goo) for *go* remains; (wuod) for *with* is unknown; they say rather (eil goo wij·i).

10. This *d* after *l* is very commonly dropped.

11. (Wops, haps) still known; (aps) unknown.

12. This *-is* plural to words in *-st*, has been heard, but not generally. The *jay* is called (joi).

13. (Driv, wik, rip) are not known; (ship) for sheep is; but a *shepherd* is always a *looker.* (luok·er). *Field* is (fil) without the *d*.

14. (Pet) for *pit*, known; (net) for *knit* unknown. (Mees, lees) known, but the use of (ee) for long *i* seems confined to these words.

15. (Hin) for *hen*, known.

16. (Kras) for *cross*, known.

17. (Skiv·lz) unknown.

Footnote to 19. *Cow* is (kew), the (e) of *set* followed by (oo), not (keu). All the (ou) dipthongs are (ew) in Kent, as they are commonly (aew), that is, a little broader, in Norfolk. The (ew) is common in London. No information has been received as to *calf*, a word very variously pronounced; but heifer is (aa·fer).

A specimen of modern Kentish pronunciation and a considerable number of Kentish words from the dictation of Mr H. Knatchbull-Hugessen, are given in Mr A.J. Ellis's "Early English Pronunciation", chapter xi 2, no. 11, Subdialect 34).

A NEW
DICTIONARY
OF
KENT DIALECT

As it is felt it would increase the value of this Dictionary to know the various sources of words and those which are still in use I have indicated this thus:

*   Still in use
\+   Parish & Shaw
†   Sanders
G   Grose
=   My own collection or words received from Kent sources as acknowledged.
P   Pegge

A

A. The letter is used as a prefix and as a word in its own right. For example: "She's always a-doing things wrong". (See Be) +

ABED. In bed. "Mary's abed with a cold". +

ABIDE. To bear; endure; tolerate; to put up with. It was generally used in the negative: "I can't abide his manners". =*+

ABITE. Mouldy; mildewed (See Abited) =

ABITED. Mildewed, when applied to decayed food. Similar to Ampery, Fenny, Mowl and Bicey. (See Bything) PG+

ABITHE. Mildewed; rotted; decayed, of timber. (See Addle) P

ACELOT. (See Harcelot) =

ACH-BONE. A rump of beef. P

ACHING TOOTH. To have an aching tooth for something was to hope or wish for it deeply. +

ACKLE. To work or failing to do so; any mechanical device or machine which would or would not operate normally or did so was said it will or would not ackle. =†*

ACT-ABOUT. To play the fool. (See Mess-About). "He got acting-about, fell down and broke his leg". =*+

ADDLE^1. Gone to decay; rotted (See Abited, Abithe). P

ADDLE^2 ADLE. + Unwell; confused; depressed; unable to concentrate.

ADDLE-PATED. Giddy in the head. (See Pothery) =

ADOING. Doing. In some of the Kent dialect speech when doing was prefixed by "a" the "g" was dropped, such as "What be ye adoin'?" (See A) =

ADRY. Dry; in a dry or thirsty condition. (See Dryth) P+

AFEARED. Affected with terror or fright; fear; frightened. +

AFORE. Before. "Its no good planting afore Jack Frost has gone". (See Fore-long) =*+

AFTERMEATH. Used for the grass which grows after the first crop has been mown for hay; a second crop of grass. Pegge stated: "after-month, that which comes and grows after the mowing; after math." In other counties known as the after-grass or after-math. (See Rowens, Roughings) P+

AFTERS. The second course of a meal; the sweet, apple tart and custard, etc. (See Seconds) =

1

AGIN. Against; over-against; near. (See Anent, Anents, Anewst) =*+

AGREEABLE. Consenting; acquiescent. "They axed me what I thought an't and I said as how I was quite agreeable." Now in general use. +

AGUE. A shivering malarial fever once common among labourers, especially those working on Romney Marsh. When my own great-grandfather, William Windle, went from his own small farm at Underdown, Mystole, near Canterbury, to work with the harvest or haymaking on Romney Marsh and its vicinity he usually afterwards was racked with the ague, or "agoo" as some pronounced it. *=

AIMES. (See Hemwoods)

AINED. Increased in price. =

AIREY. A gusty, blustery, windy day was said to be airey. =†

AITCHY, UTCHY. A little misty and cold in the morning. "Bit aitchy this morning". =

AKERS. Acorns. +

ALAMOST. Almost. P+

ALEING. An old-fashioned entertainment, given with the aim of collecting subscriptions from guests invited to partake of a brewing of ale. Pegge describes "an aleing, where mirth, ale and music are stirring; tis a custom in West Kent for the lower class of housekeepers to brew a small quantity of malt and to invite their neighbours to it, who give them something for a gratification; this they call an aleing and they do it to get a little money and the people go to it out of kindness to them." P+

ALE-SOP. A refection consisting of toast and strong ale, hot. It was the custom for the servants in large houses and other establishments to enjoy it on Christmas Day. +

ALL-A-MOST. Almost. P+

ALLEMASH DAY. Allumage Day. The day on which the French-speaking silk weavers in Canterbury began to work by candlelight; their own name for the day in autumn on which they started again to use artificial light when the hours of daylight became less and evenings were "drawing in". Probably dates back to the time of Elizabeth I when the weavers came in refuge to Canterbury where they found hospitality and were able to ply their skills. From the French à la meche (de chandelle)

Alley Bodge

ALLEY. The space between two rows of hops in the garden. *=

ALLEY BODGE. A narrow, low, small, double-ended wagon or cart with four small, broad, iron wheels, drawn by a horse with chain and traces through the alleys in a hop garden. A smaller version, with a handcart type handle, was used by pickers for haulage up and down the alleys. = (See Bodge, Trug-Bodge, Water Bodge).

ALLEYCUMFEE. A fictitious place. Anyone being too inquisitive or "nosey" and asking where you were going would be told "alleycumfee". =

ALL-ON. Continually; to "keep "all-on" adoing something" was to "keep at it, to get it over with and completed." A nagging wife keeps "all-on" talking and brow-beating her husband. =+*

ALLOW. To consider. +

ALLWORKS. The name for a labourer on a farm who was capable of and employed to do any job that required to be done. Pegge stated: "A man-servant employed by a farmer in all sorts of work he has occasion to set him about. Such as one they call an allworks; he is the lowest servant in the house and is not hired for the plough or wagon particularly as the other servants are, but to be set about anything." (See Second Man) P+

ALONGST. Alongside; on the long side of anything, alongst it. +P

ALUS. An ale-house +

AM. Used for the word "are". As "They'm gone to bed", a contraction of "they am" for "they are." (See Them, I Be) P+

AM YE. Are you. =

AMENDMENT. Manure laid on the land. =+

AMMETS. Ants. =

AMMET-CAST. An ant-hill. =

AMMITS. Ants. = There is an Ammit-hill Lane in Yalding-Laddingford area.

AMMUTS. Ants. =

AMMUT-CAST. An ant-hill. +

AMON. or Whole Amon is a hop, two steps and jump; a comparable expression was used in a children's game. A Half-Amon is a hop, one step and jump.

AMONGST THE MIDDLINS. In reasonably good health; fit. "How you be gettin' on now, Joe?" "Oh, I be amongst the middlins". (See Middling) +

AMPER. A tumour or swelling; a blemish; also means a fault, defect or flaw. (See Ampery) G+

AMPERY[1]. Ailing; sick; weak; unhealthy; unwell; beginning to decay. An ampery tooth was a decayed tooth (See Amper, Dawthery, Dicky, Hampery) P=

AMPERY[2]. Applied to cheese, timber and other items when beginning to decay and become mildewed, rotten,. sickly, weak and unhealthy. (See Abited, Fenny, Mothery, Mowl, Hampery) P

AMPERY[3]. In a poor condition; ricketty; as of a bad wagon or ladder. (See Ampery[2]) =

AMPREY. As Ampery.

AN. Used for the word "of". "What do ye think an 't?" +

AND-IRONS. The dogs, brand irons or cob-irons placed on either side of the open wood fire to keep the brands in place. + (See Brand-Irons, Cob-Irons).

ANENT. Over-against. Pegge quotes as example: "concerning an Act of Parliament made in Scotland 1653 anentis witchcraft." P

ANENTS. Against. +P (See Agin)

ANEWST. Over-against; near hand; nigh; almost; about. +P (See Anents).

ANNIT. A corruption of the query "Isn't it?" into the familiar slang "Ain't it?"; "Is it not?" Possibly brought to Kent by labourers from London working on the North Kent coast and in ports and also used in the Kent hop gardens by East London pickers and was changed by the Wealden speech into "annit". =+*

ANOINT. To give a child several smacks, a thrashing, for being naughty; also to thresh corn. (See Anointed) =

ANOINTED. Mischievous; naughty; troublesome. +

ANOTHER-WHEN. Another time. +

ANTHONY PIG. The smallest, weakest piglet of a litter, supposed to be the favourite or the one requiring most care to rear it, peculiarly under the protection of St. Anthony, and said to follow its owner everywhere. In other counties it is called by numerous names such as Ampony, Nestle-bird, Runthony, Runtling, Piggy-widden, Squab, Tiddling, Squeaker, Dolly-Pig and Tantony Pig (For Kent see Runt, Runtlet, Daniel, Dolly). St. Antony is the patron saint of swineherds and sometimes represented with a small pig at his side. +G

ANVIL CLOUDS. Large white clouds shaped somewhat like a blacksmith's anvil which were said to foretell rain. =+

ANY OLD ROAD. Any way. =* (See Old).

A-PLENTY. Enough; sufficient. "Whoa, there, that's a-plenty". =

APPERN. Apron. +

APS. An Asp or Aspen tree (Populus tremula); A Viper snake (Vipera berus).

AQUABOB. An icicle. (See Cobble, Cock-bell, Cog-bell, Ice-Candle, Icicly) +G

ARBER. The elbow. +

ARBITRY. Arbitrary; high-handed; impulsive; hard; was sometimes used for a greedy grasping person. +

AREAR. Upright; reared up. +

ARG. Argue. (See Argify) =

ARGIFY. Argue. "Doan't ye argify wi' me". =

ARKIE, ARKIES. An ear; the ears. = (See Weekers)

ARRIVANCE. Place of origin; birthplace. + (See Rivance)

ARSLET. (See Acelot, Harcelet, Harslet) =

ARTER. After. +

ARTFUL. Ingenious; clever; amusing; said of some object or invention that takes the fancy and interest by its skill in movement. A dog that begs cleverly on its hind legs was likely to be said to be "artful". "Artful" objects were such items as a "jack in the box" toy, an opera hat, a shut-knife, or a magnet. Not the usual definition of artful, i.e. cunning, deceitful, but closer to skilful. A modern use of this was heard when a man who dried a sparking plug and then rubbed it with a pencil said "That's the artful dodge of it", i.e., clever means of bringing the plug into use again. =

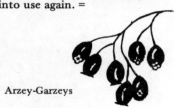

Arzey-Garzeys

ARZEY-GARZEYS. Haws; berries of the Hawthorn tree (Crataegus monogyna), also sometimes called Azzy-Gazzies. *=† (See Haazes, Harves, Quick)

AS. Was often used unnecessarily in speech, such as "I can only say as this, etc." or "I reckon as you'll find its as how it is." +

ASHEN-KEYS. The clustered winged seeds of the Ash tree (Fraxinus excelsior) +

ASIDE. Beside; by the side of. Pegge stated: "Formerly very common at Canterbury" "He stood aside him until he died." P+

ASPRAWL. Gone wrong; upset; out of order. +

ASSOCK. A large pond (See Hassock) =

ASTRE. A hearth. Lambarde in his Perambulation of Kent, ed. 1596, page 562, stated that even in his lifetime this word was nearly obsolete in Kent, though still retained in Shropshire and other counties. P+

ATWEEN. Between. =

AUGUST BUG. A beetle slightly smaller than a May Bug (Cockchafer) or the June Bug (which see) +

AV. Of. "I ha'ant 'eard fill nor fall av 'im for years." +

AWHILE. For a time; a period of time. Now in general use. *+

AWLN. A French measure of length equalling 5 feet 7 inches, used in measuring nets. +

AWVIZ. Always. Spoken in the Wealden dialect. =

AX[1]. Ask; to ask. This was a common transposition used in rural areas. "I axed a man the way". Other examples were "aks" for ask; "waps" or "wops" for wasp; "haps" for hasp. + (See Crips, Crup)

AX[2]. An axle tree; the rod or bar which connects two opposite wheels, on which the wheels revolve. + (See Yax).

AXED. Asked. =

AXE EEN MATTOCK. A hoe-like tool used for grubbing trees, bushes, etc., that had a blade on one side like a Half-Mattock and a narrow pecking blade on the other side of the eye. Modern versions have shorter blades and are called Grubbing Mattocks. = (See Double-sider Hoe, Weald Hoe, Corn Hoe, Clod Hoe, Kent Hoe, Tommy Hoe, Half-Mattock, Plate Hoe, Peck).

Axe Een Mattock

B

BACK. To carry on one's back. =

BACK-ANSWER. A change of heart =* (See Back-Word, Back-Say).

BACK OUT. A backyard or backway. =+ (See Backside, Backing Out)

BACKENING. A relapse; a hindrance; a hold-up; a throwing back. +

BACKER. A carrier, porter or unloader. +

BACKING OUT. A hop garden term meaning moving from one hop row to pick in others, instead of each person staying in their own row allotted them. This usually takes place in the last few days of picking, so that all rows of hops are cleared before moving to another set, those pickers who have finished their own rows moving into rows of other pickers that remain to be picked. =*

BACKPART. Still in use, meaning the back or end of something or someone; "part" is redundant. "I shall be glad to see the backpart of this job." +*

BACK-SAY, BACK-WORD. A change of heart, mind, plans, or decision. "I'm sorry I shall have to give you back-word on our agreement." (See Back-Answer) =*

4

BACKSIDE. A yard at the back of the house; a close. +P (See Back Out).

BACKSTAY. A flat piece of wood put on the feet, on the same principle as a snowshoe and used by the inhabitants of Romney Marsh formerly to enable them to walk more easily across the shingle in the Dungeness area. Similarly so-used and called in Sussex and formerly used on the Norfolk Broads to walk over loose beach or soft mud. Also a stake driven in to support a Raddle-Fence (See Raddle-Hedge and Raddle) +*=

BACKSTERS. Same as Backstay. + Same name used in Sussex.

BACKWAY. The yard or space at the back of a cottage. +*= (See Back Out, Backside).

BACKWENT. As Backpart, also a rear view, a glimpse. "Went" is redundant. "Who was that, Dan'l, who's gone past?" "Dunno. I only caught a backwent of him." =

BAG. To bag means to cut with a bagging hook. +

Bagging Hook

BAGGING HOOK. Also called a Brish Hook, Brishing Hook, Fagging Hook, Swap Hook. A curved cutting implement, similar to a Sickle or Reaping Hook, but with a square or blunt end, instead of a pointed end as in a Sickle. Sometimes had a broader, flatter blade. Used to "brish" or for cutting back hedges and for grass and weeds. The handle is not in the same plane as the hook itself, but raised parallel to it so that those who used it kept their hands clear of the hedge or ground and did not strike it. There are several sizes of this Hook, which causes confusion, particularly as in some areas these Bagging Hook sizes have been given local names. No. 1 Hook is more curved; No. 2 Hook is larger and less curved; Nos. 3 and 4 even larger Hooks in same pattern; No. 5 Hook very large, was used to open a road around a field of corn to allow the binder to work. Not to be confused with the long, wood handled Brushing Hook still used in forestry to cut woody weeds and climbers. (See Pea Hook, Sickle, Ripping Hook, Swap, Wheat Hook). =+*†

BAIL. The handle of a pail, bucket or kettle; a cake bail was the tin or pan in which the cake was baked. + Also used in Sussex.

BAIL RIDGER. An iron bar used instead of a back chain on a saddle on a horse's back to support the shafts. *= (See Redger, Ridger, Redger Bar).

BAILY,[1] BAILEY. The open space enclosed by a fortification; a court within a fortress. The level green area before the court at Chilham castle, i.e. inbetween the little court and the Street was so-called. A similar instance is in Fokestone where it is called The Bale or the Bayle. The Old Bailey in London is a better known example, which was formerly situated within the ancient bailey of the city wall between Lud Gate and New Gate. +P

BAILY[2]. The bailiff, on a farm, is always pronounced in this way. The Under-Baily was a person in charge of two horses. For example, in the type of farm called "a six horse place", the first four horses were under the charge of the waggoner and his mate, the other two being in the charge of the Under-Baily. +

BAILY-BOY. A bailiff-boy. A boy employed by the farmer to go over the ground of the farm daily, to see and ensure everything was in order and to do any work necessary. +P

BAIN'T, BEEUNT. For "are not", "be not", or "be you not". "Surelye you bain't agoin' yet awhile?" +

BAIN'T-YE. For "be you not?" (See Bain't) =

BAIST. The framework of a bed with webbing. + (See Beist, Boist, Byst)

BAIT. A meal taken by labourers in the fields or roadmen by the roadside. Sometimes applied to a snack between breakfast and dinnertime, or as another name for lunch. + (See Baited, Beaver, Bever, Drinking, Tommy, Progger).

BAITED. Horses fed in the stable by the waggoner and his mate were "baited". About 7 p.m. the waggoner would bait and bed down his horses for the night. = (See Bait).

BALD-PATES. A name used by country people in Thanet for the silver Roman coinage, possibly to describe the baldness or poor design of the effigy on some of the examples. + (See Borrow Pence, Dwarfs-Money, Hegs Pence and Scimminger).

BALE. (See Bow).

BALK[1]. A path on a bank or raised pathway, also a pathway that serves as a boundary. +

BALK[2]. A cut tree.

BALL SQUAB. A newly hatched or featherless young bird. +

BALLET. A ballad; a pamphlet; so-called because ballads were usually published in pamphlet form. +

BALLOW. A stick; a walking stick; a cudgel. + (See Bat).

BAM. An expletive; a swear word. =

BAND. In the Umbrella method of training hops the four strings are joined about a yard from the ground by a piece of string, the band. The strings spread out above to give the umbrella shape. =*

BANNA, BANNER. For "be not". "Banna ye goin' hopping this yer?" + (See Bain't).

BANNICK. To thrash; strike; clout, an animal or person with the hand or an implement, such as a Bat (which see) † (See Bannock).

BANNICKING. A thrashing; a beating; a "good hiding"; usually given to a naughty child. † (See Bannock).

BANNOCK. To thrash; beat; chastise; lash. + (See Bannick).

BANYAN DAY. A sea term for the day on which no meat was served to the sailors. Later used by families ashore and extended to country people. "Saddaday is a banyan day." "What do ye mean?" "Oh, a day on which we eat up all the odds and ends."

BARBEL. A sort of petticoat worn by Folkestone fishermen. + (See Barvel).

BARGAIN PENCE. |Earnest money; money given on striking a bargain; making a deal at market. + (See Borrow Pence).

BAR-GANDER. Name for the Sheldrake on the Isle of Sheppey. =

BAR-GOOSE. The Shelduck (Tadorna tadorna), common on Kent mudflats and saltings. =

BARM + BARME G. Brewer's yeast. (See God's Good, Sizzing, Siesin)

BAR-PIG. Male pig intended only for the butcher. =

BARREL DREEN. A round culvert; a drain; a sewer. +

BARTH. A shelter for cattle; a warm place or pasture for calves or lambs. +P

BARTON. The demesne lands of a manor; the manor house itself; more usually for the outhouses and courtyards. = (See Place)

BARVEL. A short leather apron used by washerwomen and fishermen; a slabbering bib (See Barbel) +P

BAR-WAY. A gate constructed of bars or rails, so made as to be taken out of the posts. (See Heave-Gate) +

BASH. To dash; smash; beat in; thump; hit. "His hat was bashed in." Now in general use. +

BASTARD. A gelding. +

BASTARD FALLOW. To cut the first crop of clover then plough the field up, leave it idle until the early autumn and then crop it. =

BASTARD RIG. The Smooth Houndfish (Mustelus vulgaris), a species of small shark as known at Folkestone where it was landed. +

BASTE. To beat; chastise; admonish; A culinary word in common use. *=

BAT, BATT. A staff; a stick; a walking stick; a wood cudgel between four and five feet thick able to be grasped and wielded; a piece of timber longer rather than broad. References are found to it in old records as a "tymber bat": 1664 "pd John Sillwood, for fetching a batt from Canterbury for a middle piece for my mill 0 10s 0d." Shakespeare in "The Lover's Complaint" wrote "So slides he down upon his grained bat", i.e. his rough staff. Pegge said "A bat, of timber, as a tymber bat in "Old Parish Book of Wye". Parish & Shaw gave the example: When some prisoners were tried in 1885 for breaking out of Walmer Barracks, the constable giving evidence said "One of the prisoners struck at me with a bat", which he explained as being, in this case, "the tarred butt-end of a hop pole." Sanders gives it as "a heavy piece of wood generally two inches in diameter, several of which are usually incorporated in a well-made wood faggot". It is also the name for the long handle of a scythe; a small water trough for horses to drink from (See Tanks); the stick used for keeping the traces of a plough-horse asunder is called a "trace bat" or a "spread bat"; a large pole, as used in wirework hop gardens; the name for a "stone" or "rubber" used to sharpen scythes, and the name for a log for the fire. P+†= (See Libbat, Libbet, Rubber, Sally Batt, Sharper).

BATS. The legs. "She's got a good pair of bats on her". =

BAULKING UP. Belching up wind; burping. =†

BAULLY. A boat + (See (Bawley).

BAVEN, BAVIN. A little faggot; a faggot of brushwood bound with only one wiff, while a normal faggot was bound with two; brush faggots with the brushwood at length, or in general brushwood. =PG+ (See Faggot)

BAVEN TUG, BAVIN TUG, BAVIN WAGON, POLE TUG. A type of Kent wagon used for transporting bavins, also for carrying Sweet Chestnut hop poles to the hop garden. = (See Bobbin Tug, Tug).

BAWLEY. A small fishing smack used on the coasts of Kent and Essex, about the mouth of the Thames and Medway. Bawleys are generally about forty feet in length, thirteen feet beam, five foot draught and fifteen or twenty tons measurement. They differ in rig from a cutter, in having no boom to the mainsail, which is consequently easily brailed-up when working the trawl nets. They are half-decked with a wet well to keep the fish alive. In the past a taunting rhyme: "Hawley, bawley — Hawley, bawley, What have you got in your trawley?" when said to a bawley-man supposedly had the same anger-arousing effect on him as a rag to a bull, or the poem of the "puppy pie" did upon a barge-man. +=

BAY. A dam built in ditches to retain water when required; a high bank of a river to hold back flood water; when a bank was constructed either side of the river for this purpose they were called "bays". = (See Deekers).

BAY-BOARDS. The large folding doors of a barn do not reach to the ground and the intervening space is closed by four or five moveable boards which fit in a groove and are called "bay-boards". +

BAYER. Bear; bare †

BE. For "are", "am". "Where be ye?" P +

BEAN-HOOK. A small hook with a short handle used for cutting beans. + (See Bagging Hook, Pea Hook, Sickle).

BEARER. Narrow strap on the side of a horse's neck as part of harness decoration, sometimes having tiny brass ornamentation. *=

BEARERS. The men who bear or carry a dead person's coffin to the burial service and grave. In Kent the bier is still sometimes called a "bearer". Now in general use. +*

BEARBIND, BEARBINE, BAREBINE. The Convolvus or Field Bindweed (Convolvus arvensis). Pegge states: "Bearbind, a weed called by others Bindweed". P+=

BEASTS. A name for the first two or three meals of milk after a cow has calved + (See Bestins, Biskins, Bismilk, Poad-Milk)

BEAVER, BEAVOR, BEVER, BEVOR. A light meal, not necessarily accompanied by drink, taken between breakfast and dinner or between dinner and tea. In rural areas also meant a cold meal eaten in the open, in a sheltered place if available by the hedgeside, etc., by farm labourers, deekers, and other workmen, about breakfast-time. Possibly a corruption of the French "bouvoir", to drink and may have originated in Chatham Dockyard, where it is still used, after French Napoleonic prisoners of war were employed. From them it was "anglicized" by dockyardmen and eventually it spread into north-east Kent and elsewhere. Variations are used in other counties. +*=† (See Bait, Elevenses).

BEAZLED. Very tired, exhausted; alternatively bested by a problem. =

BECAUSE WHY. Why; the why and wherefore, used in speech, sometimes arguments. +P

BECKETT. A strong, tough piece of cord by which the hook is fastened to the snood in fishing for Conger Eels. +

BEDSTEDDLE. A bedstead; the wooden framework of a bed which supported the actual bed itself. =*+ (See Baist, Steddle).

BEE-LIQUOR. Mead; made of the washings of the combs, from fermented honey and water. P+

Beetle

BEETLE. A wooden mallet, used with iron wedges to split wood and for other purposes. Each side of the beetle's head is encircled by a strong band or ring of metal to prevent the wood from splitting. The saying "as deaf as a beetle" refers to this mallet and is used similarly to the expression "as deaf as a post". +

BEETLE HOGS. Hedgehogs. Deliberately set free in cottages to rid them of Black Beetles, usually Cockroaches. =

BEFORE. "Carry it before you," i.e. with you. P

BEFORE-AFTER. Until after; an event that will not occur until the passing of a considerable period of time. "I won't see him before-after Christmas now". +

BEGGY. Used by schoolchildren to describe an item of equipment that they considered to be almost worn out or at least in poor condition. *=

BEHOLDEN. Indebted to; under obligation to. "I wunt be beholden to 'em". =

BEIST. As Baist; also a temporary bed made up on two chairs for a small child. +

BELATED. To be late, after time, particularly at night. "I must be off or I shall get belated". +

BELEFT. For "believed". "No-one would have beleft it". +P

BELOW LONDON. An expression that meant "not in Kent"; anywhere beyond the city of London and boundary of Kent. (See Foreigner, Furriner, Sheeres, March-Man). +

BENDER-AND-ARRS. Bows and arrows. +

BENTY. A bird's nest made of various grasses, principally the Bent Grasses, usually applied to that of the Blackcap (Sylvia atricapilla). =

BENERTH. The service which the tenant owed the landlord by plough and cart. +

BERBINE. The Verbena, a cultivated plant. Not to be confused with Barebine, Bearbind, Bearbine. +

BERTH[1], BIRTH[1]. A place or station; a good birth, used by seamen to describe a bunk or sleeping place. Used elsewhere in this meaning. G*=

BERTH[2], BIRTH[2]. To lay down floorboards. To birth or berth a floor is to place or lay down a floor. Pegge said: "Flooring brods are called in Kent berthing-brods. A person well-seated by the fireside is said to have got a good birth. At sea birthing the hammocks is placing them." P+

BESOM. A naughty mischievous child; a maiden or unmarried woman of moral instability or with a temperamental character. †=

BEST. To best, get the better of. "I shall best ye" + (See Bested, Bestid)

BESTED. To get the better of. = (See Bestid, Worst).

BESTID. Destitute; forlorn, poverty-stricken. (See Bested) +P

BESTINS. Formerly used in East Kent for two or three of the first meals' milk after a cow has halved. P (See Beasts, Biskins, Bismilk, Poad Milk).

BET. Beat *†

BETTER-MOST. The best; much superior to. *† (See Bettermy).

BETTERMY. Used for bettermost (which see); superior. +

BEVON, BEVINGS. Faggots, mostly the type used as stack bottoms or steddles (which see). (See Baven). =

BIB. Name given to the Pout or Whiting Pout (Gadus luscus) by Folkestone fishermen. +

BIBBER. To tremble; shake nervously, or with grief. "I saw his underlip bibber". +

BIB-BOB. To swing or bounce about. =

BICEY. Mouldy; as Abited, Abite. (See Bythy)

BIDE. To stay. "Just you let that bide." Still used universally as "Let's bide our time" +

BIER-BALKS. Church ways or paths along which a bier and coffin may be carried. + (See Lyste Way).

BIGAROO. The Whiteheart Cherry. Still used for the Bigarreau cherry. =

BILL, BILL-HOOK. A sharp hand implement with a hooked top used to sever woody growth, cut and lay hedges, trim and split branches. There is a type peculiar to Kent, but other counties have their own variations. =

Two Kent Billhooks

BILLET[1]. A spread bat or swingle bar to which horses' traces are fastened. +

BILLET[2]. (See Libbat)

BILLYCOCK. A black felt hat, with a band of braid ribbon and a white bone buckle at the side. A known use was as part of the apparel worn by the coachman of a four in hand at Mystole House, Chartham, Canterbury, in the late 19th century. Word passed into general use and used as a 19th century colloquial term for a low-crowned flexible felt hat with a wide curving brim. "Muster William looked spry as he rode by in his billycock." =*

BIM. Bed. "We were always told 'Tis time for bim'."

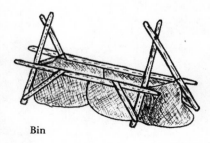

Bin

BIN. The receptacle used for containing the hops after being picked and before being "measured". About six feet long and two feet wide, comprising a collapsible wooden frame from which hangs the bin cloth. =

BIN MAN. (See Pole Puller)

BINDER. A long stick used for hedging; a long pliable stick of any kind. Also applied to the sticks used in binding on the thatch of houses or stacks. Walnuts were threshed with a binder (Not to be confused with Libbat). +

BINE. One of the stems of hops growing from a "hill" and up a string. Hops develop on a bine or the stem as grapes grow on a vine. (See Hop Bind). Also the stem bearing pods of peas, either trailing or up sticks or strings. =*

BING-ALE. Ale given at a tithe feast. Pegge states "The liquor which the fermor of a parsonage gives to the fermours and to the servants (at two separate entertainments, servants first and masters afterwards) at the end of the year when he has gathered their tythe." +P

BIRDES NESTES. Birds' nests. A very old East Kent pronunciation. +

BIRTH. (See Berth) G.

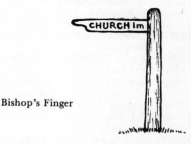

Bishop's Finger

BISHOP'S FINGER. A guide post, so-called because it shows the right way. (See Pointing Post, Throws, Went). +

BISKINS. Used in East Kent for two or three of the first meals' milk after a cow has calved. +P (See Beasts, Bestins, Bismilk, Poad Milk).

BISMILK. Used in West Kent. +P (See Beasts, Bestins, Biskins, Poad Milk).

BITCHERING. Said of a bitch when she is proud. P

BITTER-COLD. Very cold and icy; piercing cold (See Cold, Hand-Cold, Finger-Cold) =

BLACK BRINDS. Oak trees less than six inches in diameter or 24 inches in circumference if allowing for the bark; used for fencing posts. †

BLACK RIND. The name for an immature oak tree that remains undeveloped and small in size. +

BLACKIE. A black bird, usually the Blackbird, but sometimes used for a Rook or Crow. +

BLACK-TAN. Good for nothing; useless, idle person. +

BLAR, BLARE. To describe animal noises; to bleat; to low; to bellow. +*

BLARING. Shouting about; excited. Now in universal use. *= (See Boldrumptious).

BLEACH. Sickness is said to bleach a person, to bring them low. Pegge comments: "I suppose because it is apt to make people look pale and white." P

BLEAT. Corruption of bleak; cold; cheerless. +†

BLEAT WIND. Wealden corruption of bleak wind, a very cold, piercing wind. † (See Bleat).

BLESS MY SOUL. An exclamatory utterance. (My Great Chart grandfather often said it, preceded by Lor' (Lord) — A.M.) Also said as "Bless My Soul and Body". = (See Dear Hearts-Alive, Saint's-Alive).

BLESSING. Fortunate; a piece of luck. = (See Mercy).

BLIGH[1]. Lonely; dull. "The poor chap's awful bligh." +

BLIGH[2] BLY. A faint resemblance; similarity to an object or person; a general likeness. A contraction of "belike". Resemblance to a parent was also known as "tyvered" not to be confused with "tyver". G+ (See Favour, Spit, Shay).

BLIV, BLUV. A corruption of believe; believed. "I bliv the sky's turning to rain." +

BLOOD. A term of pity or commiseration. In Kent the expression "poor blood" was used, particularly by elderly people, in the same way as "poor old body", "poor soul", were used elsewhere. "They poor bloods were out in the fils in all that snow and must have bin nearly fruz". +

BLOODINGS. Black puddings. +P

BLOOMAGE. The plumage of a bird.+

BLOUSE[1]. A red-faced countrywench. += (See Boldrumptious)

BLOUSE[2]. To sweat; to perspire freely; a state of heat which brings high colour to the face. +

BLOUSING. Red and sanguine; applied to the colour of the face caused by sweating in great exertion and heat. "He had a blousing colour." +

BLOW. The wind; used to describe the forceful strength of the wind. "That nor-easter last night was a tidy old blow." *=

BLOWING-UP. A term used to describe wind increasing in strength, sometimes preceding rain or a storm. *=

BLUE BOTTLE. The Cornflower (Centaurea cyanus). Now used elsewhere. =

BLUE BOTTLES. Bluebells or Wild Hyacinths (Endymion nonscriptum) + (See Red Bottle, Yellow Bottle).

BLUE-SLUTTERS. Name given by Folkestone fishermen to very large jellyfish. +

BLUNDER[1]. A heavy noise, as of falling or stumbling. +

BLUNDER[2]. To move awkwardly and noisily about, as, when a person moving in a confined space knocks an object over or throws others down. Still in use generally.

BLUSTROUS. Blustering, boisterous, noisy, strong winds or waves. +

BOAR CAT. A tom cat. +

BOBBERY. A squabble; a row; a fuss; a disturbance; an argument + (See Set-out).

BOBBIN. A bundle of firewood, smaller than a faggot and larger than a pimp, where each stick should be about eighteen inches long. + (See Baven, Bavin, Faggot, Kilnbrush, Rib, Wiff).

BOBBIN-TUG. A sort of cart on a light framework of wheels, somewhat like a timber wagon. Used for carting bobbins about for sale. It had an upright support at each of the four corners to keep the bobbins in place. + (See Baven Tug, Tug).

BOBLIGHT. Twilight. +P

Bo-Boy

BO-BOY. A scarecrow, dressed as a human figure, in old clothes, hat and with pole arms and straw face. + (See Rook Starving).

BOB'S A-DYING. When a child or person has been upset or is crying or fretty. = (See Grizzle).

BODAR. An officer of the Cinque Ports whose duty it was to arrest debtors and convey them to imprisonment in Dover Castle. +

BODGE[1]. A container; a type of wooden basket used by gardeners; a scuttle-shaped box for holding coal, carrying ashes, etc. Also loosely applied to any container from a cup (of tea) to a cartload (of dung). In Sussex known as a Trug-basket but in Kent known as a Trug-bodge (See Trug, Trug-Bodge, also Alley Bodge, Water Bodge). The bodge now holds an indefinite quantity but formerly was used as a peck measure (See next entry). +=

BODGE[2]. An uncertain quantity, usually about a bushel or a bushel and a half. Sometimes a small or medium quantity of corn or meal to carry out to animals as food. "There's a bodge of corn, nearly a bagful." +

BODGE[3]. A low, narrow, four-wheeled cart pulled on a chain by a horse and used to take dung, etc., through hop alleys during summer when the bines were growing. Also a go-cart or "barrow" made by nippers with a box and some pram wheels. (See Alley Bodge) =

BODILY-ILL. A person ill with a fever, shingles, bronchitis, etc., is described as bodily-ill. Of a person who had cut a finger, sprained an ankle or broke a leg it would be said "Oh, he's not, as you may say, bodily-ill." +

BOFFLE[1] To baffle; confuse; bother; tease; obstruct. +

BOFFLE[2]. A confusion; a blunder; something managed in a confused, blundering, awkward, inconvenient way. +

BOIST[1]. A little extempore bed by the fireside for a sick person. Boist originally meant a box with bedding in it, such as the Norwegian type of bed. (See Baist, Beist, Byst) P+

BOIST[2]. A makeshift bed or hut, used by hop-driers or charcoal burners. =

BOLDRUMPTIOUS. Presumptious. + (See Polrumptious).

BOLT. Swallow food quickly; greedily. (See Gollop, Hog, Scorf, Waffle).

BOLTER. A young wild rabbit, so-called until about six months old. †

BOND. The wiff or wisp of twisted straw or hay with which a sheaf of corn or truss of hay was bound by hand. + (See Wimmeler).

BONE[1]. To bone fruit trees meant to cut all the side shoots back "tight", i.e. close. =

BONE[2]. To steal; to pinch or thieve. =

BONELESS. A corruption of Boreas, the north wind. In Kent when the wind blew violently it was said "Boneless is at the door." Originally the boreas was "the wind from the mountains." +

BOOBY-HUTCH. A clumsy, badly designed covered carriage or seat. +

BOOT IRON. An iron plate strapped on to the sole of the boot of their digging foot to protect the boot when digging with a Hop Spud. =

BOOTSHOES. Half boots; thick boots. A once common measurement of grass was to say its "Bootshoe High." + (See High-Lows).

BOP. To hit; to throw anything down with a resounding noise or clatter. "George was violent drunk so the constable bopped him to quieten him down." +=*

BOROW. A tithing. The number of ten families who were bound to the king for each other's good behaviour. An ancient administrative unit consisting formerly of ten households living close together. +

BORROW-PENCE. An old name for ancient coins; probably coins found in the tumuli or barrows. + (See Bald-Pates, Hegs Pence, Scimminger, Bargain Pence).

BORSHOLDER. A constable's assistant; a petty constable; a headborough or chief of each tithing in a hundred. At Great Chart there used to be held a custom of electing a "dumb borsholder". It was made of wood, about three feet long, with an iron ring at the top and four rings at the sides, by means of which it was held and propelled when used, presumably, as a ram to break open the doors of houses believed to contain stolen goods. Similarly, at the manor of Chart in Wateringbury the same custom took place to elect in place of a man the "dumb borsholder", a man acting for it and answering for it at the court. This "dumb borsholder" was also a staff of wood, three feet long, with an iron ring at the bottom and four more on the sides. In the top was fixed a square iron spike, four and a half inches long. It was also used to break open doors of houses, without a warrant from a Justice of the Peace, if it was suspected that persons or goods were

11

unlawfully concealed in any of the twelve houses over which the "dumb borsholder" had jurisdiction. In this case the same twelve householders took it in turn to act as the deputy borsholder for a year and while in office received the sum of a penny for each of the eleven other house-holders. +

BORSTAL. A pathway up a hill, generally a very steep one; a winding way up a hill. P+

BOSSET. Worn on one side. A pair of shoes with the heels worn on one side are run over or bosset. =

BOSS-EYED. Cross-eyed; squinting; pur-blind. +*=

BOSTAL. As Borstal. +

BOSTLER. A borsholder or constable +

BOTTLE. Not much bottle, i.e. not much good. =

BOTTOMING. To bottom; digging out or to dig out the silt from the ditches until the bottom or bed is reached. =

BOULT, BOULTED. To cut pork into pieces for the purpose of pick-ling it. +P

BOULTING TUB. The tub in which pork was pickled. +

BOUNDS. Still used in the phrase "no bounds" to mean uncertainty. "No bounds where he is". +*=

BOUT. A period of time; a turn; a "go"; a long task of hard work. Now in universal use, particularly to des-cribe a drawn-out illness or ailment. "He had a long bout of flu."

Two Forms of Bow

BOW. A length of pliable stick, usually Hazel, fixed to the scythe to gather corn while reaping and fitted when a Creet or Cradle was not available. A staple was driven into the bottom end of the sneath, the hazel rod was pushed into the staple and then the rod bent outwards and then upwards, the upper end being tied to the sneath to make the bow. *= (See Creet, Sickle and latter's Scythe reference).

BOY-BEAT. Beaten at anything by a person younger than oneself. "I was boy-beat by young Billy." +

BRACK. A tear, rent, split in clothes; a crack.+

BRAKE-PLOUGH. A plough for brak-ing or clearing the ground between growing crops. +

BRAKING. Clearing the rows between rows of beans or other crops with a shim or brake plough. +

BRANCH. A head, tail, or part of a large head of hops. =*

Brand Iron

BRAND-IRONS. The fire dogs or cob-irons which confine the brands on an open hearth. +P (See And-Irons, Cob-Irons)

BRANDY COW. A cow that is brind-led, brinded or streaked. +

BRARMER. Good; special. Used else-where. =

BRAUCH. Rakings of straw. (See Brauche) +

BRAUCHE, BRAWCHE. Rakings of straw to kindle fires. +G

BRAVE. Large. "That poplar is grow-ing to a very brave size." +

BREAD-AND-BUTTER. In Kent these three words were used as one substantive and it was usual to prefix the indefinite article and to speak of a bren-butter, a bren-budder. + (See Breads-Butters)

BREAD-AND-CHEESE. The young green shoots of Hawthorn in Spring-time, eaten by children in the past as food when playing "Mothers and Fathers." =

BREAD-AND-PULL-IT. Dry bread; a dry crust eaten as a child's punish-ment. If children asked what was for dinner they were told "Bread-and-Pull-It" (See Terms, Expressions, Sayings and Proverbs) =

BREADS-BUTTERS. Similar to Bread-and-Butter (which see), but used to describe several slices of bread and butter. "There are still the breads-butters to pass round." =

BRECKIE, BREKKY. The word breakfast shortened and corrupted. Usually used by parents to their young children. †

BRENT. Steep, high formation of the land. An area of Faversham is still known as The Brents. +

BRET[1]. To decline; alter; fade away; decay. Standing corn that was so ripe that the grain fell out was said to "bret out." + (See Brit).

BRET[2]. A piece of the wood torn off with the strig in gathering fruit. Similar to Brut in definition and use. + (See Spolt, Spalter).

BRICKBAT. A piece of a brick. P (See Bat).

BRIEF[1]. Common; plentiful; frequent; rife. P

BRIEF[2]. A petition drawn up and carried round for the purpose of collecting money. Formerly money was collected in churches on briefs, for various charitable purposes, both public and private. In some churches Brief Books are still occasionally preserved which contain the names of the persons or places on whose behalf the Brief was taken around, the object, and the amounts collected. The objects include events which may seem strange to us, such as the ransoming of British travellers and baggage seized by Mediterranean pirates, the relief of flooded inhabitants in the Low Countries and similar exigencies, as well as charitable works in Britain. +

BRIMMING SOW. The same condition in a sow as the description applied to the bitch as being "on heat", a cow as "bulling" and a mare as "hossing"; a sow "in season." = (See Cluck).

BRIMP. The Gadfly which torments sheep and cattle; also used for the Horse-fly. Pegge states: "The bre'fly that torments bullocks; bre' is for breeze; OE brise, the Gadfly." P+= (See Nimble Dick).

BRIMS. As Brimp +

BRIMSEY. As Brimp +

BRISH[1]. A nimble, spry person; used mainly to describe an elderly person active for their age. = (See Peart).

BRISH[2] To brush, cut, trim, or mow over lightly; to "brush" a hedge or verge; to trim a hedge with a Brishing Hook — Bagging Hook. =

BRISH[3]. To touch lightly in passing. "He just brished me". = (See Brish[1], Brish[2])

BRISHING HOOK, BRUSH HOOK. Usually used for a Bagging Hook (which see) but also occasionally a long handled curved blade tool to brish or brush a hedge especially if a high hedge. =

BRISHINGS. Trimmings from a hedge. = (See Brish, Bagging Hook).

BRIT. To knock out; drop out; rub out; applied when grain is over-ripe and drops out or when hops "shatter", break to pieces. + (See Bret, Brut).

BROACH. A spit; also a piercer; "to broach or tap a cask", to "broach a subject", i.e. to open it, to begin. +PG* = Commonly used now in several counties.

BROCK, BROK. An inferior horse. + (See Brockman).

BROCKMAN. A horseman; a man who maintains horses. +

BROKE. A rupture. + (See Brook).

BROOD. Wide; broad. A garden would be 20 yards lord and 10 yards brood. =

BROOK[1] To brook one's name is to answer in one's disposition to the purport of one's name. Similar to "Like by name and like by nature". =

BROOK[2]. Something broken; fractured, i.e. broken ground, fen, marshland. =

BROOKS. Low marshy or moory ground, but not always containing running water or a spring. +P

BROOM-DASHER. A maker, dealer or seller of brooms. Dasher is also combined in the word haberdasher, a seller of smallwares or articles. Broom-dasher was also used as a designation of a careless, dirty and slovenly person. (See Dash) +

BROWN-DEEP. Lost in reflection; gazing without seeing; day-dreaming. +

BROWSELLS, BROWZELLS. The remains of the fleed of a pig after the lard had been extracted by boiling; also bits and pieces of various cooked meats mixed with fat to form a hard "cake"; crisp residue after fat pork has been rendered down for lard. The "cake" was eaten on its own or with bread, and village butchers also prepared and sold the "cake". Pegge stated: "The small bits of skin remaining after the lard is tried (boiled down) which the common people eat and are very fond of it." Known as scrutchings in other counties. =+†

BRUCKLE. Brittle. +

BRUFF. Blunt; rude in manner; rough; similar to present "gruff". +

BRUMPT. Bankrupt; broken; penniless; similar to skint now. "I am brumpt" meaning "I have no money". +

BRUNGEON. A brat; a neglected child; a waif. +

BRUSH. To trim hedgerows, cut thistles, etc.; mow thin, rough grass + (See Brish).

BRUSS[1]. It is spoken of bees when they fly about and appear strong and active. P

BRUSS[2]. Brisk; petulant; proud; a "forward" person. +

BRUT[1] BRUTTE To browse or nibble off young shoots. Cows, if they can, or sheep in an orchard, will "brut" the low hanging leaves and young wood of trees. From the French brout — a shoot of young wood, and brouter — to nibble off such shoots. P+

BRUT[2]. To brut, rub off, brit or break off the young shoots, bruts, of stored potatoes. + (See Chat, Brutting, Nurity, Spear).

BRUT[3]. To grow or shoot, applied to buds or potatoes + (See Spear).

BRUTTED. The broken off tips of hedges and bushes or tops of plant crops; also used for pasture only lightly grazed. =* (See Brut, Brutting).

BRUTTING. The breaking off of shoots, leaves and fruit either when putting in, setting or removing a ladder, or while picking. Cherry pickers who do a lot of brutting are not looked upon kindly by the grower. Also to brut potatoes. *= (See Chat).

BUCK[1]. To wash. +

BUCK[2]. A pile of clothes ready for washing. Farmers used to wash the clothes of their farm servants or in lieu allowed them a guinea a year. The lye, soap and washing utensils were kept in the bucking chamber or bunting house and there were also piled the clothes and other linen waiting to be washed as soon as there

was enough for one buck. Shakespeare used the word buck-basket for what is now called a clothes or linen basket, in "Merry Wives of Windsor", Act 3, Sc. 5: Fal: "They conveyed me into a buck-basket." Ford: "A buck-basket!" Fal: "By the Lord, a buck-basket; rammed me in with foul shirts and smocks, socks, foul stockings and greasy napkins..." +

BUCK[3]. To fill a basket. +

BUCK BASKET. A clothes basket. =

BUCK-FISTED. Clumsy; awkward. * (See Cack-Handed, Fumble -Fisted, Ham Fisted, Unhandy).

BUCK WASH. A large washing tub, formerly used in farmhouses, when, once a quarter, they washed the clothes of the farm servants, soaking them in lye. +

BUCKING. A kind of washing, the bucking being done by beating the clothes in the water on a stone with a pole flattened at the end. Pegge also states a buck was a tub. P

BUCKING CHAMBER. The room in which the clothes were bucked or steeped in lye, prior to washing. +

BUD. A weaned calf, of the first year, that has not yet grown into a heifer. So-called because the horns have not grown out, but are in the bud. P+

BUFF. Flowers growing in a clump, tuft, or "hassock". +

BUFFLE-HEADED. Thick-headed; stupid; ignorant. +

BUG[1]. To bend. P+

BUG[2]. A general term for any winged insect, usually flies or beetles, i.e., May Bug, Lady Bug, June Bug, July Bug, Rain Bug. At the lifetime of Pegge was also in general use. P+

BUG[3], BUGGY. Outwardly unstable; in a bad mood or ratty. Anyone with "the bug" was short-tempered with other people. *†

BULL HUSS. The Large Spotted Dogfish or Nurse Hound (Scyllium catulus) + (See Huss, Robin Huss, Spur Fish).

BULL-ROUT. The Goby (Gobius minutus). +

BULLING. Applied to a cow (See Brimming Sow). =

BULLOCK. A fatting beast of either sex. +

BULLOCKS. Accrding to Pegge "Said of bulls, cows and oxen."

BUMBLE. To make a humming noise.

Hence Bumble Bee for the Humble Bee. +

BUMBLE -FISTED. Clumsy when performing a manual task. + (See Buck Fisted, Cack Handed, Ham Fisted).

BUMBLESOME. Awkward; clumsy; ill-fitting. +

BUMBULATION. A humming noise. + (See Bumble)

BUNNY-MOUTH. (See Rabbit's-Mouth) *=

BUNT[1]. To shake to and fro. +

BUNT[2]. To sift the meal or flour from the bran. +

BUNT[3]. To butt or nudge heavily, applied to cattle and horses. +

BUNTING. A Shrimp. +

BUNTING HOUSE. An outhouse where the meal was sifted. + (See Bunt, Bunting Hutch, Byst).

BUNTING HUTCH. A boulting hutch, the bin in which the meal is bunted or bolted. A Bunting Oast was also called a Byst. +

BURR[1]. The female inflorescence or blossom of the Hop, or flowers of the horse chestnut. "The hops are in burr." *+

BURR[2]. The rainbow-like halo or circle around the moon that foretells rain. It was believed that the larger the burr the nearer the rain. + (See Sun Dog.)

BURR[3]. Something fused and inseparable; was used to describe a coagulated mass of bricks which by some accident had refused to become separated, but were a sort of conglomerate or mass. + (See Burr[1] and 2, Clinkers.)

BURR[4]. The Wealden form of Bare and Bear. †

BURY. A rabbit's burrow. +

BUSH. Used specially and particularly to describe the Gooseberry, i.e., "under a gooseberry bush". Also applied to Currants but not so frequently. P+

BUSINESS. Pegge says "Otherwhere mostly in a contemptuous depreciating way, as "a poor business", but in Kent they say "a great business", for a large undertaking, as a large farm." P

BUTCHERS. A method of training hops in a hop garden. *= (See Umbrella, Upright)

BUTT[1]. A flatfish, better known as the Flounder (Pleuronectes flesus).

On the mudflats of the Medway they were picked up by hand, known as Griping (which see), as they lay on the mud bottom at low tide. The fishermen would work along and close by the channels feeling the mud bottom with their hands until they felt the shape of the fish, then it was siezed with one hand behind the head, the other body side of the tail, and swept out of the mud into an open sack that was tied around the waist of the fisherman. They were caught in the river at Sandwich by spearing them in the mud like Eels. Now little demand for Flounders, although the author enjoyed their delicious white flesh many times as a boy, when caught by griping in the Medway by his father. Largely shunned by present-day fish eaters because they say the flesh tastes too strongly of the mud the Flounders are in. Occasionally caught for fish-processing factories. +*

BUTT[2]. The name for the Turbot (Rhombus maximus) formerly used by fishermen at Margate. +

BY-BUSH. In ambush or hiding. "I just stood by-bush and heard all their plans". +

BYSACK. A satchel or small wallet; a kind of wallet, for a man to carry anything from market in; a small sack or satchel which a man carries by or beside him. P+

BYST. A settle or sofa. A Bunting Oast was sometimes also known as the Byst. + (See Baist, Beist, Boist)

BYTHE. The black spots on linen produced by mildew. + (See Abited, Bythy, Bicey)

BYTHY. As Bythe, spotted with black marks left by mildew. "When she took the cloth out it was all bythy." +

C

CACKY. Animal or human excreta. *= (See Turd, Treddles)

CACK-HANDED. The difficult instead of the easy way of achieving something; awkwardly; fumbling and clumsy; an inconvenient or sloppy way. Sometimes applied to someone left-handed. "I had to tackle it cack-handed." Used elsewhere. *= (See

Buck Fisted, Ham Fisted, Cag-Handed, Fumble Fisted, Swop Footed, Unhandy)

CAD. A journeyman shoemaker; a cobbler who has finished his apprenticeship. A contemptuous name used for any assistant, applied to a junior or inferior servant. Now used generally for a vulgar, bad-mannered person with no feelings or moral sense. +

CADE. A barrel containing six hundred herrings; any parcel or quantity or pieces of beef, less than a whole quarter. + (See Card)

CADLOCK. The plant Charlock (Brassica sinapistrum). +

CADE-LAMB. A pet lamb, a house lamb. + (See Sock Lamb)

CADEY, CADUS. Hat. =

CAGGY. Muddy, mucky, sticky. = (See Claggy)

CAG-HANDED. Left-handed. = (See Swop-Footed, Cack-Handed)

CAILES, + CALES. P Skittles; ninepins. Pegge says "as they call them at Canterbury. O.E. cailes or kayles, ninepins." +P (See Keals)

CAKE BAIL. A tin or pan in which a cake was baked. + (See Bail)

CALIVER. A large pistol or blunderbuss. + (See Dagg)

CALL[1]. Used to described necessity, but always with the negative prefixed, i.e., "There's no call for you to get into a rage." +

CALL[2]. To consider. "He is called an honest man". P

CALL-OVER. To find fault with; to abuse; to denigrate; to deflate with argument; to upbraid or reprimand; to bawl out. +

CALLOW. Naked; bare; bald; with little covering. To lie callow was to do so in a cold, exposed manner with few bed clothes as a cover. It was used of underwood thin on the ground; unfledged birds were said to be "a callow brood" and undeveloped, inexperienced youth was also known as a callow time of life. +P

CALLYWAGSERS. Dried beans; haricot beans. =

CANKER BERRY. The fruit of the Wild Rose (Rosa canina), the hip. Also known as the Canker Rose. Shakespeare wrote in his Sonnets, liv. "The canker-blooms have full as deep a dye, As the perfumed tincture of the roses". P+

CANKER ROSE. The Wild Rose (Rosa canina), the Dog Rose. P+

Canterbury Hoe

CANT[1]. A push, shove or throw. "I gave him a cant just for fun". P+

CANT[2]. A portion of cornfield or woodland; a corner of a field. In the past the bailiff drew his cant furrows through the growing corn in Spring. These were recorded in his cant-book with the measurement of the cants. During harvest-time he added in the book where relevant the prices paid for cutting each of them. A wood was parcelled out in cants for either cutting or selling. Pegge states: "A corner of anything; as a cant, a cut of a loaf when the corner is cut off. When a wood is thrown into fellets (portions) or a field of wheat dispos'd into parts to be hired out to the reapers, they call them cants" (See Fellet, Wented). Having a tough or easy assignment was to have a "tidy cant" or a "pretty good cant" P+=

CANT[3]. To tilt over, to upset; to throw out. "The form canted up and over we went". +

CANTLE. As Cant[2]. P

CANTELL. An indefinite number; a cantell of people, cattle, sheep, etc.; diminutive of Cant (which see). A corner or portion of indefinite dimension; a cantell of bread, cheese, wood, timber. P+

CANTED OUT. Thrown, tilted or tipped out, such as from a cart, bed, etc. G (See Cant[3].)

CANTERBURY BALSAM. Name used in the locality of Canterbury for the wayside and woodland plant, Annual Mercury (Mercurialis annua). =

CANTERBURY BELLS. The garden flower commonly grown, but the name was also formerly used for the Wild Campanula or Nettle-leaved Bellflower (Campanula trachelium). There is a possibility the name was originally given to the plant because of the similarity of the flowers to the small bells that were used on the trappings of the pilgrims' horses on their way to the shrine of St. Thomas a Becket at Canterbury. +

16

CANTERBURY HOE. A medium shafted hoe with a heavy iron head with three flattish prongs or speens, these being half an inch wide with three inches in width between the inner edges of the prongs or speens. Sometimes a two-pronged hoe is called a Canterbury Hoe although its correct name is a Kent Hoe. The larger Canterbury Hoe was an ideal tool for use by men who were being paid to hoe piece-work so they could cover more ground; also used for drawing earth over potatoes. *=† (See Clod Hoe, Kent Hoe, Tommy Hoe, Corn Hoe, Half-Mattock, Axe Een Mattock, Weald Hoe, Plate Hoe, Peck, Doublesider Hoe).

CAP. Part of the flail which secured the middle band to the handstaff or swingle, as the case may be. A flail has two caps, i.e. the handstaff cap, usually made of wood, and the swingle cap, made of leather. Formerly used for threshing corn by hand. +

CAPONS. Red Herrings. + Now in universal use, but formerly a nickname used by the Ramsgate fishermen.

CAPTURED. A word used to describe the destruction of or damage to vegetables and flowers by frost. "Jack Frost captured my dahlias last night". =

CAR'. To carry. "You wunt car' that fur". +

CARD[1]. A card of beef, a clod, the latter being "the coarse part of the neck of an ox. In Kent a card or cade of beef is any parcel or quantity of pieces under a whole quarter." In this example probably card is an inferior spelling for caad. P

CARD[2]. Similar to Cade. A barrel containing Herrings. + (See Cade)

CARFE. A cutting of hay; a quarter of a stack cut through from top to bottom. +

CARPET-WAY. A green way; a smooth grass road or lane; a lyste way. P+

CARRY-ON. To be in a passion; to act unreasonably; to do as one pleases. "You can't carry-on how you like here". +*= Still in general use.

CARVET, CARVETT. A thick hedgerow; a roadside copse; a shave; a piece of land carved out of another. P+ (See Shave, Shaw)

CASMER. Cabbage. =

CAST[1]. Thwarted; defeated; having lost an action at law. "They talk of carr'ing it into court, but I lay he'll be cast". +

CAST[2] CASTIES. An accumulation of earth thrown up above ground level by a Mole, also the excreted soil by Earthworms and the earth and material above and composing the nests of Ants, usually the Common Red Ant (Myrmica rubra), these being called a mole-cast, - molehill; a worm-cast (now in general use) and ant- or emmet-cast- an anthill. Several heaps were called casties. P+†*=

CATCH. The catch was a very small bushel, less than half a basket which was recorded as a bushel and allowed as a favour to the hop pickers with the last measuring (See Measurer) on a Saturday. =

CATER[1]. To cut or move diagaonally; to plough a field diagonally so the rain runs to the furrows; to cut across diagonally, caterways. *=+ (See Caterways).

CATER[2]. The Anglo-Saxon word for Grasshopper, used in Kent and from which the word cater, to move or cut diagonally arose. A Grasshopper is prone to hop diagonally so if a person moved at an angle they were also said to Cater. During the reign of Queen Elizabeth a London silversmith named Cater used to engrave a tiny grasshopper on examples of his craft as his sign or mark, some of which still exists. = (See Cater[1])

CATERWAYS, CATERWISE. From corner to corner; crossways; diagonally, slantingly; to walk diagonally across a field. Still used by farmers in the West Peckham area to describe the diagonal planting of hop gardens and orchards. Caterwise or Cater-Corner was said of an article, object, etc., placed across the angle of a room, etc. +=* (See Wented)

CAVING. The refuse of beans and peas after threshing; used for horse "meat" : food. Name principally used in West Kent. Called Tauf, Toff, in East Kent (which see, also Gullidge). +

CAWL. A hen coop; a wooden cage for broody chickens. +

CAXES. Pieces of bean stalk about eight inches long, used for catching Earwigs in Peach and other wall fruit trees; dry hollow plant stalks. + (See Cecksies).

CECKSIES. A piece of Elder hollowed out to catch Earwigs. = (See Caxes).

CEREMONY. A fuss; a bother; a commotion; something troublesome to plans; a disturbance. Still in use. *+= (See Bobbery, Set-Out).

CHALLOCK. Charlock (Brassica sinapistrum) = (See Kilk, Kinkle)

CHAMPIONING. A Christmas custom, when boys and men dressed as Mummers, singing carols and songs, went round the villages "championing". Possible name derived from the reference to St George the Champion, a leading character in this Yuletide Mummer's Play. It was also held in Sussex, other characters being Father Christmas, a Turkish Knight, and a Doctor. In Wiltshire the Mummers were called John Jacks and there was a fifth performer with an imitation humpback called John Jack. It is curious that in other parts of England this Mummers' Play took place at Easter, as still does in Midgley, Yorkshire. This is believed to have an ancient pagan origin, later adapted by the Christian church to symbolise the triumph of Good over Evil. But it is puzzling that St. George, whose saint's day is in April, should be connected in Kent with a Christmas play. (See Lerry, Lorry) +=

CHANGES. Changes of clothing, especially of underclothing, body linen, shirts or shifts. "I have jest put on clean changes". P+

CHANGK. To chew. +

CHARNAIL, CHARNELL. A hinge; possible char-nail, a nail to turn on. +

CHARRED. Drink that is soured in the brewing. If in brewing the water is too hot when it is first added to the malt, the malt is said to be charred and will not give its strength, hence beer that is brewed from it will soon turn sour. The word charred thus first applied properly to the malt and then passed to the drink brewed from it. To char is to turn and beer is still described as being "turned". P+

CHART. A rough, waste common. Pegge states: "A common rough ground over-run with shrubs, as Brasted Chart, Seal Chart, and indeed there runs a tract through this county which one may call the Chart of Kent; Westram (Westerham), Brasted, Whitley Shrubs (?), etc. Hence the Kentish expression "charty ground". Other Kent places with this name: Little Chart, Great Chart, Chart Sutton. P+*=

CHARTY. Rough uncultivated ground, like a chart. +P

CHASTISE. To catechize; to accuse; cross-question; to examine. +

CHAT[1]. A rumour; report; story; gossip; to talk idly; pass conversation. + (See Nabble)

CHAT[2]. To sort small potatoes; to chat potatoes is also to brut or break off shoots, as in brutting. =

CHATHAM CAP. A cap with a peak at the side. =

CHATHAMESE. The name for the local dialect peculiar to Chatham and the surrounding district and once quite distinctive from the Kent dialect of other areas. Originates from the time when the building of the first wooden ships for the Elizabethan Navy began on the river Thames and Medway. Chatham's population was then small and hundreds of tradesmen — carpenters, shipwrights, mastwrights, rope and sail makers were imported from small shipyards on both banks of the Thames. Many of these men were Cockneys or East London inhabitants and their accent, combined with the local tongue, gradually created "Chathamese". =

CHATS: Small, undersized, inferior potatoes. +*=

CHATSOME. Talkative +

CHATTING. Talking; gossiping. *= (See Chatsome, Guesting).

CHAVISH. Peevish; fretful. +

CHAW. Farm hand. =

CHEE. A pole or straight stick used for staking beans; as a chicken perch; a perch as a roost in the chicken houses. "Going to chee on a chee stick" was a hen roosting on a perch. "Cheeing" was also used as roosting: "There is a covey of Partridges cheeing at the bottom of the field". += (See Gee, Hen-Chee, Hen on a Chee Stick).

CHEE-BAT. A perch in a henhouse. = (See Chee).

CHEEGE. A frolic +

CHEER. Used in the greeting "What cheer?" instead of "How do you do?", or "How are you?" London corruption is "Wotcher". Now used universally. Probably it came into North Kent where it was commonly used formerly through Cockney or London workmen's influence. +*=

CHEERLY. Cheerfully. +

CHEESE BUG. A Wood Louse. + (See Monkey Pea, Pill Bug, Pea Bug, Slater).

CHEF. The part of a plough on which the share is placed and to which the reece is fixed. +

CHERRY APPLES. Crabs or Choke Cherries. +

CHERRY BEER. A type of drink made from Cherries. Cherry Brandy? Pudding-pies (which see) and cherry-beer were usually eaten and drunk at the Easter feast. +

CHICKENSTRAP. Corruption of "Kicking Strap" around a horse's hind quarters to dissuade it from kicking out; part of the harness when a horse is in a trap or a light-heavy cart. =

CHIDLINGS. Chitterlings; the smaller intestines of a pig; cooked pigs' entrails. +* In general use.

CHILLERY. Chilly; rather cold. +

CHILL-WATER. Lukewarm water. + (See Cold)

CHILTED. A variant of chilled; meaning badly affected by the cold; health indisposition caused by exposure to cold, damp or draughts; cold to the touch. + (See Chillery).

CHIMLEY. Chimney. *=

CHINCH. To point or fill up gaps between bricks, tiles, etc., with mortar. +

CHIOOP. To belabour; to grumble at; to nag at; to noisily tell off; to moan at. If a man was late home for dinner, perhaps through being in the public house or where he should not have been, his wife would chioop at him. Sometimes also said as Chipe. (I have heard this stated at Gee-up. "His wife won't half give him gee-up when he gets home".

CHIP. A light, punnet-like type of basket of twelve pounds with a metal handle to contain cherries for market. = (See Trug, Punnet).

CHITTER. The "Jenny" Wren (Troglodytes troglodytes). +

CHIZZEL, + CHIZZLE. G Bran.

CHOATY. Chubby; broad-faced; plump-looking. "He's a choaty boy". P + G

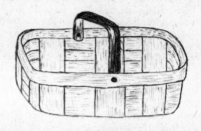

Chip

CHOCK. To choke; to fill tight. Anything over-full, full to the brim, is still said to be "chock-full" or "choke-full". P+

CHOCKERS. Hob-nailed, sprigged or steel-tipped kind of workmen's boots or heavy footwear. †*= (See Choggers, Choppers)

CHOFF. Stern; morose. +

CHOG. An apple core; a lump of rough wood; a grubbed-out hop hill was also a chog. =

CHOGGERS. As Chockers. =

CHOICE. Careful of; to set great store by anything. +

CHOP. To swap; to exchange. "Don't keep chopping and changing". =

CHOPPERS. As Chockers; Choppers was used in North Kent when such heavy boots were used to kick a person's feet from under him in a brawl or to hack or trip a man in a game of football. If a football player regularly used this method of fouling by chopping them over with his Chockers or Choggers he was nicknamed "Chopper". =*†

CHOP-STICKS. Cross-sticks to which the lines are fastened in Pout fishing. +

CHRIST-CROSS. Now Criss-Cross. "Christ-Cross Row" was the name for a child's alphabet on a horn book; name from the cross which was placed at the beginning of the row of letters; also the name for the signature of a person who used this mark, made by crossing two lines, because they could not write. +=

CHUCK[1]. A chip; a chunk; a short, thick clubbed piece of wood, for burning. P+

CHUCK[2]. The chips made by sharpening the ends of hop poles. +

CHUCK[3]. A large, thick piece of bread and cheese. +

19

CHUCK-HEADED, CHUCKLE-HEAD-ED. Stupid; doltish; simple-minded; wooden-headed. P+ (See Buffle-headed, Looby)

CHUFF. Chubby; fat. P+ (See Choaty)

CHUFFER. Able to eat a considerable quantity of food at one time; someone with a large appetite. †

CHUMMIE. A chimney sweep. +

CHUNK[1]. A hunk; a piece; a portion. Now in general use. P+*= (See Chuck, Hunk, Snowl)

CHUNK[2]. A log of wood or other piece of timber. +

CHUNTER, CHUNTERING. To grumble; grumbling. †

CHURCHING. To describe the church services generally and not the particular service for mothers after they have given birth to a baby and it is taken for baptism. The latter definition is still used. +

CLABBY. Hard. Tortoiseshell is clabby-crusty. =

CLAD. A hard clod of earth. (See Clad-hoppers) =

CLADDERS. Throwing clods. A man cleaning out and removing refuse and mud from a pond caught one of several children throwing clods or lumps of earth at him and said to her: "Ye be one o' de girl cladders bairn ye?" i.e. "You are one of the girls throwing clods, ain't ye (be you not)?" =

CLADHOPPERS, CLODHOPPERS. Large, heavy boots worn for agricultural work, dyking, etc. In general use now. †*=

CLAGGY. Muddy; mucky; sticky. = (See Caggy)

CLAM. A rat trap, like a gin. +

CLAMP, CLUMP. A heap of turnips, mangolds or potatoes covered with straw and earth to preserve and protect them during the winter. (See Ring, Ringe). Pegge states it was also used for a heap of bricks ready for burning. P+*=

CLAMS. The marine rock and wood boring molluscs, the Pholas family, the Piddocks. +*=

CLAPPERS. Planks laid upon supports for pedestrians to walk on when roads were flooded. +

CLAPSE. A fastening; derived from clasp. + (See Waps).

CLARR. Claw; to grab; to snatch. =

CLAT. A Romney Marsh word meaning to remove the clots of dirt, wool, etc., from between the hind legs of sheep. + (See Dag)

CLATTER. To throw out wildly or in a noisy manner. = (See Cluther)

CLATTING. Removing soiled wool from sheeps' hindquarters with hand shears. = (See Dag, Dagging).

CLAVEL. A grain of corn free from the husk. + (See Clevel)

CLAYT. Clay or mire. G+

CLEAN. Wholly; entirely; completely. "He's clean gone that's certain". +

CLEANSE. To tun or put beer up into the barrel. P+

CLEDGE. Clay; stiff loam or land. + (See Dough).

CLEDGY. Sticky or stiff, usually applied to the condition of the soil, cledgy land being stiff land. GP+

CLEVEL, CLEVELS. As Clavel; a grain of corn free from the husk. Shaw states how it was a popular belief in East Kent that each clevel of wheat bears the likeness of Him who is the True Corn of Wheat (St. John xii, 24). He was told by an old man at Eastry, 1887, that the Brown Wheat shows it more than the White, because it is a bigger clevel. To see this likeness the clevel must be held with the seam of the grain from you. This is a similar belief to that of the mark of the Cross on the donkey's shoulder and the mark of the thumb and fore-finger in the head of a haddock. +G†*=

CLEVER. In good health. In reply to the question "How are you today?" it used to be replied "Well, thankee, not very clever yet", i.e., not very active, not able to do work requiring much exertion. +*=

CLIMBERS. Travellers Joy, Wild Clematis, Old Man's Beard (Clematis vitalba), that climbs rapidly up and over hedges and verge trees in the countryside. +

CLINKERS. The hard refuse cinders of a stove, forge or furnace, which have fused together in large lumps. In general use. + (See Burr)

CLIP. To shear a sheep. +=*

CLITE, CLYTE. Clay or mire (See Clayt) GP

CLITEY, CLYTEY. Clayey soil; clay-like; puggy; sticky. (See Dough) =

CLIVER. Cleavers or Goose-grass (Galium aparine). +

CLODGE. A lump of clay. +

CLOD HOE. A heavy, two-pronged

hoe with various purposes, such as making furrows, weeding, to heap up earth in rows of potatoes and when reversed could be used to hit and break up lumps or clods of earth to a tilth.† Also called a Clump Hoe (which see). (See Kent Hoe, Canterbury Hoe, Tommy Hoe, Corn Hoe, Half Mattock, Axe Een Mattock, Weald Hoe, Plate Hoe, Double-sider Hoe, Peck).

CLOMP. To stomp about noisily, especially in heavy boots. †*=

CLOSE. An enclosed yard or fenced-in field adjoining a farmhouse; a small lane; originally peculiarly used in Kent for a farmyard but now in general use for any enclosure. P+

CLOUT[1]. A clod or lump of earth in a ploughed field. +

CLOUT[2]. A blow with the palm of the hand; a smack. +*= (See Clump, Cuff, Dob, Larrup, Spat, Swipe).

CLUCK[1]. Broody. A hen that wants to sit being broody was said to be cluck; on cluck. A cluck hen : a broody hen. += (See Brimming Sow, Noony).

CLUCK[2]. Unwell. Originally used for livestock that were ailing, in particular hens, later used for humans who felt "a bit cluck", drooping and off-colour. P+ (See Noony)

CLUDGY. Heavy, of soil. Used by Hasted in "History and Topography of the County of Kent. =

CLUMMY. Clammy; hot, sticky weather. =

CLUMP[1]. As Clomp. †*=

CLUMP[2]. A heavy blow or smack. *=+ (See Clump Hoe, Cuff, Dob, Larrup, Swipe).

CLUMP[3]. To nail a new sole onto the old one on a shoe. †

CLUMP HOE. A two pronged hoe. So-named because it could also be used for clumping or knocking large sods or clods of earth to break them down; also called a Clod Hoe (which see). =†

CLUNG[1]. Withered; dull; out of temper; also used to describe a dullish, stubborn, stick-in-the-mud sort of person. +

CLUNG[2]. Damp, as hay when not quite ready. = (See Clung[1])

CLUNGEY. Used to describe limp and sticky hop branches caused by being left over-exposed to the sun or to being left detached from the bine. =

CLUNK. The same meaning as Clump (which see) in relation to heaviness; noisy movement; to fall heavily; give a naughty child a hard clout or smack. *=

CLUTHER[1], CLUTTER. A litter; heaps of bric-a-brac, but not necessarily rubbish or objects of no use. Anything untidy or in a muddle was in a clutter. "I wish he'd throw out some of this clutter" +*=

CLUTHER[2], CLUTTER. Variant of Clatter. A great noise; to make a noise generally, as by dropping things accidentally or knocking them together. "There was such a clutter when the pan shelf fell down". +*=

CLUTHER[3], CLUTTER. Used of the special sound made by Rabbits in their burrow just before they bolt out the hole. "I 'eerd 'im cluther", i.e. "I heard him make a noise" implying "therefore, he will soon make a bolt for it." +

COAL SHOOT. A coal scuttle. +

COARSE. Rough, windy, snowy weather. + "The weather's turning coarse". (See Corse)

COADCHER. Wealden for Cold-Cheer meaning a cold meal or a hot meal that had been allowed to go cold. The original dialect was Cold-Cheer but was corrupted to Coadcher, another example of laziness of speech due to Cold-Cheer taking too long to pronounce. †

COB. To throw gently or lightly. +

COBBELL, COBBLE. An icicle. + (See Aquabob, Cock-Bell, Cog-bell, Icily, Ice Candle)

COBBELIS. Icicles. = (See Cobbell)

COBBO. A freshwater fish, the Miller's Thumb or Bullhead (Cottus gobio) G (See Corbeau)

COB-IRONS. And-iron; irons standing in the hearth and intended to keep the brands and burning coals in their place; also the irons by which the spit is supported. + (See And-Irons, Brand-Irons)

COB-NUT. A game which consisted in pitching at a row of nuts piled in heaps of four, three on the bottom and one on top. All the nuts knocked down were the property of the pitcher. A large nut used for pitching was called the "Cob". Also played in Gloucestershire where it possibly originated. G (See Cob)

COCK-BELL. An Icicle. The "Bargrave MS. Diary", describing the weather in France in the winter of 1645 says: "My beard had sometimes yce on it as big as my little finger, my breath turning into many cock-bells as I walked". +P (See Cog-Bells, Cong-Bells)

COCKER. To spoil; to indulge; to pamper; to cosset; still in use in this definition; also used to describe selfish, cocky, priggish, spoilt children. +

COCKLE. A stove used in drying hops. +

CODDLE. To cuddle; to fuss over or mess about with; also work in a slow, desultory fashion. †

CODDLING. Fussing about with; messing about over some task or thing. †

CODDLER. A person who fusses. †

CODS. Pods, as in pea pods. =

CODWARE. Pulse growing in cods or pods. G (See Kidware, Pod-ware)

COGUE. A dram of brandy; a small drinking cup, used especially at sea. From the Welsh cawg, a bowl. P+

COG-BELL. An icicle. +P (See Cock-Bell)

COG-BELLS. Very short icicles hanging from tree twigs, buildings, etc., especially if they are dripping in a thaw and thus have a resemblance to Cong-Bells: (which see) drips from the human nose. †+=

COILER-HARNESS. The trace harness + (See Quiller, Quoiler, Vill Horse).

COLD. Used in the phrase "out of cold", meaning water is "Out of cold" when it has been slightly warmed and the chill taken off it. Not very warm but lukewarm. (See Chill-water). Also used in Finger-cold and Hand-cold (which see). P+

COLD PACKED. Term to describe slack-dried hops which when left in the kiln pack together in lumps. =

COLLAR. Smut in wheat. +

COLLAR-MAKER. A saddler whose chief work was on farms and who who was so-called because he chiefly made or mended horses' collars. +

COMB. An instrument used by thatchers to beat down the straw and afterwards smooth it. + Universal now.

COMBE. A valley. Occurs in a number of place names, such as Swanscombe, in Kent. P+

COME. Used in speech to refer to an approaching date or time to mark a previous event. On such a day or at such a time when it arrives. "It'll be seven wiks come Friday sin he were took bad." +

COME 'ITHER. Come hither; come here. An instruction by a waggoner to his horse. *=

COME OUT, COME OUT OF. An expression used in the sense of to belong to; where a person inhabits. Two old men the worse for drink and shouting; "We don't care if we do come out the spike" (which see). =

COMPOSANT. The bluish, luminescence, like a ball of fire, sometimes seen on the masts, yards and projections of ships at sea, as a result of electricity in the air; said to be a sign of coming squalls. Several may be seen on different parts of the same ship. +

CONCLUDE. To decide. "So he concluded to stay at home for a while." + In general use now.

CONE. To crack or split with the sun's heat, as timber is apt to do, as though a wedge has been inserted in it. P+

CONE-WHEAT. Bearded Wheat. +

CONG-BELLS[1]. (See Cock-Bell, Cog-Bells) Icicles. Sanders states Cong-Bells also applies to the icicles formed by frozen breath on a man's beard or moustache (See Cock-Bell) †=

CONG BELLS[2]. Drips of mucous from the nose caused by a cold in the head or by moisture droplets that have made their way into the nose from the eyes when weeping due to bitter cold winds. Cong is probably a corruption of the slang Conk for a nose, bells being used as the name for the drips of water or mucous, supposedly resembling bells, or small icicles (See Cog-Bells). Sometimes the N in Cong was dropped through laziness in the Wealden speech to make Cog-Bells (which see) for mucous drips according to Sanders. †

CONJURE. Not meaning to exercise magic tricks and sleight of hand but allied in the sense it means skilful in a task , or able to achieve such a task. "It was proper pretty to see they ship dogs conjure the sheep into they folds". "Missus, can you conjure up something to eat." †

CONNIVER. To stare; gape; look at. Curiously opposite in meaning to universally used "connive". +

CONQUERING. Bringing something under control; reducing their number. It was used when cutting down thistles, nettles, etc. "He's going so fast he'll soon conquer them". =

CONTANCROUS. Cantankerous; peevish; perverse; prone to quarrelling. P

CONTRAIRY. Disagreeable; unmanageable; cussed. Used elsewhere. +

CONTRAIRIWISE. On the contrary; exact opposite. +

CONYGARTHE. A rabbit warren. Lambarde, 1596 — "The Isle of Thanet and those easterne parts are the grayner; the Weald was the wood; Rumney Marsh is the meadow plot; the North Downes towards the Thaymse be the conygarthe or warreine." +

COOCH-FIRE. A bonfire (See Dencher-Pout) =

COOCH-GRASS. Couch Grass (Agropyron repens). Parish & Shaw commented: "A coarse, bad species of grass, which grows rapidly on arable land, and does much mischief with its long stringy roots". +*= (See Gootch Grass).

COOFER. To kill. =

COOFERED. Killed; dead. =

COOL-BACK. A shallow vat or tub, about twelve or eighteen inches deep, wherein beer was cooled. +

COORT. A small cart. G

COP[1]. A shock or sheaf of corn; a stack of hay or straw; a cock; a hay-cock; alternatively to heap anything in a pile; to throw together to make a rising pile, such as a pile of pea bine. P+

COP[2]. To catch; to sieze; also not much cop was not much good in quality. =

COPE. To muzzle an animal. To "cope" a ferret or fierce dog meant to guard or "sew up" its mouth. Pegge states "to cope a ferret, to sew up the creature's mouth". P+

COPSE. A term in marshy districts to describe a fence across a dyke which has no opening. +

CORBEAU. The fresh water fish, Miller's Thumb or Bullhead (Cottus gobio). +

CORD-WOOD. A pile of wood, such as split roots and trunks of trees stacked ready for use as fuel. A cord of wood measured eight feet long by four feet high by four feet thick. +

Corn Hoe

CORN HOE. A hoe with a very wide, large blade or plate, like a Plate Hoe in shape, on one side, six to seven inches wide, while on the opposite side of the eye was a narrow blade about one to one and a half inches wide. Used when fields of corn were hoed all over between the drills, the small blade being used to cut out docks, thistles, corn-cockle, etc., between the corn plants. = (See Clod Hoe, Double-sider Hoe, Axe Een Mattock).

CORSE[1]. A large cleaver, the largest used by a butcher. P

CORSE[2]. A long-shaped cutting chopper, blade equal width at top and bottom near handle, used for splitting firewood and small objects; not an axe. †=

COSSET. To caress; to fondle; to pet. +

COSSETY. Used to describe a child that has been petted and expects to be fondled and caressed. +

COST. A cost of lamb was a forequarter of lamb; a "rib". P+ (See Ribspare).

COSTER. A variety of Kent Apple. Hence coster-monger, an apple seller. =

COTCHELL, COTCHULL. Upset; distressed; disturbed from normal. =†

COTCHERING. Gossipping. +(See Chatting, Guesting).

COTERELL. A raised mound in marshes to which shepherds and lookers and the sheep can retire when the salterns are submerged by the incoming tide. +

COTTON. To agree together or please each other, or to come to a decision after an explanation. "They cannot cotton no-how". "I can't cotton on to what you mean". To "cotton on" to something means to understand. P+*=

COUPLING BAT. A piece of round wood attached to the bit or ringle of two plough-horses to keep them together. + (See Bat)

23

COURT[1]. A small cart (See Coort). P

COURT, COURT LODGE. A manor house, where the court leet of the manor was held. Now used often incorrectly to describe a new building, but sometimes this has been built on the site of an old one entitling it to this description. Parish & Shaw state "Thus Eastry Court is the old house, standing on the foundations of the ancient palace of the Kings of Kent wherein is held annually the Court of the Manor of Eastry". +

COURT-CUPBOARD. A sideboard or cabinet used to display the silver flagons, cups, beakers, ewers, etc., i.e. the family plate; distinguished from the "livery cupboard" or wardrobe. +

COURT FAGGOT. A name given to best and choicest kind of faggot. +

COVE KEYS. The Cowslip (Primula veris). Also known in Kent as Lady-Keys, Culver-Keys, Paigle, Pegle, Horsebuckle (which see). +*=

COVE. A part of a building; the shelter which is formed by the projection of the eaves of a house acting as a roof to an out-building; a shed; a lean-to or low building with a shelving roof, joined to the wall of another. Pegge states "when the eeves of the house are brought down lower, to shelter or cover a room underneath; a low building joyning to the wall of another, upon which the rafters lean and at the upper end are supported by it." PG+

COVED. Used to describe a room, as for example, in an attic room, where the walls are not perpendicular, but slant to form the sides and roof; something with sloping sides was said to be coved. +

COVEL. A water tub with two ears. +

COVEN. Sloped; slanting; applied to a sloping ceiling, a coven ceiling. + (See Cove, Coved)

COVERTLID, COVERLYD. A counterpane; the outer covering of the bed which lies above the blankets. +

COW[1]. A pitcher. +

COW[2], COWL. The moveable wood top on the chimney of the hop oasthouse or malt kiln, usually made and erected by Kentish wheelwrights. Pegge states "The wooden thing put over the chimney of a hop-host or malthouse, which turns with the wind, and prevents smoking; it means cowl, as "a friar's cowl."" P+*=

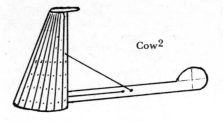

Cow[2]

COW-CRIB. The square manger for holding hay, etc., which stands in the straw yard and is so constructed as to be low at the sides and high at the corners. +

CRACKLING. The crisp of roast pork. In universal use now. =* (See Crup)

CRACK-NUT. A Hazel nut. Still in use to denote this nut from other nuts, Brazil Nut, etc. +*=

CRAMMER. A lie; an untruth. =

CRAMP NAME. Used to describe Christian names considered pretentious. =

CRAMP WORD. A long or difficult word to understand, spoken by persons from other counties. "Our new parson, he's out of the sheeres, and he uses so many of these here cramp words". +

CRANK[1]. To mark crosswise. +

CRANK[2]. Merry; cheery; pleased. "Missus is mighty crank today". +G

CRANK[3], CRANKY[1]. A boat or ship over-masted, apt to roll and in danger of over-setting and capsizing; once a common sea term also. =

CRANKY[2]. Used to describe someone light-headed from drinking; an eccentric person; someone not entirely mad or lunatic but unstable or given to out-of-ordinary behaviour. *= (See Crank[2], Cranky[3])

CRANKY[3]. Simple; foolish; dull-witted; mad; crazy; sometimes used of an imbecile. "Poor lad, they had to take him away 'cause he went cranky". *= (See Cranky[2])

CRAP. For crop. "a crap of corn". P

CRASS. Much out of temper; irritable. = (See Curs, Grand-Crass)

CRAY RING. The ring on the sneath

Cray Ring

of a scythe into which the blade is fixed and wedged. *= (See Sickle, Tray Ring).

CREAM. To crumble, shatter. Hops when they are too ripe or dried and crumble to pieces are said to "cream". P+

CREATING. Making a fuss over nothing important; deliberately causing a disturbance or commotion; becoming annoyed over a trifling thing usually; making a fuss in anger. *=

CREEPING JESUS. A person who shuffles about; shy and quiet in movement; possibly originated from monks walking about with a slow gait. When a person crept up on you and made no noise to indicate their coming it was said to them "You are a creeping jesus". *= (See Preter Grievous)

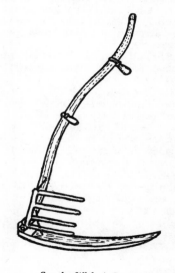

Scythe With A Creet

CREET. A cradle or framework of wood, placed on a scythe when used to cut corn. + (See Bow).

CRIPS. Crisp. A common transposition used in rural areas. + (See Ax)

CRIPT. Depressed; out of spirits; feeling forlorn. + (See Cruppish)

CROCK1. To put away; hide; lay by; save up; bread used to be "crocked". "Ye'd better by half give that butter away, instead of crocking it up till its no use to nobody". +

CROCK2. An earthenware pan or pot found in most kitchens and used for keeping butter, salt, etc. Large crocks with lids were used for containing bread, cake, etc. A well-known superstition referring to this object is that if a person goes to the place where the end of a rainbow rests they will find a crock of gold buried. P+*=

CROCK BUTTER. Salt butter which has been put into earthenware crocks to keep during the winter. Alternatively, during summer months when milk was plentiful for buttermaking through grass being more lush than in winter, the surplus butter was salted, placed in crocks and buried deep in the earth or put in underground ice-chambers or ice "houses" to keep, being taken out in winter for consumption or sale. +

CROFT. A vault. +

CROOCH. Crouch; to bend. =*

CROP. The craw or maw of a fowl or bird, such as a Pigeon. P*=

CROSHABELL. A courtesan; a low woman; a prostitute; a woman who sells her favours. +

CROW. The fat adhering to a pig's liver; "liver and crow" was a common term and they were eaten together. P+

CROWFISH. The Common Three-Spined Sticklebat (Gasterosteus aculeatus). + (See Prickybat, Tittlebat)

CRUMMY. Filthy; dirty; rough-looking; untidy; used to describe a person, his or her clothing, a room, furniture, etc. †*=

CRUNDLE. Crumble; to crumple; to crush; break into small pieces; to disintegrate. †

CRUNDLED. Crumbled; crushed. †

CRUNDLING. Crumbling. †

CRUP1. The crisp, hard skin of a roasted pig or of roast pork; a crisp spice-nut. P+*= (See Crackling)

CRUP2. Crisp; used to describe snow or frost on grass, etc. "You'll have a nice walk as the snow is very crup". +

CRUP3. A nest. "There's a wopsies crup in that doated (rotten) tree". +

CRUP4. Pettish; peevish. "You are very crup". P (See Cruppish)

CRUPPISH. Peevish; out of sorts; run down; tired out. A man who has a hangover from drinking the previous night would sometimes say in the morning "I feel cruppish". +

CUBBY BIRD. The Jenny or Ginny Wren. =

CUCKOO. A fool; a simpleton. "Poor lad. He's a cuckoo". =

CUCKOO BREAD. The wild plant, Wood Sorrel. (Oxalis acetosella) +

CUCKOO CORN. Corn sown to late in the Springtime. +

CUCKOO FLOWER. A wild plant Lady's Smock or Milkmaids (Cardamine pratensis). Sometimes was also applied to Cuckoo Pint (Arum maculatum). *=

CUCKOO'S BREAD AND CHEESE. The seeds of the wild plant, Mallow (Malva sylvestris) +

CUCKOO'S EYES. A wild plant Germander Speedwell (Veronica chamaedrys). *=

CUCKOO'S MATE. A summer visiting bird, the Wryneck (Jynx torquilla torquilla). Now in general use. *=

CUFF. A lightly administerd hit, smack, or blow. = In general use now. (See Clout, Clump, Dob).

CULCH. Lumber; stuff; rubbish; rags; bits of thread; any and every kind of refuse, i.e. broken slates, stones, littering a place. Broken seashells laid on the oyster beds during breeding them for the spat to adhere to is still known as culch. P+G*= (See Pelt, Sculch, Reffidge, Scutchell).

CULL[1]. The culls of a flock are the worse examples, picked out to be parted with. "To cull" still means to pick and choose, select. P+G*

CULL[2]. Another name for the fresh water fish Bullhead or Miller's Thumb (Cottus gobio). G (See Cobbo, Corbeau).

CULVER KEYS. The wild plant, the Cowslip. P+ (See Cove Keys).

CUMBERSOME. Awkward, inconvenient; unwieldy; clumsy; heavy. +* Still used generally.

CURRANT BERRIES. Red or Black Currants. P+ (See Gayzels).

CURS. Cross; surly; shrewish; possibly variant of Crass (which see). P+

CUT. Nearly drunk; tipsy; light-headed; sometimes used to indicate completely intoxicated. "He's three parts cut", i.e. "He's nearly drunk". *=

CUTTING DIDOES. Cutting capers; playing tricks and pranks; fooling about. = (See Didos)

CYPRESS, CYPRUS. A material like crepe. +

D

DABBERRIES. Gooseberries. A corruption of Dewberries, a name sometimes given to Gooseberries. P+

DABBING OUT. To wash clothes occasionally; to do it on several days instead of all at once. The latter is common practice now, with the convenience of washing machines, but not in the past when Monday was washing-day and then fuel was expended for boiling water. A "dabber out" was looked down on by other wives. "She is one of those women who is always dabbing out."=

DADDLES. The hands. Spoken to a child "Come and have your daddles washed." = (See Dandymen, Peepers, Weekers, Handy-Pandies, Donnies).

DAFFY[1]. A large number or quantity was described as "a rare daffy of people, etc."; occasionally also used to describe a small quantity of spirits. +=

DAFFY[2]. Daft, silly; mentally unbalanced; stupid. = (See Cuckoo, Cranky)

DAG[1]. To remove the clots or dags of wool, dirt, excreta, from between the hind legs of sheep. + (See Clat)

DAG[2]. A lock of wool that hangs at the tail of a sheep and becomes bedraggled in dirt, etc. + (See Dag[1], Daggings, Dag-Wool)

DAGGING. Removing soiled wool from sheeps' hindquarters with hand shears. = (See Dag[1], Clatting).

DAGGINGS. The fouled clippings of wool from the tail area of a sheep. = (See Dag[1], Dag[2], Dag-Wool)

DAG-WOOL. Waste wool, cut off in trimming the sheep. + (See Dag, Daggings).

DAGG. A large pistol. + (See Caliver)

DAMPING. Meaning it is lightly drizzling but not actually raining drops. +*=

DANCE. A rarity. "It's dance to him". P

DANDYMEN. The hands. Usually used by a mother to a child. = (See Daddles, Handy-Pandies, Weekers, Peepers)

DANG. An alternative for "Damn" as a cuss word. + Used in other counties.

DANGLE. As Dang; an expletive, damn. =

DANIEL, DANNEL †, DANNULL. The smallest piglet in the litter was called the Daniel, or one of the other variations. Possibly as a reference to Daniel in the lion's den, in the case of the Daniel piglet it being the weakest having to survive against the rival stronger piglets. Less often used incorrectly to describe the smallest in a litter of kittens or puppies. †=* (See Anthony Pig, Dolly, Runt, Runtlet, Runtling).

DARVEL. Sanders refers to this word as Wealden-cum-gipsy for Devil, a combination of both Kentish Wealden dialect and Kentish gipsy language. †

DASH. To dash, to make besoms and brooms; hence name Broom-dasher (which see) =

DAT. That. =

DAWDY. Neat, dainty. "That's a dawdy little tool". =

DAWTHER1, DODDER1. To tremble or shake; to move in an infirm unsteady manner. "He is getting on now and caan't do s'much as he did but he manages just to dawther about in the shop a little otherwise". P+

Dawther

DAWTHER2, DODDER2. A pretty grass, sometimes still gathered for ornamental purposes. It has loose panicles of flowers and seems to tremble with every slight breath of wind, hence its associated dialect name with Dawther, Dodder for a trembling, shaking elderly person. The grass is more widely known elsewhere as Quake Grass, Quaking Grass (Brizia media) or Totter Grass. P+=* (See Doddling Grass, Doddering Grass).

DAWTHERY. Doddery; shaky; trembling; feeble. Used of elderly people

He begins to get very dawthery". + (See Doddery, Ampery, Hampery)

DE. The. "De old mare's going home".

DEAD-ALIVE. Dull; uninteresting; monotonous; when applied to somewhere, a remote village, for instance: "Its a dead-alive place"; or to mean dull, simple sometimes stupid, when applied to people: "He's so dead-alive". +*=

DEAD-MEN. The large thick poles at the edge of a hop garden set to lean back and take the strain of the whole garden. They are anchored by wire hawsers. *=

DEAL1. A part; a portion. Anglo-Saxon dael, meaning a part, portion, and Anglo-Saxon daelan, meaning to divide, thus it is still used in the expression "to deal cards", i.e. to give fair portion or issue to each. P+*=

DEAL2. A nipple, of a sow, bitch, vixen, etc. Pegge states it as "nipples". P+ (See Deals)

DEALS. The nipples of a sow, bitch, vixen, rat; cows' teats. = (See Deal2)

DEAR HEARTS-ALIVE. An exclamatory utterance. = (See Gracious Hearts-Alive, Hearts-Alive, Saints-Alive).

DEATH. Deaf. P+

DEATHNESS. Deafness. +

DEEK. A dyke or ditch. P+ (See Dick)

DEEKERS. Workmen who dig, clean and maintain ditches (deeks), dig "grips" (furrows) to drain off surface water and build "bays" to dam ditches and retain water. + (See Bay, Deek, Grip).

DEN1. Then. =

DEN2. (See DENE) P+

DENCHER. A slow bonfire. It was considered wrong and not usual, as it is now the practice, to allow a fire to blaze away on a field, such as a stubble field. To dowse or dencher it so that it smouldered made the ash residue more valuable as fertilizer it was supposed, in the past. = (See Denture, Dencher-Pout)

DENCHER-POUT, DENSHER-POUT. A pout or pile of weeds, rubbish, refuse, stubble rakings, made in the fields for burning. + (See Cooch-Fire, Pout)

DENE, DENNE. A wooded or wood-lined valley with pasturage; also anciently a measure of land. The word "den" occurs frequently as the terminating part of village and parish names, such as Benenden, Bidden-den, Horsmonden, Smarden, Tenter-den, etc. Pegge states: "a dene of land" as from Somner's Antiq. Cant. edition 1703: "The manor of Len-ham, consisting of 20 ploughlands and 13 denes". Though this be not peculiar to Kent alone . . . for there is scarce a county in England but what has some town or village, whose name is compounded of this word . . . yet I think there is no-where such a nest of them as in the County of Kent, where they are found in many places, but nowhere so thick sown as in the Weald, etc. etc." From Anglo-Saxon denu, a valley, a den. P+

DENIAL. A hindrance; a set-back; detriment; draw-back. "It's a denial to a farm to lie so far off the road". P+

DENTURE. Variation of Dencher (which see). To "denture" a field the turf was cut off, put in heaps and burnt. Where this happened the field was sometimes named Denture Field. In Sussex a Densher Plough was an instrument for turf cutting. (See Pout) =†

DERACINATE. To pluck up by the roots. =

DESTINY. Destination. He's already set off for his destiny". =

DEVIL-IN-THE-BUSH. The garden flower Nigella or Love-in-a-Mist. +

DEVIL'S THREAD. The parasitic wild plant, the Lesser Dodder (Cuscuta epithymum), which grows in fields, waste places, verges, its clinging threads tangled around the stems of its host plant, such as Furze, Thyme, Heather and Clover. Also has the names of Hellweed, Devil's Root, Hell Root used formerly by botanists and rural people. +

DEWLAPS. Coarse woollen stockings buttoned over others to keep the legs warm and dry. +

DIBBER. (See Dibble). Usually used for planting out cabbage plants, etc. P+*=

DIBBLE. An implement, pointed at one end, sometimes with a handle at the other, for making holes in the soil wherein plants or seeds are set. Until the early 17th century it was a method used as an alternative to broadcasting the seed and by using a

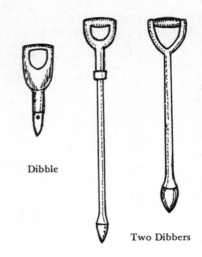

Dibble

Two Dibbers

dibble or dibber the corn could be sown in straight rows that were easier to hoe out weeds. Corn dibbers were usually made of iron or wood, the iron ones having either an iron or wood handle. P+*=

DICK, DIK. A dyke or ditch. P+ (See Deek, Water Table).

DICKY1, DICKEY. Out of sorts, feeling poorly; unwell; miserable; sluggish +*= (See Cruppish)

DICKY2. A term of endearment. =

DICKY-HEDGE-POKER. The shy gar-den bird, the Dunnock, Accentor or Hedge Sparrow, (Prunella modularis occidentalis), so-named because of its unobtrusive ways of food gathering in hedge bottoms and among plants and shrubs. +*= (See Jimmy Hedge Moper)

DIDAPPER, DIVEDAPPER. The Dab-chick or Little Grebe (Podiceps ruficollis), a water bird of ponds and lakes, dabble being the diminutive of dab, dabble meaning to play in the water, while dapper means dip-per, from the diving actions of the bird on the water when hunting for food. Sometimes the word is erron-eously applied to the Moorhen, an-other water bird. P+

DIDDLE-O. Simple-minded; senile. =

DIDOS, DIDOES. Capers; pranks; tricks. "Dreckly ye be backturned there he be a-cutting all manners o' didoes." + (See Cutting Didos)

DIED-ON. Passed away; already dead. =

DILLIN. Used by schoolchildren in a

derogatory sense to describe another pupil with whom they are displeased. =*

DIMPSEY. Twilight. =

DIN-A-LITTLE. Corruption of "within-a-little"; almost; nearly. "I knows din-a-little where I be now". +

DINKY. Sweet and fresh; clean. "The washing smells nice and dinky". =

DIP. A tallow candle made by dipping the wick in the melted tallow. Now used generally. =

DISABIL. Unkempt; untidy; with clothes, hair, etc., in disorder. Almost certainly a Kent dialect word that has a French origin, from French Déshabillé; deschevele, dishevelled. +

DISGUISED. Tipsy; slightly drunk; intoxicated. "I'd raather not say as he was exactly drunk but he seemed as though he was jes' a little bit disguised".

DISH-MEAT. Spoon meat, i.e., soft food which does not require cutting up and can be eaten with a spoon, usually for invalids or young children. Meat spooned up in a stew. GP +=

DISHWASHER. The bird, Pied Wagtail (Motacilla alba yarrellii), found in or near wet and damp places, rivers, lakes. +P*= (See Peggy, Peggy-Dishwasher)

DISSIGHT. Something which makes a person, place or object unsightly; a blemish; a defect. "Them there ruined cottages are a great dissight to the street". +

DO. To "do" for anyone meant to keep house for them. In modern slang it means to cause them an injury or harm in some way. +*-

DOATED. Rotten; decayed; usually applied to timber or trees. + (See Doited).

DOB. To put down, also to clump, hit, smack, beat. +*=

DOBBIN1. Temper. "He lowered his dobbin", i.e. "lost his temper". +

DOBBIN2. Unhappiness; tearfulness; about to cry. It was usually applied to a child, especially a baby, when it changed from a smiling expression to about to cry, or actually crying. "There, there now. Don't hang your dobbin down" : "There, there now, don't cry like that". Possibly this variation arose from the way a horse (See Dobbin3) puts its head down over a hedge or fence when sometimes standing still and may look rather lonely, sad and unhappy, the baby about to cry lowering its chin before crying as the horse lowers its head. =

DOBBIN3. Name for a horse, sometimes a patient old farm horse; used as a familiar or nickname, instead of a human Christian name. "Come on, dobbin, time for your bait". = (See Dobbin2, Baited). Now in general use.

DODDER. (See Dawther1, Dawther2).

DODDERING GRASS. The Quake Grass (Briza media). = (See Dawther2, Doddling Grass).

DODDERY. Shaky; unsteady. = (See Dawthery)

DODDLE. To dawdle †=* (See Mooch)

DODDLING GRASS. The Quake Grass (Briza media) = (See Doddering Grass, Dawther, Dodder).

DODDLUMS. A game of skittles where the ball is held captive by a cord hanging from a post and the skittles are arranged on a tray upon a table. =

DODGER1. A night cap. +

DODGER2. A tool used for extracting and removing weed plants, such as thistles. = (See Spud)

DODMAN. A Snail (See Hodman-Dod, Snag). =

DOG1. To follow; to "dog" a person was to follow close in their footsteps, on their heels, like a dog does; to track someone; to persevere until caught. =* Still in universal use.

DOG2. An instrument for pulling up hop poles. (See Hop Dog, Hop Jack)

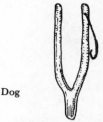

Dog

DOG3. An instrument made of natural forked Ash four feet or so long, used with a hook or length of tied string by thatchers for carrying the straw or yelms up to the required place on the roof when thatching; also known generally as a Jack, Bow or Yack. +=*

DOGGED. Well-dressed. A woman "dogged up" to go out would be wearing her best clothes and hat, with make-up; equally applied to men. =

DOG-TIRED. Very tired; worn-out; exhausted. =

DOG'S DAISY. A very common plant of fields and waste places, the Stinking Mayweed (Anthemis cotula). Supposed to have this dialect name because it blooms during the Dog-Days, but flowers from June to September. Not to be confused with the Dog Daisy (Chrysanthemum leucanthemum), the Ox-Eye Daisy being its better known name. +

DOINGS. Small tasks and odd jobs. When a person only kept a small farm and let himself and his team and implements out for hire for such tasks to farmers wih larger farms he was said to do doings for people. P+

DOITED. (See Doated). +

DOLE1. The stump of an old tree left in the ground; a boundary-stone +

DOLE2. A set parcel or distribution; an alms. + (See Deal)

DOLE3. A bale or bundle of nets. +

DOLEING. Almsgiving. "To dole out" or "doleing out" was to be handing out or making a charitable gift, whether in food, money, etc. + (See Deal, Dole).

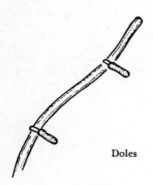

Doles

DOLES. The short handles which project from the bat of a scythe and by which the mower holds it when mowing. The parts of a scythe are 1. the scythe proper or cutting blade; 2. the trai-ring and trai-wedge by which it is fastened to the bat; 3. the bat or long staff by which it is held when sharpening and which is cut peeked so that it cannot slip and 4. the doles as already described. +

DOLE STONE. A landmark or boundary post + (See Dowal, Dowl)

DOLING. A fishing boat with two masts, each carrying a sprit-sail. Boys in his "History of Sandwich" describes them as "ships for the King's use, furnished by the Cinque Ports." +

DOLLOP1. Commonly known now to mean a lump of something soft or semi-fluid, such as a dollop of cream, or a piece or portion of something such as pudding or cake. +*=

DOLLOP2. A long length of Bramble growth. =

DOLLOP3. A canvas bag of a special type used by Kentish smugglers on the backs of their horses. Parish & Shaw state: "A parcel of tea sewn up in canvas for smuggling purposes". +=

DOLLOURS. Alternative spelling to Dolours, used to describe the wind when it falls or abates. G (See Dolours, Blowing Up)

DOLLY. The smallest pig in a litter. = (See Daniel, Anthony Pig, Runtlet)

DOLLYMOSH. To demolish; destroy; entirely ruin or spoil; to scotch a plan or scheme. If something was accidentally broken, such as a cup being dropped, it was said to be "dollymoshed". +

DOLOURS. Used to express the moaning of the wind when blowing up for rain. P+ (See Blowing Up)

DOLPHIN. The Aphis or Greenfly that attacks roses, honeysuckle and other garden flowers, shrubs, fruit trees and vegetables. Also applied to the Blackfly that is a pest on beans. P+

DONNARD. A half-bushel measure for corn, etc. =

DONNIE, DONNY. A hand. Used only in speech concerning babies or very small children. † (See Daddles, Dandymen, Shake-a-Donnie)

DONNIES. The hands. Used as Donnie. † (which see).

DOODLE-SACK. The bagpipes. + Used elsewhere.

DORICK. A frolic; a lark; a spree; a trick. "Now then, none of your doricks". +

DOSS1. To sit down rudely. +

DOSS2. A dose, such as of medicine. = (See Dost)

DOSSET. A very small quantity of any liquid. +*=

DOST. A dose, such as of medicine. = (See Doss)

DOUBLE-SIDER HOE. A hoe with Half-Mattock shaped blades on each side of the eye about six inches long, but one blade being wider than the other. = (See Axe Een Mattock).

Double Sider Hoe

DOUGH. A thick clay, resembling bread dough. P+

DOVER-HOUSE. A necessary house, a lavatory; a convenience; a wash-house. + (See Necessary House)

DOWAL, DOWL. A boundary stone or post. + (See Dole Stone)

DOWELS. Low lying marshes. +

DOWN. A stretch of high open ground, usually chalkhill. The term is not only applied in Kent, but is more frequently used in this county, with reference to the chalk downland and North Downs. It is also applied as the terminating part of several village and parish names in Kent, i.e. Harble-down, Leysdown, etc., also Chart-ham Downs, Barham Downs, etc. There is also the maritime term, The Downs, for open sea off Deal. P*=

DOWNWARD. The wind is said to be "downward" when it is in the south. P+ (See Out, Upward)

DOWTY. A decaying, rotten tree. "That tree is a bit dowty". =

DOXEY. A girl or woman with a low reputation was referred to as a "doxey". =

DRAB. To drub; flog; beat; pummel; strike. +

DRAG. A pile of thorn bushes wired into a bundle and weighted with a heavy stone, slat or timber, then harnessed to a horse for dragging across a field in Springtime. = (See Dredge)

DRAGGLETAIL. A slut; a slatternly female; a dirty, untidy, unkempt and slovenly woman. The nastiest insult that formerly could be spoken to or written about a woman living in a rural community in Kent was to call her a draggletail, due to a draggle-tailed sheep having a filthy excreta covered hind quarters and tail; also meant a long-tailed sheep; and a long-tailed old-fashioned skirt.

Dragon's Tongue

DRAGON'S TONGUE. The purple and yellow Stinking Iris, Gladdon or Roast-Beef Plant (Iris foetidissima), that occurs in woodland on the North Downs, chiefly near Boxley. +*=

DRAUGHT. The bar, billet or spread bat, to which the traces of all the horses were fixed when four were being used at the plough. +

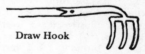

Draw Hook

DRAW HOOK. An implement for cleaning out dykes and freeing them of weeds, consisting of a three-tined fork, bent round so as to form a hook and fitted to a long handle. +

DRAW-WELL. A hole or well sunk for the purpose of obtaining chalk. +

DRAY. A term applied to a place where there is a passage through or across the slime and mud. +

DREAN1. A drain. +

DREAN2. To drip, after being soaked wet through during rain. "He was just dreaning wet when he came in". + (See Sobbed)

DREANING, DREENING. Wet through; soaked to the skin, wring-ing wet; draining. =

DRECKLY-MINUTE. Immediately; directly; at once; without delay; straight away; contracted from "dir-ectly this minute". + (See Minute)

DREDGE1. A bush harrow; to drag a

bundle of bushes over a field like a harrow. + (See Drag)

DREDGE[2]. To catch with a drag-net, the word peculiar to Oyster fishermen. P

Dressing Knife

DRESSING KNIFE. A sharp knife used to cut bine bases and rootstock, when dressing the roots by cutting away any diseased roots and pruning them by reducing the numbers of underground runners. The knives were often made from old Sickle or Scythe blades by the user. = (See Tommy Hoe).

DRIFT. A unit of a hop garden comprising a certain number of rows of hop hills and bines. *= (See Hill).

DRILL. To waste away; to become weaker; sickly; applied to plants, animals or humans. "It's terrible to see poor master becoming so drill". +

DRINKING. A refreshment between main meals used by the ploughman and labourers consisting of a piece of bread and some cheese and a bottle or mug of beer. When they came off the fields at ten in the morning and six in the evening for this they "took their drinking". PG

DRIV. To drive. "I want ye to driv the cattle". +

DRIVE-BUNDLE. Pegge states: "A drive-bundle, when a horse first carries one, and then returns to fetch another; that is, in carrying on double-horse". P

DRIZZLE. To bowl a ball close to the ground. + (See Trull)

DROITS. Rights; dues; customary payments. PG+

DROKE. Duckweed, the green plants that very commonly form a covering surface on still, standing water, such as small ponds. +

DROPHANDKERCHIEF. The game usually also known as "Kiss in the Ring". +

DROP-ROD. To go "drop-rod" was an expression used of carrying hay or corn to the stack, when there were two wagons and only one team of horses. The load of one was then left at the stack and the horses taken out of the rods or shafts and sent to bring the other wagon from the field to the stack. +

DROSE, DROSLEY. To gutter; spoken of a candle flaring away and causing the wax to run down the sides. "The candlestick is all drozed", i.e. "covered with running grease". +

DROSINGS. Dregs of tallow. + (See Drose)

DROVE WAY. A road for driving cattle to and from marshes and meadows where they pastured. +

DROZE. As Drose. The candle drozes, the candle melts in burning. G

DRUG. To hang out washing to drip if weather not right to actually dry it. =

DRUMMER. An adult rabbit that "drums" with its hind legs and feet on the ground when it is surprised and runs to its burrow entrance to warn other rabbits within the vicinity of danger. †*=

DRUV. Driven. "We wunt be druv against our will". +

DRYTH[1]. Thirst; drought. "I call cold tea very purty stuff to squench your dryth." +P

DRYTH[2]. Dry; soil that had dried after winter, rain, etc. When it had become dry and hard farm workers commented "The dryth is in the ground." =

DUBBY. Lavatory. =

DUFF[1]. A dark-coloured clay. +

DUFF[2]. A variant of the word dough and used for a pudding made with flour and water. When plain it was called "Hard Duff" or "Hard Dick". When fruit was included it was called "Spotted Duff" or "Spotted Dick". Word still used as Plum Duff. *=

DULL. Blunt; said of knives, saws, axes, anything with a cutting edge; to make blunt. "As for fish-skins, tis a terr'ble thing to dull your knife", used in this meaning by Folkestone fishermen. =

DULLING UP. Becoming overcast, dull and cloudy. =

DUMBLEDORE. A Bumble Bee or the Dor Beetle; also means to boom or hum, as does such a Bee. +

DUMMYERKER. Suet duff, meat, fruit, jam, or even home-made bread or cake that was a bit too solid were all "dummyerkers". =

DUMMYORKER. Cake. = (See Dummyerker)

DUN-CROW. The Hooded Crow (Corvus cornix)

DUNK. To throw down, up, or upon; to dump; to place. †

DUNNAMANY. Meaning "Don't know how many". An example of the fusion of a sentence to form one word. +† (See Dunnamuch)

DUNNAMUCH. Meaning "Don't know how much". + (See Dunnamany).

DUNTY. Stupid; confused. It was also applied sometimes to mean, stunted, dwarfish. +

DURGAN-WHEAT. Bearded Wheat. +

DWARFS-MONEY. Ancient coins. A term more commonly used on the coast. + (See Bald Pates, Borrow Pence, Hegs Pence, Scimminger)

DWINDLE. A sickly child. "Ah, he's a terrible poor little dwindle, I doan't think he won't never come to much". + (See Dicky, Cruppish, Flue)

DYKERS. Workmen who make, clean and maintain dykes and ditches. + (See Deekers)

DYSTER. The pole of an ox-plough. + (See Neb)

E

EAR. To ear, to plough. P+

EARING, ERYNG. A day's ploughing; ploughing time. "Eryng of land three times" — Old Parish Book of Wye. "And yet there are five years in which there is neither earing nor harvest" — Gen. xlv. 6. P+

EARTH. To cover up with earth. In use still to describe earthing up or covering potatoes. +*=

EARYWIGS. Earwigs. = (See Pincherwig, Pinchywig)

EAXE. An ax or axle. + (See Ax)

ECHE. An eke or addition; supplement; augment; to increase. For example, an additional piece to a bell rope, to eke it out and make it longer. Also to make something, such as food or drink, divide between a large number by careful distribution,

to eke it out. Still in general use. +*=

ECKER. To stammer; to stutter. +

ECKERPIE. The Magpie (Pica pica) that makes a stuttering, chattering cry. = (See Ecker, Megpy).

EDDISH. Stubble. = (See Ersh, Gratten, Podder-Grotten)

EELM. The Elm Tree (Ulmus procera) + (See Ellum)

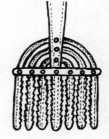

Iron Eel-Shears

EEL-SHEAR, EEL-SHEER. An iron pronged spear on an eight to ten feet long pole handle used by thrusting it into ponds and ditches to catch Eels in the serrations. +=

EEN¹, END. To cross a field one way in cultivation; to go to the other end of the field and back. =

EEN². An end; the end. =

E'EN A'MOST. Almost. It was generally used in speech with emphasis. +P (See All-a-Most)

EEND. A ploughing term; the end of a plough furrow; two furrows making one eend. +

EFFET. Name used for any of the three species of Newt; an Eft.From Anglo-Saxon efete. P+*+ (See Evit)

ELDERN. The Elder tree (Sambucus nigra) and its wood. +

ELEVENSES. A drink or light refreshment meal taken about eleven o'clock in the morning. In Sussex this was called "Elevener", similar to the Kentish Leavener (which see); in Essex it was called "Beevors" similar to the Kentish Bever, Beaver, Bevoir. Still commonly used universally. +*= (See Bait, Bever, Beevoirs, Leavener, Nuncheon).

ELLINGE1. Solitary; lonely; far from neighbours; ghostly; melancholy. From Ango-Saxon ellende. P+ (See Uncous, Unky)

ELLINGE2. A rough, dirty, wet night was said to be "ellinge". =

ELLUM. The Elm tree (Ulmus procera) = (See Eelm, Elvin)

ELVE. (See Hulve) =

ELVIN. The Elm tree (Ulmus procera) P+ (See Eelm, Ellum).

EMMET. An Ant. +P*= (See Ammets, Ammits, Ammuts, Horse Emmets)

EMMET-CASTES. Ant hills; ant heaps. + (See Casts, Casties)

ENNIT (See Annit) =

ENOW. Enough. "Have ye got enow?"+

ENTETIG. To introduce. P+

EPS. The Aspen tree or Asp tree (Populus tremula)

ERNFUL. Lamentable; sadly; sorrowfully. "Ernful bad" was lamentably bad; "Ernful tunes" were sorrowful tunes. P+G

ERSH. The stubble remaining after the corn has been cut. P+ (See Eddish, Gratten)

ESS. A large Earthworm. +

EVERYTHING SOMETHING. Something of everything; a mixture; all sorts of things. "She called me everything something", i.e. "She called me every name she could think of". Occasionally still used. +*=

EVIT. Used for a Newt; pronounced usually as Effet, with the "v" soft. = (See Effet)

EWE-LOCK. A coupling used for connecting an alley-bodge or a trailer to a horse or rear of another vehicle for towing. =

EYESORE. A disfigurement; something which offends the eye of the beholder; spoils the appearance of an object or view; a detriment. "That heap of rubbish is a terrible eyesore." In universal use. (See Dissight) +*=

EYLEBOURNE. An intermittent spring that overflows, usually at the end of the winter rains, flooding roads and lower land before finding its way into the Stour. "There is a famous eylebourne which rises in this parish (Petham) and sometimes runs but a little way before it falls into the ground" — Harris' "History of Kent". (See Nailbourne) In other counties these overflowing springs are known as Winterbournes. (The Petham eylebourne still periodically overflows — A.M.) P+=

FACK. The first stomach of a ruminating animal, from which the herbage is resumed into the mouth when the animal chews the cud. P+

FADER. Father. Extract from the Will of Sir John Spycer, Vicar of Monkton, A.D. 1450 : "The same 10 marc shall be for a priest's salary; one whole yere to pray for my soule, my fadyr soule, my modyr soul, and all crystyn soules". — Lewis. +

FAGS, FAGGS. A cant word of affirmation; in good faith; indeed; truly; of good intent. In "A Winter's Tale" Shakespeare uses "I' fecks" : in faith, where the word was apparently in the process of abbreviation. +P

FAGGING HOOK. (See Bagging Hook)

FAGOT, FAGGOT. A kind of firewood. = (See Baven, Bobbin, Pimp, Kiln-Brush, Sere, Wiff)

FAIRISIES, FAIRISEES. Fairies. This reduplicated plural of fairy — fairyses — caused confusion concerning the use of the story-book "fairies" and the Pharisees of the Bible. +P (See Heg, Pharisees)

FAIRY SPARKS. Phosphorescent light; electric sparks sometimes seen on clothes at night (we know this as static electricity)originally attributed to the fairies. Also called Shellfire (which see) (See Composant) P+

FAKEMENT. Pain; distress; uneasiness. +

FALL1. To fell a tree; to cut down. +

FALL2. A portion of growing underwood ready to fell or cut. + (See Fellet)

FALL3. Old wagoners used to say "We ball our horses at the rise, of the sap in Springtime, and in the fall, of the leaves in autumn". Ball was a physic or medicine ball for conditioning. (Although used now as a term for autumn in North America it is possible the word was taken there by English settlers — A.M.) = (See Fall1, Fall2)

FANTEEG. A state of worry; in a dither; excitement; passion; a fluster. +

FANTOD. Similar to Fanteeg; uneasy; restless; fidgetty; on edge; dithery. +

FARDLE. A bundle; a little pack. + Shakespeare refers to fardels in "Hamlet" : "Who would fardels

34

bear?" a fardel being a package, a cumbersome burden. +

FARGO, FAGO. A bad smell, such as emanated from a full earth privy. † (See Fogo, Hoogo)

FAT. A vat; a large open tub; a ton or tun. + (See Ton, Tun)

FATHER SHEAVES. Before the horse-drawn reaper could start, the outside edge of the field of corn, by the hedge or ditch, was first hand cut with a scythe. This corn was tied by hand with straw bands and the sheaves, being large and heavy, were called Father Sheaves by the harvesters. +

FATTEN. Dialect for a weed or weeds of any variety, but possibly it may be a corruption of Fat Hen, more commonly known as Good King Henry (Chenopodium bonushenricus) a plant often growing in abundance in neglected agricultural land and by the wayside. It was eaten in the past as a substitute for spinach. +=

FAVOUR. To resemble; have a likeness to another person, usually a parent, grandparent or relative. "he certainly favours his father, especially across the eyes". In universal use. +* (See Bly, Bligh, Spit)

FAZEN. The fazen eel was a large brown eel and was so-called at Sandwich and other ports to distinguish it from the Silver Eel.

FEAR. To frighten. P+

FEASE1. To fret; worry. + (See Frape)

FEASE2. A feasy, fretting, whining child. +

FEASY. Whining; peevish; troublesome; + (See Fease, Tattery)

FEETENS. Foot prints; foot marks; hoof prints. +

FEIGHNIGHTS. A word used by children at play in games of tag or chasing games when a rest was required to get the breath back. The child would cross the first two fingers of both hands, stand on one leg or climb on an obstacle, such as a wall, and shout "feighnights", so that while resting the child could not be "touched" or "it" in the game. This originated from the Middle English "feign" or "fains I", meaning to shirk a duty or excuse oneself from some task. =

FELD. A field + (See Fill, Fild)

FELLET. A portion of woodland divided up for felling; a portion of felled wood. + (See Fall, Cant)

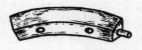

A Fellie with dowel and two holes for spokes

FELLIES. Felloes; part of a cart wheel. =

FELLOWLY. Familiar; companiable; free. P+

FENAGE. Finish; stop; cancel; cease; end. †

FENNY1. Mouldy as with reference to cheese. From Anglo-Saxon finie, meaning mouldy. P+G (See Abited, Ampery, Bicey)

FENNY2. Dirty; sour; unclean. +=

FESS1. Confess abbreviated. "They made him fess he stole the apples" † (See Fessed)

FESS2. "In a fess" meant to be mentally tense. †

FESSED. Puzzled; confused; also abbreviated Confessed. † (See Fess1)

FESSED UP. Mentally puzzled or confused through hesitation or vacilation. † (See Fess2)

FESSER. Someone with a personal knowledge of a local subject. Sometimes it was used as a nickname for that person. Also an abbreviation of Confessor and Professor. †

FET. To fetch; fetched; P+

FEW. In use did not mean a small number, but rather the opposite, when used in phrases with the word good, such as "a good few", "a goodish few", to mean "quite a lot", "pretty many" or "a nice lot".

FICKLE. To fickle a person in the head is to put something, such as an idea, into their head; also meant to put suggestions, thoughts and rumours into other people's minds to spread them. P+

FID. A portion of straw pulled out and arranged for thatching. Four or five fids are about as much as a thatcher can carry up in his "dogs". +

FIDDLER. The Monk or Angel Fish (Rhina squatina); also called the Fiddle Fish because of its shape. Intermediate in size between the Sharks and the Rays. +

FILD. A field. Pronounced fill. P+ (See Feld, Fill)

FILL. A field. + (See Feld, Fild)

FILL-HORSE. (See Vill-Horse) =

FILL-NOR-FALL. An expression that was frequently used for any person missing or absent or anything else lost; no news either good or bad. "My old dog went off last Monday and I can't hear neither fill-nor-fall of him". +*=

FINGER-COLD. Used to describe the weather when the cold is not very intense or bitter, but enough to make the fingers tingle; cold to the finger touch. "We shall very soon have the winter 'pon us. 'Twas downright finger-cold first thing this morning." +*=

FINKLE. Wild Fennel (Foeniculum vulgare), a herb.

FIPPENCE. Fivepence; used for £ s. d. coinage. =

FIRE-FORK. A shovel for the fire made in the form of a three-pronged fork, as broad as a shovel and fitted with a handle made of bamboo or other wood. +

FIRK1, FIRKE1. A Wealden dialect word meaning to fool about; to muck about. †

FIRK2, FIRKE2. A Wealden dialect word meaning to scratch, to be scratched, by their thorns when picking roses or blackberries. †

FIRK3, FIRKE3. To think of and look after oneself first and everyone else second. †

FIRK4, FIRKE4. To tidy up, to poke about when putting in order. †

FLAM. To deceive or cheat; a falsehood; a fraud. +

FLAVOUR. Heat. "The sun casts a great flavour". P

FLAW. To flay; to strip the bark off timber. +*

FLAZZ. Fledged, applied to birds newly fledged. +

FLECK. Ground game such as Hares and Rabbits. "They killed over two hundred pheasants, but terrible little fleck". +

FLEED. The inside fat of a pig from which lard is made. P+ (See Browsells)

FLEED CAKES. Cakes made with the fresh fleed of a pig. +*=

FLEEKY. Flaky; in flakes. +

FLEET1. To skim any liquid, especially milk. +

FLEET2. To float. The word was used by North Kent bargemen and occasionally by "inlanders". "The Ada and Edith fleeted about four o'clock today."

FLEET3. Every Folkestone herring boat carried a fleet of nets and sixty nets made a fleet. +

FLEET4, FLETE. A creek; a bay or inlet; a channel for the passage of boats and vessels, hence the name Northfleet. Still in use on maps, being applied to sheets of salt or brackish water in the marshes adjoining the Medway and Swale. Most fleets have no communication with the tidal water except through water-gates, but they generally represent the channels of streams that have been partly diverted by drainage.

FLEET-MILK. Skimmed milk. + (See Fleet1, Flit-Milk)

FLEETING-DISH. A shallow dish for cream. + (See Fleet, Fleet-Milk)

FLIBENITE. Fly-by-night. Formerly applied in Kent to a woman of doubtful morals and mysterious habits, perhaps with a suggestion of witchcraft; now used generally for a person who gads about at night or a debtor who decamps at night without paying. =

FLIBBERTYGIBBET. A fly by night; a flighty girl. =

FLICK. Loose hair from a cat, fur from a rabbit or the coats of other animals. +

FLICKING-TOOTH-COMB. A comb for a horse's mane. +

FLIG. Strands of grass. +

FLINDER. A butterfly of any species. P+

FLINDER-MOUSE, FLINTER-MOUSE, FLITTER-MOUSE, FLINTY-MOUSE, FLITTY-MOUSE. All applied to any member of the Bat family (Chiroptera). P+

FLIT-MILK. Skimmed milk; the milk after the cream has been taken off it and separated of all its fat content. P+ (See Fleet, Fleet-Milk)

FLOAT. A wooden frame, sloping outwards, attached to the sides, head or back of a cart, enabling it to carry a larger load than would otherwise be possible. +

FLOWER. The floor. +

FLUE. Delicate; weak; sickly. It was also applied to animals, but more commonly to persons. P+ (See Cruppish, Dicky, Dwindle)

FLUFF1. Anger; wrath; choler. +

FLUFF2. Something nice, pretty, attractive; said of a pretty girl "She's a nice bit of fluff." Now widely used elsewhere, but possibly of Chathamese origin. (See Chathamese). =

FLUMP. A fall causing a loud noise. +

FOAL'S FOOT. The wild plant Colt's-foot (Tussilago farfara). +

FOBBLE. To play or fool about with or where there was a possiblity of danger or having an accident. †

FOBBLING. To play or fool about, usually applied to children. †

FOBBLER. A person who "acts-about", "plays the fool". †

FOGO. A stench; a smell. + (See Fargo, Hoogo)

FOG. The second crop of grass. + (See Aftermeath) Also used in the name for the grass, Yorkshire Fog or Meadow Soft Grass (Holcus lanatus), thus named due to its soft, downy, whitish-green leaves and stems. +=

FOLD-PITCHER. An iron implement, for making holes in the ground to hold wattles or hop poles. + (See Peeler, Pitcher).

FOLKS. A term for men-servants used in the rural areas, chiefly East Kent. "Our folks are all out in de fill". P+

FOLKESTONE BEEF. Dried Dogfish. Visitors to the fishermen's houses in Folkestone in the past would see them with strips of fish hung out to dry. The fish had had their heads, tails and fins removed. Examination of the strips with a rough skin on one side identified the fish as one of the species of Dogfish, still caught and eaten today as Huss, Rock Salmon, Robin Huss, Gurnet, etc. On being asked what was the name of the fish being dried it was usual for the fishermen to reply it was "Folkestone Beef".

FOLKESTONE WASHERWOMEN, FOLKESTONE LASSIES, FOLKESTONE GIRLS. The names given to large, heavy, black, billowy, threatening rain clouds. +

FOOTING. A custom in hop gardens where a visitor had his shoes or boots wiped with a hop bine or apron, requiring him or her to pay his footing in ale. Should they refuse then they were pushed backwards into a large hop basket so they could not get out or were kept in a hop bin until they changed their mind. = (See Shoe Money, Old Lip)

FOR. Used in the adjectival sense:

"What for horse is he;" i.e. "What kind of horse is he?" "What for day is it;" i.e. "What kind of day is it?" P+

FOR WHY. When explaining something the word Why is often prefixed with For. "I will tell you for why". =

FORE-ACRE, FORRAKER. The land at the ends of a field where the furrows cross; fore-acre or the headland of a field when ploughing. P+ (See Forical, Forracker)

FORECAST. Forethought. +

FORE-DOOR. The front door of a dwelling. +

FORE-HORSE. The front horse in a team of four. + (See Rod Horse)

FOREIGNER. A stranger to a village or area who comes from the "shires" and is not Kentish born. Different to Furriner (which see). A local definition occurred in Folkestone where, if a fisherman took as his wife a woman from outside the town or from another village, he was said to have married a "foreigner". += (See Furriner, March-Man, Below London, Sheeres)

FORE-LAY. To waylay; to stop. +

FORE-LONG. Abbreviated "before Long"; before much more time has passed; soon; quickly. "I fore-long found 'im a job". =* (See Afore)

FORE-RIGHT. Direct; right in front; straight forward. P+ (See Outstand, Upstand)

FORICAL. A headland in ploughing. P+ (See Fore-Acre, Forracker)

FORRACKER, Forraker. The land around the edge of a field; a headland when ploughing. = (See Fore-Acre, Forical)

FORSTAL, FORESTAL, FOSTAL. A paddock near a farmhouse; the house and home building of a farm; a farmyard before a house; a small opening in a street or lane, or land not large enough to be called a common; a way leading from the highway to a large house. P+

FOUR WENTS. A crossroads. = (See Went)

FOUR-WENT-WAY. A crossroads = (See Went)

FOUT. Fought. "Two joskins (farm labourers) fout one day in a chalk pit until the blood ran all over their gaberdines". +

FOWER. Four. The spelling used in old documents and parish records. +

FOY. A treat given by or to a person on their going abroad or returning home. P+

FOYING. Victualling ships, acting generally as agents for them and going to their aid when in distress. +=

FRAIL1. Peevish; hasty; irritable; cross. Not used to mean someone or something weak or ailing. P+ (See Tatter)

FRAIL2. A small basket. +

FRAIL3. A flail, used for hand threshing corn. The flail consisted of the hand-staff or part grasped by the thresher's hands; the hand-staff cap made of wood which secured the thong to the hand-staff; the middle-bun or flexible leather which served as the connecting link between the hand-staff and swingel; the swingel-cap, made of leather, which secured the middle-bun to the swingel; the swingel, which swung free and struck the corn. There was a Kent saying which referred to the hard work in threshing: "Two sticks, a leather and thong, Will tire a man be he ever so strong." +=

FRAPE1. To worry; fidget; fuss; scold. "Don't frape about it so". +

FRAPE2. A woman of an anxious, worrying temperament, who grows thin with care and worry. "Oh, she's a regular frape". +

FRENCH HOPS. (See Queen Hops).

FRENCH MAY. The garden tree Lilac (Syringa vulgaris) +

FRESH CHEESE. Curds and whey. +

FRIG, FRIGGING. Restless movement; continually fidgetting. †

FRIGGER. A fidget, usually applied to a child, unable to sit still and continually moving. †

FRIGHT WOODS. (See Frith)

FRIMSY. Slight; thin; soft; frail. Variant of Flimsy in general use. +

FRIT. Frighten. =

FRITH. A hedge, copse or coppice. An old word that also applies to a sparse, scrubby type of wood or shaw with very little or no timber of value, being inferior through growing on poor soils, competing with Furze, Heath and much undergrowth. The name Frith or Fright Wood may have been applied to a wood many years past and still bears it, although the timber may long since have become more valuable with modern methods.

FRORE. Frozen. +

FROUGHTENED. Frightened. =

FRUITING. Fruit picking. "Are you goin' fruiting?" An example of lazy Kent speech, where "pick" is omitted, rather than true Kent dialect. †*=

FRUZ. Frozen. +

FULL MEASURE. (See Race Measure)

FUMBLE-FISTED. Clumsy. (See Buck-Fisted, Cack-Handed, Ham-Fisted, Unhandy). =

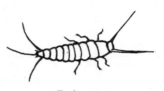

Furbrat

FURBRAT. The Silverfish (Lepisma saccharina), an active silvery-white scaled insect that occurs in pantries, kitchens and bakehouses where it is attracted by sugary or starchy food. Also known occasionally as Firebrat in Kent and other counties. Children who spent a lot of time in front of a fire in winter were also called Firebrats or Furbrats. †

FURNER. A baker. From the French fournier. P+

FURRICK. (See Furrige)

FURRIGE. To forage; to hunt about and rummage and put everything into disorder and untidy while looking for something. +

FURRIN PEASIES. "Foreign" pea pickers; strangers who lived beyond the parish where the peas to be picked were situated and came to work with the local people to harvest the pea crop. † (See Foreigners, Home Peasies, Furriner)

FURRINER. Not a foreigner in the true sense but meaning a person, a stranger, living outside of the parish boundary and who came to visit in the parish. Each parish was "foreign" to the others in former days the inhabitants of different parishes being "foreigners" to each other, even if they lived only a few miles apart. (See Foreigner, Furrin-Peasies) †

FURTHER YET. Further still; not at the end of some task. =

FURS. Furrows. =

FUT IT. To walk. *=

Gaberdine or Smock-Frock — c.1870

G

GABERDINE, GABBERDIN, GAB-BATIN. A coarse, loose frock; a smock frock, sometimes called a Cow Gown, worn by labouring men, waggoners, particularly on farms in agricultural counties, including formerly in Kent. + (See Slop).

GADS. Rushes and Sedges that grow on wet, marshy ground. +

GAFFER. A master; employer. "Here comes our gaffer". Later in wider use in rural counties, one being Sussex. +

GAGEY. Weather that is unsettled and changeable was said to be gagey; uncertain; showery. = (See Shuckish)

GAIRN. A garden. A hop-gairn was the name for a plantation or garden of hops. G

GALEY. Boisterous; stormy. A galey wind blows in gales, fits and intervals. P+

GALLEY BIRD. The Green Woodpecker (Picus viridis virescens). *=

GALLIGASKINS. Trousers. +

GALLON. Used as a dry measure for corn, flour, bread, potatoes. In Kent these dry goods were always sold by the gallon. +

GALLS. Jellyfish. + (See Miller's Eyes, Sluthers, Stinger, Water-Galls)

GALORE. Plenty; abundance. Now in general use. +*= (See Golore)

GAMBREL, GAMBLE STICK. A stick used to spread open and hang up a pig or other slaughtered animal. +

GAMMY1. Sticky; dirty; unclean. †

GAMMY2. A diseased, injured, hurt, broken or cut part of the body, but mostly applied to the limbs. "Jim's laid up with his gammy leg he broke last week". *=

GANCE. Thin; slender; gaunt. "Them sheep are doin' middlin', but here and there a one looks rather gance". +

GANGWAY. A passage through; an entry; a thoroughfare; also a sea term. Now in universal use. GP+

GANT. Gaunt. P

GARBAGE. Not, as now, used to describe refuse, but in the past was a sheaf of corn, a cock of hay, a faggot of wood, or any other bundle of the product or fruits of the earth from cultivation. +

GARMY. Sticky. = (See Gammy1, Garmed Up)

GARMED UP. Smeared or unpleasantly smothered with something; a child eating jam and bread with jam smeared around its mouth is garmed up with it. =*

GARP. To gawp; to gape; to stare overlong at another person or persons especially if they are in conversation with others or doing something private or personal; the gaper also may have and keep their mouth open while staring in a foolish, vacant, bad-mannerd way. † (See Garped, Garping, Gawp, Gawping)

GARPED. As Garp. Gaped; gawped; stared at. † (See Garp, Garping, Gawp, Gawping).

GARPING. Gaping; staring. † (See Garp, Garped, Gawp; Gawping).

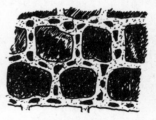

Garret

GARRET. To drive small wedges of flint into the joints of a flint wall. +

GARRETED. Used in the phrase "Not rightly garreted" describing a simpleton, a mentally unbalanced person or a weak, silly, sometimes childish, adult. The modern version is "Not right in the head" or "Not right in the top story". A garret was another name for an attic or small room on the top storey of a building.

GARRETY, GARROTY. Wild; mad; crazy. =

GASCOIGNES. According to Pegge "small black cherries". P

GASKIN. The Gean (Prunus avium), a wild cherry, but not the Wild, Dwarf or Bird Cherry. The heart-shaped fruit is either red or black, sweet or bitter, with a staining juice. Believed to be the original wild stock of the modern Black Hearts and Big-gareux cherries. In the past it was gathered in the wild to send, with cultivated black cherries, to add flavour in the manufacture of a "port wine", cherry brandy type of drink. Name also used with reference to the Wild Damson or Sloe from which a wine was also commonly made. =+

GATE. A way or passage down from or through cliffs, rocks and high ground to reach the sea. It has been incorporated into the names of several Kent seaside places — Margate, Ramsgate, Kingsgate, Sandgate, West-gate) P+

GATHER. To understand. "I gather what you mean". =

GATTERIDGE TREE. The Spindle tree (Euonymus europaeus), also called Pegwood and Prickwood, usually more a large shrub than a tree. +

GAU, GEU, GOO. An exclamation expressive of doubt, surprise, astonishment. The Cockney variation is "Cor" in "Cor, blimey" still in common use in Kent and elsewhere in southern England. +*=

GAUSE. Thin; slender. +

GAVELKIND. An ancient tenure in Kent, by which the lands of the father were divided among all his sons and not only the eldest inherited; or the lands of a brother, dying without issue, divided among all the surviving brothers. A custom in which all female descendants were completely excluded and illegitimate children inherited with the legitimate children. P+

GAWP. A feeble-minded, silly or foolish person. † (See Garp, Garped, Garping)

GAWPING. Staring. Probably corruption of gaping in universal use. †*= (See Garp, Garped, Garping, Gawp)

GAY. Lively; active; hearty; in good health. "The old mare was very gay this morning". +

GAYZELS. Blackcurrants. + (See Currantberries). Also sometimes used for the Wild Plum (Prunus domestica) +

GAZELS. As Gayzels. +

GEAT. A gate. +

GEE1. A roost; a lodging. "To go to gee", i.e. "To go to roost". Pegge says it was pronounced as chee. Applied to fowls. P+ (See Chee)

GEE2. An instruction to a horse to go away, to move faster; also given as "gee up". A command to a horse to go to the off side. Latter used in West Kent chiefly. += (See Mether, Wai, Why).

GEG. To reach prior to vomitting. As a child may put something in its mouth to tickle its throat and make it reach. (See Gog) =

GENTAIL. An Ass. +P

GENTLEMAN. A person who from age or any other cause is incapacitated from work. "He's a gentleman now, but he just manages to doddle about his garden with a weeding spud". +

GETOVER. A stile, usually one without a footboard, a spile or slat of wood nailed horizontally each side of the fence to step on. =

GETTING ON. A term to describe someone who is becoming elderly. Anyone in their fifties and sixties was said to be "getting on". *=

GIBLETS. Clothes in rags and tatters. +

GIFTS. White specks which appear on the finger nails and are supposed to indicate something coming or an event in the future, but are in reality sometimes a sign of poor health and mineral or vitamin deficiency. The belief about these is now widespread and foretells thus: A gift on the thumb indicates a present; gift on the forefinger indicates a friend or lover; a gift on the middle finger indicates a foe; a gift on the fourth finger indicates a visit to pay; a gift on the little finger indicates a journey to go.

GIG. A billet or spread bat, used to keep the traces of the plough-horses apart. +

GILL. A streamlet, rivulet or beck; also applied to a narrow wooded valley with a stream of water flowing through it. P+

GIMMER. A mistress; female employer. "My gimmer always wore those blue and white checked aprons". +

GIN. Given. "I cou'd a gin de man a smack". +

GINNY. Jenny, used for the Wren. =

GIRL. A very small frame or clothes horse for drying clothes or linen. = (See Maid, Tamsin)

GIT. Get. "Git olt uv it tighter". =

GIVE. To give way; to yield; to thaw. "It gives now", i.e. "it is thawing". The phrase "Its all on the give" meant that a thaw had begun. It is still occasionally used referring to something giving way under pressure" : "Its beginning to give". +=* (See Givey)

GIVE OVER. To leave off; to cease; to stop. "Give over will ye! I wunt uv no more an't". Still a common expression, particularly in northern England counties. *=

GIVEY. Earth which has been frozen hard and then as it thaws breaks up and becomes soft was said to be givey. + (See Give)

GLEAN. A handful of corn tied together by a gleaner. + (See Gleaners)

GLEANERS. Women who followed the reaper and binder and stookers to gather up stray ears of corn and straw so that little was wasted. = (See Lease)

GLIMIGRIM. The drink better known as Punch. +

GLIN. A light or lamp. =

GLINCE, GLINCEY. Slippery; icy. "The road is terrible glincey". + (See Glins)

GLINS. Slippery; pronounced glince. P

GO. To get about and do one's work. "He's troubled to go", i.e. "He has great difficulty in getting about and doing his work." "He's gone in great misery for some time", i.e. "He has gone about his work in great pain and suffering". +

GOAL-RUNNING. An old Kentish sport, particularly in the eastern part of the county. It was a complicated game of "tag". Two barefooted teams stood along a baseline with two flags 20 yards in front. Each member of the team in turn raced round his flag and tried to avoid being touched by his opponent. It has been revived from time to time on the Romney Marsh. =

GOB. To spit; to hawk. "I hate to see men gobbing". *= (See Hawk)

GOD'S GOOD. Yeast; barm. It was once a pious custom to invoke a benediction by making the sign of the Cross over the yeast. In the days of superstitious beliefs when the success of anything was precarious housewives used to bless or exorcise it and having beaten the yeast or barm into the ale when it was in the vat they always crossed it with two long strokes with the hand from side to side. God's Good was probably the form of blessing or exorcising or the first two words of it spoken during the blessing. P+ (See Barm, Siesin, Sizzing)

GOFF. A common type of apple. This word may have applied to one especial variety or to any apple tree that produced a prolific crop. +

GOG. As Geg. =

GOING. The departure. "I didn't see the going of him". +*=

GOING TO'T. Going to do it; as: "do this or that", the answer is "I am going to't". It was also spoken in full: "I am going to it" and formerly very frequent in some parts of Kent speech. P+

GOL. A young gosling. +

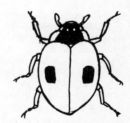

Golding

GOLDING. A beetle, the Ladybird (Adalia bipunctata — Two-spot) or (Coccinella seven-punctata-Seven-spot); also the name of a variety of hop. P+ (See Marygold).

GOLLOP. To swallow greedily; to gulp; eat fast; to bolt food in a hurry. +*= (See Bolt, Guzzle, Hog, Scorf, Yaffle)

GOLLS. Goslings or very young geese. P (See Gol)

GOLORE. Plenty; plentiful. P (See Galore)

GOMMED. Gummed; plastered; stuck up. "He was all gommed up with mud". =

GONE BACK. Hops that are only just

dried sufficiently when some moisture is re-absorbed from the atmosphere. =

GONE OFF. Used to describe milk that has gone sour or other food that has become rancid or bad, such as jam, bacon, butter, etc; also hops that have become soft and withery when unpicked. *= (See Rasty, Reasty).

GOO. Go. †

GOODING. A custom of going about the streets and calling at houses asking for gifts on December 21st, St. Thomas' Day. + Pegge says: "to go a gooding", when the poor of a parish go about for an alms, the week before Christmas". Custom thought to have last survived in the district surrounding Maidstone.

GOODMAN. A Kent and Sussex surname that occurred in dialect. It was used as an old title of address to the master of the house and was commonly referred to in parish registers. Thus we read: "1707, Jan. 13 Buried Eliza, ye wife of Goodman Curteis". "1708, Jan. 14 Buried ye old Goodman Wood". In St. Matthew XXIV, 43, it reads "If the Goodman of the house had known in what watch the thief would come he would have watched".

GOODY. Similar to Goodman. The title given to an elderly widow and was contracted from goodwife. Also frequent in parish registers: "1706. Dec. 17 Buried old Goody Mills". "Payed to Goody Gorge 6 pence". +

GOOD 'OPPIN'. A fine, late summer's day is still described in the West Malling area as it being "good 'oppin' ", i.e. a good day for hopping (hop-picking in the hop garden) = (See Hopping)

GOOED. A corruption of Goed, gode, for gone. †

GOOING. Going. †

GOOSEBRING. Gooseberrying; gooseberry picking. An example of lazy Kent speech, like Fruiting (which see) rather than true dialect. †

GOOSEGOG. Fruit of the Gooseberry; a gooseberry. Used mainly by children. *= (See Goozy)

GOOZY. A fruit of the Gooseberry. = (See Goosegog)

GO-TO. To set. "The sun goes-to". P+

GOOTCH-GRASS. Cooch Grass (which see). =

GORSTER. To laugh in an uncouth manner. = (See Goyster)

GOSS. Furze, Gorse (Ulex europaeus), that grows on heaths. P=

GOUD-UP. Exhaustion; tiredness after hard work. =

GOULE. Bog Myrtle (Myrica gale), a shrub growing in bogs and damp ground. Also known as Sweet Gale, Sweet Willow and Candle-berry Myrtle. +

GOYSTER. To laugh aloud noisily and in a vulgar manner. A goystering lass, girl or wench was of a romp or "tomboy" type. Incidentally tomboy we use today was formerly used as boy-maid or a lad-lass. P+G

GRABBY. Grimy; filthy; grubby; dirty. + (See Gammy, Grubby)

GRACIOUS HEART-ALIVE. A Kent exclamation of utter surprise. Sanders states this may be of Roman Catholic origin with the Gracious Heart part of it and suggests its earliest beginning was due to someone crying out the religious call of "Gracious Heart-Alive!" over some supposed dead person having been found to be alive; or made an appearance after a long time away, or presumed missing or dead, but found alive. † (See Dear Heart-Alive, Hearts-Alive).

Graft

GRAFT. A small spade for digging grips. Not a Spud. =

GRAN. Very. = (See Great)

GRANABLE. Very. + (See Great)

GRANADA. A golden pippin. P+

GRAN NIGH. Very nearly. Today the expression would be "Darn near."

GRAND. Very; greatly; Grand-Crass, very much out of temper; Grand-Rich was very rich. G (See Gran, Crass, Great)

GRANDLY. Greatly. "I want it grandly". P+

GRANDMOTHER'S NIGHT CAP. A garden flower, better known as Monkshood (Aconitum napellus) or Columbine (Aquilegia vulgaris). In other counties it is known as Granny's Bonnet. +

GRAPE-VINE. Parish and Shaw stated: "A vine which bears grapes. In other counties when they say vine they mean a grape-vine, as a matter of course; so when they use the word orchard, they mean an apple orchard, but in Kent it is necessary to use distinguishing terms, because we have apple orchards and cherry orchards, hop vines and grape vines." Pegge stated: "Grape-vine, a vine; Wild of Kent and Sussex. Orchard in Derbyshire is always spoken of apples, but in Kent they say apple orchards because of the cherry orchards". Formerly grapes were grown widely in Kent, one area being at Littlebourne, for the monks at Canterbury.

GRATTAN, GRATTEN1, GRATTON, GROTTEN . Stubble; a stubble field after the corn harvest. P+*= (See Gratten2, Ersh, Eddish, Grotten, Podder-Grotten)

GRATTEN2. To feed on a gratten or stubble field; to turn out chicken, pigs, etc.; "grattening" was to turn them out to find their own food by foraging; the stubble after corn harvest. *=

GRAUM. To grime; dirty; blacken. + (See Gammy, Grabby)

GREAT. Very. "Great Much" was very much; was commonly pronounced "gurt". + (See Gran, Granable, Grand) P+

GREAT CHURCH. The name for Canterbury cathedral. "That fil belongs to the Great Church", i.e. part of the possession of the Dean and Chapter of Canterbury. +

GREATEN. To enlarge. +

GREEDS. Straw thrown on to a mixon or dung heap. P+

GREEN BAG. The bag or sack in which the hops are brought from the garden after picking to the Oast. + (See Poke)

GREEN. Pegge states; "To take a horse a green, i.e. to the field or to green meat; as when they say "he goes a green", i.e. he goes to grass. A green is an open piece of ground and generally a common or waste." P (See Green Meat)

GREEN MEAT. In Summer the clover or lucerne was cut green for horses and Cows. Cut by labourers with scythes and wooden rakes, who loaded it on a cart and carried it back to the stock where it was fed off the cart as required. *=

GREYBIRD. A Thrush, usually the Song Thrush or Mistle Thrush. +

GREY-HUNTER. A person who caught badgers, an animal wrongly thought to be a pest and so killed as much as possible on estates; also part of the gamekeeper's job in the past. =

GRIDGIRON. Gridiron. +

GRINNY-GROGGING. Open mouthed; gaping; foolish, grinning. "What are you staring at you grinny-grogging a'porth?" =

GRINSTONE. A grindstone. + (See Grinstun)

GRINSTUN. A grindstone. = (See Grinstone)

GRIP. A dry ditch; a furrow to drain off surface water; in North Kent also applied to the natural channels, a few feet in width, in the saltings on the coasts. +*=

GRIPING. The name given along the North Kent coast to the practice of groping at arm's length in the soft mud of the tidal streams for Flounders and occasionally Eels. Care had to be taken in picking up Flounders due to the pointed bonelike extremity behind the Flounder's head with which they defend themselves and a careless slip by the fisherman in grasping the fish could mean a badly gashed hand or arm. =+* (See Butt)

GRIST. Corn ready to be ground or has been ground, flour, meal, etc. Used in the saying "All grist to the mill", used in the sense of gain. +*=

GRISTING, GRYSTING. The flour which is obtained from the lease-wheat. + (See Gristhead, Lease-Wheat)

GRISTHEAD, GRISTHOOD. "Grist to his mill" (See Grist) meant everything to be a source of gain, to turn everything to one's advantage. The saying "He does not earn enough to buy the gristhood" was used in the sense of "He's unable to support a wife." = (See Grist, Gristing)

GRIT. To set the teeth on edge; to grate; "grit the teeth" meant to take a firm resolve to do something. +

GRIZZLE. To fret; complain; grumble; be tearful; whining; weeping. "For goodness sake don't grizzle so". "She's such a grizzling woman". +*= (See Bob's A-dying)

GROG. Ale with ginger and brown sugar, drunk by waggoners. etc. =

GROSS. Gruff; deep-sounding. +

GROUSING. Grumbling; nagging. *= (See Joutering). Now in general use.

GROTTEN, GROTTON. (See Gratten) P+

GROVETT. A small grove or wood. +

GRUBBED UP, GRUBBED OUT. An orchard or wood where the trees have been felled and the roots hauled out so that land could be used for another purpose was said to be grubbed up or grubbed out. = (See Stub)

GRUB UP. To clear a wood or orchard. = (See Grubbed Up)

GRUBBY. Dirty; unclean; said of clothes: "I only wore it once and it soon got grubby." "You are grubby and no mistake". Now in general use. +*= (See Gammy, Grabby)

GRUMBLE. Chide; chastise a child with speech who has been careless or naughty; not so violent in use as "Creating" or "Grousing". A child chided would reply "Don't grumble me so". = (See Creating, Grousing, Joutering)

GRUPPER. That part of the harness of a cart horse which is called in other counties the quoilers, the breeching. + (See Quiller).

GRUPPER-TREE. That part of a cart horse's harness which is made of wood, padded next the horse's back and which carries the redger. Used in East Kent. +

GUESS-COW. A dry or barren cow. +P

GUESTING. Gossipping. P+ (See Nabble, Nabbler, Chatting, Cotchering)

GUESTLING1. The Ancient Courts of the Cinque Ports held at Shepway, near Hythe, and other places. "In July, 1688, the Common Council of Faversham commissioned their deputy mayor, two jurats, the town clerk and a commoner "to go to a guestling, which was summoned from the ancient town of Winchelsea, to be holden at the town and port of New Romney, on Tuesday, July 21st," and "there to act on the town's behalf, as they should find convenient". They were absent at the guestling five days" — Archaeologia Cantiana, xvi, page 271. +

GUESTLING2. An ancient watercourse at Sandwich in which it was the custom to drown prisoners. =

GUILE-SHARES. Shares of "wreckage"; division of spoils; cheating shares. By pretending to assist the masters of stranded ships and save the cargo or merchant's goods foyers converted the latter to their own use by calling them guile-shares, guile meaning deceit, craftiness, wiliness. Presumably dishonest foyers who took off goods then swindled the owners out of them. + (See Foying, Palter)

GULLIDGE. The sides of a barn boarded off from the middle; where the caving is generally stored. +

GUMBLE. Anything which was a poor fit or too large; usually applied to shoes or clothes. +

GUNNER. A wildfowler, but chiefly used to describe one who earned his living by shooting wildfowl, for market, on the North Kent marshes. +

GURT. Great. + (See Great)

GUTTER-GRUB. One who delighted in doing dirty work and getting himself or herself in a messy, filthy condition; a low person; a variant of Guttersnipe in common use. +

GUTTERMUD. The black mud of the gutter, thus any dirt or filth. "He came in black as guttermud". + Pegge stated; "To dirty; as when one falls from a horse into the dirt". P+

GUT-WEED. Corn Sow-Thistle (Sonchus arvensis)

GYPER. Juice, gravy. =

H

HAAZES. Haws. Fruit of the Hawthorn tree. (Crataegus monogyna) + (See Arzy-Garzeys, Harves)

HA'ANT. Haven't you. "Ha'ant you heard the news?" =

HACKLE. The expression used "hackle to it" meant "put your shoulder to the wheel", "get stuck into the task". A shirker won't "hackle to it". =

HADN'T OUGHT. Ought not. "He hadn't out to do it like that". + Still in universal use. (See No Ought)

HAGESTER, HAGISTER. The Magpie (Pica pica). PG+

HAGG-A-DAY. A door-latch, opened from exterior only, by putting blade through door to lift latch. =

HAGGED. Haggard; thin; lean; shrivelled.

HAIR. The horse-hair cloth on the Oast floor laths above the fires where the hops were dried. +

HALF-AMON. A hop, one step and a jump. P+ (See Amon)

HALF-BAPTISED. Privately baptised. + "Can such things be!" exclaimed the astonished Mr Pickwick. "Lord bless your heart, sir", said Sam, "Why where was you half-baptised? - that's nothing', that an't." "Pickwick Papers", chapter xiii, Dickens.

Half Mattock or Peck

HALF-MATTOCK. A hoe with a single triangular shaped blade or plate widest at its cutting edge. Sometimes also called a Peck (which see) = (See Clod Hoe, Tommy Hoe, Corn Hoe, Axe Een Mattock, Weald Hoe, Plate Hoe, Peck, Double-sider Hoe).

HALM, HAULM, HELM. Stubble gathered after the corn is carried, especially pea and bean straw. Still used for the stalks or stems of potatoes and other vegetables. +

HALMOT. The hall mote; court leet or manor court; from the Saxon healmot, a little council. +

HALF-SIEVE. A half-bushel basket, lined with blue paper, into which cherries were put for transporting to market. At the top were crossed hazel twigs acting as retainers to keep the destination label and cherries held down safely. Later despatched in 12 lb. "chips" — flat bottom, tray-like baskets. =

HAME. Pea straw. + (See Halm)

HAM-FISTED. Awkward; clumsy. =* (See Buck-fisted, Cack-handed, Fumble-fisted, Unhandy)

HAMPER. To injure or throw anything out of alignment. "The door is so hampered it won't close". +

HAMPERY. Shaky, ricketty; crazy, doddery; weak; feeble; sickly; loose †+ (See Ampery, Dawther, Latchetty)

HANDBILL. A billhook; one-handed tool. A proper Billhook being a long-handled tool. "When I was a nipper, 5-6 years old, I saw an old cocky cutting a tall hedge. He was using a Handbill type tool on a pole four to five feet long. I asked him what it was. He replied: 'This ere long 'un be a Pole Hook and this ere little 'un be a Handbill'." — R.B.) =

HAND-COLD. Cold enough to chill the hands. + (See Bitter-Cold, Cold, Finger-Cold)

HANDFAST. Able to hold tight. "Old George is middlin' handfast today," said of a good catch made at cricket. +

HANDFUL. An anxiety; a burden; a worrisome, responsible task or duty. "to have a handful" was to have as much as a person could do or bear. "That child is a tidy handful I can tell ye". Still in general use. +*=

HAND-HOLD. A hold for the hands; somewhere to grip when climbing. "Tis a plaguey job to climb up there, as there ain't no hand-hold". Still in general use. +*=

HANDSTAFF. The handle of a flail. + (See Frail)

HANDY-PANDIES. The hands. =* (See Dandymen, Daddles)

HANK, KINK. A skein of silk, thread or wool. An expression "A man has a hank on another person" meant "He has them entangled in a skein or string" or involved in his schemes. Possible similar useage to the expression where someone easily led or involved is said to "be on a string". P+

HAPPENS. Possible; probably, "Now happens you may not know". = (See Haps).

HAPPY-HO. Apropos; similar; coincidental. "My father was drownded and so was my brother. Now that's very happy-ho" meaning that it was a curious coincidence. +

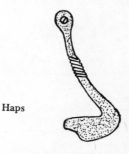

Haps

HAPS1, HASP. A hasp or fastening of a gate. P+ (See Hapse, Wops)

HAPS2. Perhaps. "Now haps you don't know". Sometimes used to mean Happens. +

HAPSE. To fasten with a hasp; to fasten or secure. In the Weald hapse was used for the verb and hasp for the noun, i.e. "Hapse the gate after you". "I can't, the hasp is gone". +

HARCELET, HASLET. The heart, liver and lights of a hog. P+ (Acelot, Arslet, Harslet)

HARD FRUIT. Apples, pears, etc., as opposed to Stone Fruit — plums, damsons, etc. and Low Fruit — currants, raspberries, etc. + (See Stone Fruit)

HARDHEWER. A stonemason. P+

HARKEE. Listen; hark! Corruption of Hark ye! † (See Harky). Also had the double meaning "Keep silent, keep quiet and listen, both at the same time."

HARKY. Hark. "Harky at the bells, they'm sound clear". + (See Harkee)

HARSLEM. Asylum. "When he got to settin' on de hob and pokin' de fire wid's fingers, dey thought 'twas purty nigh time dey had him away to de harslem." +

HARSLET. (See Harcelet) +

HARVES. Haws. + (See Haazes)

HARVEST. To gather in the corn; to work in the harvest fields; to go harvesting — cutting and stooking corn. "Where's Harry?" "Oh, he's harvesting 'long with his father." +P

HARVESTER. Originally a person from outside the parish who took employment assisting with the harvest, such persons usually being hired farm labourers. Later the name was applied to all those who helped gathering in the corn harvest. +P

HASSOCK1. A large pond. +*=

HASSOCK2. Provincial name for Kentish Ragstone (See Hassocks) and probably water collected as a pond in the quarry pits and so the name became associated with both pond and stone. =

HASSOCKS. Stone chippings used instead of gravel for making up paths and private minor roads; also a corruption of Tussocks, the large tough clumps of rough grass which grow in isolated positions in fields and roadside grass verges. †

HASTY. Heavy; violent. It was often used to describe rain. + (See Heavenshard)

HATCH. A gate in the road. A half-hatch is where a horse could pass but not a cart P+

HATCH UP. To prepare for. +*=

HATCHING UP. Preparing for. "I think he's hatching up some trickery". *=

HAUL. To halloo; to shout. +

HAULM. (See Halm) =

HAULMS AND FIGS. Hips and Haws; the fruit of the Dog Rose (Rosa canina) and Hawthorn (Crataegus monogyna). +

HAVE. To take; lead. "Have the horse to the field". P+

HAW. A small yard or enclosure. + Chaucer has it for a churchyard.

HAWK. To make a noise as the throat is cleared of phlegm; to spit; to Gob (which see). "He was hawking and spetting for near an hour after he first got up'" +*=

HAWMELL. A small close or paddock. +P (See Haw)

HAYNET. A long net, often an old fish net, used in cover shooting to keep the birds and flock from running out of the beat. +

HE WON'T BE SAID. Used of someone who won't give way, admit failure or give up; also means "He is obstinate and argumentative". =

HEADS. The numerous, often entangled, branches at the top of hop bines, sometimes left entwined around the top of the hop pole or wire when the bine is pulled down. The pole-puller has to come with a hop goad and take down the heads for the pickers. *=

HEAF. The gaff-hook used by fishermen at Folkestone. + (See Prule).

HEAL. To hide; to cover up anything; to roof in; to secrete. "Alright. I've only just got this 'ere row of taters to heal". + (See Hele)

HEART. A condition; encouragement; spoken of earth: "My garden's in better heart this year." Also used when describing misfortune or lack of encouragement: "So many things keep agoing wrong it doan't give me no heart to do more". +

HEARTENING. Strengthening. "Home-made bread is more heartening than bakers' bread". +

HEART-GRIEF. Severe grief; depressive grieving. +

HEARTH. Hearing; hearing distance. "In hearth", within hearing. "I called out as loud's ever I could, but he wasn't nowheres within hearth". P+

HEARTS-ALIVE. An expression of astonishment and surprise at some unusual, strange or startling news or event. + (See Dear Heart-Alive, Gracious Hearts-Alive)

HEAVE. To throw; to heave a card is to play it, it being, as it were, lifted up or heaved, before it is laid down upon the table. To heave or lib a libbat (which see) was to throw it to knock down nuts. P+ (See Hull, Lib, Lob)

Hedge Slasher

Heave-Gate

HEAVE-GATE. A gate which does not operate or swing on hinges but which has to be lifted, heaved out of the sockets or mortises, which keep it in place and make it appear like a part of the fence. P+ (See Bar-Way).

HEAVENSHARD. Heavily; said of rain. "It rained down heavenshard". + (See Hasty)

HEAVER. A Crab; the name being used by Folkestone fishermen. "Lord, sir. Its hard times. I've not catched a pung or a heaver in my stalkers this week (See Pung, Stalkers). The mansuckers and sluthers gets into them and the congers knocks them all to pieces". + (See Hever, Ponger, Punger, Man-sucker, Sluther)

HEAVY-EYED. Having the eyes almost closed with sleep, exhaustion, or with being ailing and ill; usually influenza made a person "heavy-eyed". =

HEAVY1. Used to describe a hop bine. A "heavy" bine has many hops on it, particularly a bine with a head bearing lots of branches of large hops; also a "heavy" crop of fruit is a good one with much fruit. A "slight" bine or "light" bine of hops is straggly, with few hops or small in size on it. ∗

HEAVY2. A measurer who quickly filled the bushel measuring-basket with hops and with a hand pushed them down to the mark indicating the 1-bushel level the hop pickers said was measuring "heavy" in favour of the farmer. = (See Light)

HEDGE POKER. The Dunnock or Hedge Sparrow (Prunella modularis occidentalis) = See Dicky Hedge Poker, Jimmy Hedge Moper)

HEDGE SLASHER, HEDGING SLASH(ER). A curved, sharp bladed, fairly long pole-handled tool used for hedge brishing, cutting brambles, etc. = (See Slasher)

HEED. Head. +

HEEL. To cover a stack with a sheet, tilt, or cover a mangold or swede clamp, with litter, straw, etc. (See Heal). A mackintosh or raincoat was also called a Healer. =

HEEST. Hoist; to lift up. A wagoner or blacksmith when he wanted a horse to lift a foot would grip the fetlock and say "Heest up". =

HEEVE1. A bee hive; a hive P+

HEEVE2. To hive bees. P+

HEFT. The weight of a thing, as ascertained by heaving or lifting it. "This here heeve'll stand very well for the winter, just feel the heft of it" +

HEG. A hag; witch; a fairy. + (See Fairisies, Pharisees)

HEGS PENCE. Old coins found in Kent were called Hegs Pence by the country folk. + (See Heg, Bald Pates, Dwarfs Money, Borrow Pence)

HELE, HEEL. To cover. From Anglo-Saxon helan. P+ (See Heal)

HELER. Anything which is laid over another object or item, such as the cover of a thurrock or wooden drain. + (See Heel)

HELLWEED. Lesser Dodder (Cuscuta epithymum). (See Devil's Thread) It was given this name presumably because of its unusual method of parasitic growth. Formerly a serious pest in clover, sainfoin or lucern crops, but now less common and also now controllable. +

HELTER-KELTER. Head foremost, all together. P

HELVING. Gossipping; "hung up by the tongue". "Where have you been helving?" + (See Chatting, Cotchering, Guesting, Nabbling)

HEM. Exceedingly; very. "Hem queer old chap, he is!"

HEM-A-BIT. Not a bit. "There's hem-a-bit of cake left". †

HEMM. A mild swear word. "A hem of a great thing." "A hemming great lump." =

47

HEM-OF-A-WAY. A long way; a very considerable distance. †

HEMWOODS. Part of a cart horse's harness which goes round the collar and to which the tees are fixed; called aimes (hames) in West Kent + (See Tees)

HEN AND CHICKENS. The Ivy-leaved Toadflax (Linaria cymbalaria) common on walls and ruins. Known also as Roving Sailor, Mother of Thousands, in other counties and generally. +

HEN-CHEE. A roost for hens. "The hens are going to chee". = (See Chee, Gee)

HEN ON A CHEE STICK. A hen roosting on a perch in a hen-house. = (See Chee, Gee, Hen-Chee)

HERE AND THERE A ONE. Very few and scattered. + "There wasn't nobody much in church today, only here and there a one".

HERN1. Hers. = (See Hisn, Ourn, Theirn, Them, Therren, Yourn)

HERN2. Wealden dialect for Heron (Ardea cinerea) † (See Hernshaw, Kitty Hearn, Kitty Hearn Shrow)

HERNRY. Heronry, the nesting site of Herons. †

HERNSHAW. The Heron. + (See Hern2, Kitty Hearn, Kitty Hearn Shrow)

HERRING-FARE. The season for catching herrings, which begins about the end of corn harvesting. +

HERRING-HANG. A lofty, square, brick room, made smoke-tight, in which the herrings were hung to dry. + (See Spits)

HERRING-SPEAR. The noise of the flight and calls, "Seep", of the Redwings (Turdus musicus), whose migration to here takes place about the herring fishing time. The Folkestone fishermen in the past liked to hear them as it was believed by the fishermen they caught more fish when the flight and calls were heard. Made at night when on migration, arriving early September, departing March. +

HETCH. Move. (See Hitch, Hotch, Itch) †

HETCH UP. Move up; also means to lift up something. † (See Hitch Up, Hotch Up, Utch Up)

HETCHED UP. Moved up. † (See Hitched Up, Hotched Up).

HETHER. Hither. "Come hether, my son". P+

HEVER. A Crab, so called at Dover. P (See Heaver)

HEYCOURT. The High Court or principal Court of the Abbot's Convent of St. Augustine's, Canterbury. +

HICKET. To hiccup or hiccough. P+

HIDE. A secret site where smugglers used to hide their smuggled goods. There were many such places on the Romney Marsh and along the Kent coastline and inland, such as along the Medway Estuary. +

HIDE AND FOX. Another name for Hide and Seek, a children's pastime. In Hamlet, iv, 2.32: "Hide fox, and all after", i.e. let the fox hide and the others go to seek him P+

HIDELEST. Most idle. " 'E was the hidelest radical yew ever set eyes on."=

HIDEY-HOLE. As Hide, a smugglers' secret hiding place. =

HIGGLER, HIGLER. A "middleman" driving a horse and cart with crates in it who went around the countryside, visiting villages, farms and poultry-keepers, to buy up their eggs and poultry, for re-selling. So-called because he "higgled" or "haggled" over the price to be paid, to try and get a bargain. "I am fattening these cockerels for the higgler". +=

HIGH-LOW. An abbreviation of high and low, as in to search high and low; to seek in numerous places. †

HIGH-LOWS. A pair of laced shoes. =

HIKE. To turn out; to clear away; to remove. "He hiked him out purty quick". +

HILL. The small continuous mound or ridge in which hops are planted; a single plant in the hop garden which is trained up four to six strings, but in the past when hops were grown up poles each hill had two or three poles depending on the type of hop; also a heap of potatoes or mangolds. The name originated several centuries ago when hops were grown up poles set in hill-like mounds of soil several feet high. +*= (See Drift).

HINK. A hook at the end of a stick, or forked cleft of a thin branch, used for drawing back the peas on the bine, while it was being cut with the Pea Hook. The Pea Hook and Hink were always used together; also used with a Bagging Hook to hold back grass and weeds while being cut, or to hold corn when used with a Reaping Hook. +=(See Pea Hook)

HIRE. To rent. To "Hire" a house, farm, etc. meant to rent it as we say today. =

HISN. His. (See Hern, Ourn, Theirn, Yourn)

HIS-SELF. Himself. +*=

HITCH. Move; pull, draw up. † (See Hetch, Hotch)

HITCH OVER. Move over; push over. † (See Hitch, Hitched Up)

HITCH UP. Move up; also to push up, pull up, hold up, lift up. † (See Hetch Up, Hotch Up, Utch Up)

HITCHED UP. Moved up; joined. †*= (See Hetched Up, Hotched Up).

HITCHING. Moving; walking; also holding. †=*

HOATH,[1] HOTH. A heath. A word which is found in several Kent parish and village names, i.e. Hothfield, Hoath, Oxon Hoath. P+

HOATH[2]. Bracken. An old cocky, chap, used to tell me "When I was a young man we cut Heath (Heather) and Hoath (Bracken) at threepence a lump, so many lumps to a wagon load."—R.B. = (See Hoath[1])

HOBBLE. An entanglement; difficulty; puzzle; scrape; trouble; an awkward situation. "I'm in a reg'lar hobble". + (See Hole)

HOBBL'D. Puzzled; put to a difficulty; baffled; in a scrape. P+ (See Hobble)

HOBBLER. (See Hoveler)

HOBGROB. To eat messily. "Don't eat your food so hobgrob". =

HOB LAMB. A lamb that has been bottle-fed and reared when its parent died or had more lambs than she could feed. † (See Sock Lamb)

HOCKATTY KICK. A lame person. +

HOCKER-HEADED. Fretful; passionate; not to be confused with Hog-Headed or Pig-Headed. P+

HODENING. A custom once common in Kent at hop picking time and Christmas Eve. (See Hoodening). Even after the custom was discontinued the singing of the carols in the Christmas season was still known as Hodening for many years afterwards, until this reference also died out. In recent years variations of the custom have been revived successfully in East Kent.

HODMAN-DOD. A Snail. = (See Dodman, Snag). In other counties this word was applied to mean a scarecrow or a variety of oddities and curiosities, natural or otherwise. (See Bo-Boy)

HOG. To be a glutton over food; to eat greedily; to "hog it" in the mouth, i.e. to overfill it; most probably derived from the way hogs feed hungrily.= (See Bolt, Guzzle, Gollop, Scorf, Yaffle)

HOG-BACKED[1]. Roundbacked; round-shouldered; hunch-backed. Present day use is shaped like a hog's back or having a hog back. +*=

HOG-BACKED[2]. Applied to a vessel when, from weakness, the stern and stem fall lower than the middle of the ship. +

HOGEY-BOGEY. A couldn't care less attitude. =

HOG-HEADED. Obstinate; awkward; cussed. + (See Pig-Headed, Hocker-Headed)

HOG PAT. A pig trough made of boards. +

HOGSHOP. All over the place; strewn around; untidy. =

HOICK, OICK. To tug or remove without much bother. "Hoick that weed out". =

HOILE. The beard or stalk of Barley or other corn. + (See Iles)

HOLE. An awkward situation; a scrape; a clash, such as with the law; difficulty; a troublesome situation. "I've got meself in a proper hole this time." =*

HOLL, HULL. To throw; to hurl. P+ (See Heave, Hull, Lib, Lob)

HOLLACKING. Ungainly; awkward; clumsy; especially in a young person.=

HOLLARD. An oak hollard was a dead bough when the bark is off it and it is as hard as iron so it burns well. =

HOLLY BOYS AND IVY GIRLS. A Shrove Tuesday custom in which children took part. Two figures were made. The local boys made a figure in the form of a boy from Holly, while the girls made one in the form of a girl from Ivy. The girls, after a rumpus, then stole the "Holly Boy" from the boys, took it somewhere outside the village and ceremoniously burnt it. In the meantime the boys had stolen the "Ivy Girl" from the girls and also burnt it, to the accompaniment of loud cheers, in another part of the village. The custom was more frequent in West Kent. P+

HOLP. Helped; gave; delivered. +P (See Houp)

HOLP-UP. Overworked. "I dunno as I shaant purty soon look out another place. I be purty nigh holp-up here, I think".

HOLT. A woodland. A word which is also found in several Kent place names, i.e. Bircholt, Knockholt. P+*=

HOME-PEASIES. Local pea pickers living close to the place where the peas were to be picked, as opposed to the Furrin-Peasies (which see) who lived outside the parish. Home-Peasies were supposedly more reliable as workers than Furrin-Peasies and grumbled less about pay and working conditions. This word has the same context as Home Pickers, the name for local hop or fruit pickers used in mid-Kent, the Ashford Valley and Weald areas. †

HOME PICKERS. Local hop and fruit pickers. † (See Home-Peasies)

HOMESTALL. The enclosure of ground immediately connected with a mansion house; the place of a mansion house. Probably original of Homestead. Pegge described it as "the house the family lives in". P+

HOMMUCKS. Great, awkward feet; applied to feet sprawled out when a person is sitting in a chair. "Get your hommucks out of it afore I trip over 'em". +

HOOD. Wood. =

HOODEN. Wooden. =

HOODING. Pegge described it as "a country masquerade at Christmas time, which in Derbyshire they call guising (supposedly a contraction of dis-guising) and in other places mumming." P (See Hoodening)

HOODENING. The "Hooden Horse" custom; a masquerade or mumming held at hop picking time and Christmas in Kent, though at different times and with varied names in other counties. According to Parish & Shaw: "In the custom of Hoodening a farmer used to annually send round the neighbourhood the best horse in the charge of a waggoner. Later, instead, a man was used to represent the horse, being supplied with a tail and with a wooden (pronounced ooden or hooden) figure of a horse's head and plenty of horsehair for a mane. The horse's head was fitted with hob-nails for teeth; the mouth being made to open by means of a string and in closing made a loud crack." (See Hoodening). The Hooden Horse was accompanied by a Fool who kept the spectators in a good humour and by Mollie who, using a birch broom, swept in front of the horse and thus drove away the evil spirits. Sometmes the Horse was also accompanied by a waggoner to lead "him" and either hand-bell ringers or various local musicians. Calls were made at various places in the village when the "mumping" or begging took place. It was supposedly good luck to give a sum to the Horse, the money being devoted to the church or parish poor, while the Horse and its accompanying party were invited into the houses for a glass of refreshment and some cake, at which the Horse's presence bestowed "good fortune" on all the household. Sometimes the Horse man beneath the covering got so inebriated with the numerous glasses of various alcoholic drinks that "it" got really lively by the time the Hoodening was at an end. This custom is becoming increasingly popular in East Kent and there are Hop Hoodening and Christmas Hoodening events that take place, some adapted to modern times, one group responsible for its popularity being the East Kent Morris Men.

HOOGO, HOOGOO. A bad smell; a stench; possibly a corruption of the French haut gout. "Where be that hoo-go comin' from?" + (See Fargo, Fago, Fogo)

HOOK. An agricultural tool for cutting, of which there are several types and sizes, i.e. Bagging or Brishing; Ripping, Pea, etc. + (See under relevant names)

HOOT. Command to a horse to go to the right. = (See Whoot)

HOP1. To pick hops. +*=

HOP2. Wood fit for hop poles. +

HOP-BIND, HOP-BINE, HOP-VINE. The Stem of the Hop (Humulus lupulus), either dead or growing. +*= (See Bine, Grape-Vine)

HOP-CAT. Larvae of the Pale Tussock moth (Dasychira pudibunda), found feeding on hop foliage. Recognised because it has several tufts of hairs, like shaving brushes, along its back. =

Hop Dog[2]

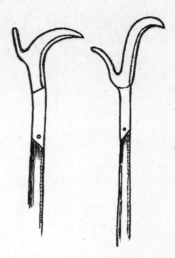

Hop Goad or Hop Hook

HOP-DOG[1]. Larvae of the Peppered moth (Biston betularia). Not to be confused with the Hop Cat (which see). The Peppered moth's green, brownish green or purplish brown caterpillar is found feeding also on the foliage of Hops. Another name for it is Land Measurer because of its method of crawling up a twig, looping its body every inch or so as it progresses. +*= (See Measuring Bug)

HOP-DOG[2]. An iron instrument used by the Pole-Puller for drawing the hop-bearing poles out of the ground. It was a V-shaped piece of iron attached approximately 18 inches from the end of a 5 to 7 feet long pole, the "V" having a series of teeth cut by the blacksmith who made it. The "teeth", when the instrument was used, gripped the bottom of the hop pole and with the lower end of the Hop Dog's pole resting on the hop hill, enabled the Pole-Puller to lever the pole loose from the ground so it could be taken to the pickers who picked in the old style with the pole and hops resting on the bin. += (See Hop-Jack)

HOP-DOG[3]. The name of an iron bar implement. = (See Hop-Pitcher)

HOPE. A place of anchorage for ships. Still in use. *+=

HOPKIN. A supper for the "hopping" workers after the hop picking season was ended. Name survives in a kind of small cake called Huffkin, formerly made for this particular "hopping" feast. P+ (See Huffkin, Wheatkin)

HOP GOAD or HOOK. An implement used by the Pole-Puller to cut and retrieve pieces of the bine left high on the wires after the bine has been

pulled down by pickers or to disentangle bines grown together on top of the poles. (See Heads). A pole, up to 12 feet long, as the handle, had at the top a curved billhook-type cutting blade, with a spike on the back or heel, used as the hook to lift off or push off the hop bearing bine pieces. The hooks varied in style according to district. =*

HOP-JACK. An implement like a large pair of pincers which were used to pull resistant poles from the earth, in gardens where the hops were trained up poles and not strings. = (See Hop-Dog[2])

HOPPER. A hop picker. Still in use. "I seed the poor hoppers coming home all drenched". +*=

HOP PEDDLER. A small single-tined tool used in hop cultivation. = (See Peddler, Tommy Hoe)

HOP-PEELER. A heavy pointed iron bar used to make holes in the earth for setting hop poles in. = (See Hop-Pitcher)

HOPPING. Hop picking. The season of hop picking. "A fine harvest, a wet hopping" — East Kent proverb. +*=

HOPPING HATS. It was formerly the custom in the hop gardens to decorate hats when the last hops had been picked. Coloured paper, feathers, straw, ribbons, wild flowers and leaves were used and the wearer of the best decorated hat received a prize when

51

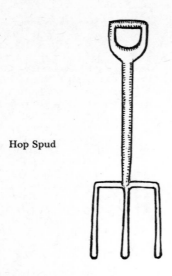

Hop Spud

the hopping feast or Hopkin was held (which see). =

HOPPINY. Descriptive of the weather typical of the hop picking season. "That's proper hoppiny s'morning' ".

HOP-PITCHER. A heavy, three-feet long iron bar with a drawn-out bulbous point and wood T-handle used to make holes for setting the hop poles in, also called a Dog; Hop-Dog, or a Fold-Pitcher. The Hop-Pitcher was thrust in the earth and worked around to make the required hole depth, there also sometimes being an adjustable iron foot attached to it to help the user penetrate the ground and judge the hole depth. The Pitcher when used for making holes for stakes, fence posts, etc., was sometimes shorter than one used for making hop pole holes. + (See Hop-Peeler)

HOP SAMPLING KNIFE. A double bladed knife used to cut a square out of a hop pocket to obtain a sample of the pressed hops therein. = (See Hop Sampling Pincers)

HOP SAMPLING PINCERS. A pair of pincers with up to eight tines, used to withdraw a sample of pressed hops from a pocket. = (See Hop Sampling Knife)

HOP SPUD. A large, heavy, wide spaced three flat-tined fork, with a bend at the base of the handle, used to dig the "slips", the land around the hop "hills", after winter ploughing. +*= (See Spud, Spudder)

HORN. A corner of a field, land or building.+

HORN FAIR. An annual fair held at Charlton, then in Kent, now in S.E. London, on St. Luke's Day, 18th October. It consisted of an "unruly and riotous" mob who, after a printed summons, dispersed through the adjacent towns, met at Cuckold's Point near Deptford, and marched from there, in procession, through Deptford, Greenwich to Charlton, with horns of different kinds upon their heads. At the Fair ram's horns were sold and every sort of toy made of horn and the gingerbread figures sold even had horns. It was also the custom for men to go there to the Fair dressed in women's clothes. +

HORNICLE. A Hornet (Vespa crabro) P+

HORSE[1]. The arrangement of hop poles, tied across from hill to hill, upon which the pole-pullers rested the poles for the pickers to gather the hops into the bins or baskets. + (See Hop-Dog[2].)

HORSE[2]. To tie the upper branches of the hop bine to the pole. +

HORSEBUCKLE. The Cowslip (Primula veris). + (See Cove Keys, Lady Keys, Peigle)

HORSE EMMETS. Large Ants, possibly those which appear at swarming time in sultry summer weather. + (See Emmet)

HORSE FLY. A Dragonfly. =

HORSE KNOT. A wild plant, Knapweed (Centaurea nigra), sometimes also known in rural counties as Hardweed and Hardheads. +

HORSE-LOCK. A padlock. +

HORSENAILS. Tadpoles. +P

HORSE PEPPERMINT. A member of the Mint family, Horse Mint (Mentha sylvestris), found on damp waste ground.

HORSE ROAD. A very old dialect term originating from the time when it was common to make a journey on horse-back, the road being divided into the foot-road for pedestrians and the horse-road for riding travellers. A later adaptation from this has been the universal "carriage-way" or "carriage road" and "footpath". +

HORSES. Used in the expression "To set horses together", i.e. to agree. "George and his old woman can't set their horses together at all." +

HORSEWAY. A country lane or road, a path or track used by horses to and from a field or woodland. A modern example is Bridle-Path. = (See Horse Road)

HORT. Hurt. "Have yer hort yerself?" P+

HOSSES. Horses. =

HOSSING. Applied to a Mare. = (See Brimming Sow)

HOT UP. To heat. "Just hot up the kettle". =

HOTCH. To move awkwardly or with difficulty in an irregular and scrambling way; mainly used of infirm eldderly or crippled persons; used also to describe a trotting sort of walk. When a man walking quickly with a boy by his side keeps the latter on the run he is described as keeping him "hotching". Hotch is also a variation of Hetch and Hitch, meaning to move. "I hustled through the crowd and she hotched after me" +*= (See Hetch, Hitch, Itch, Utch-About and Ruggle-About)

HOTCH UP. Move up. †*= (See Hetch Up, Hitch Up)

HOTCHED UP. Moved up; also means worried, unable to cope with, at a loss; and other quite different meanings: penned in, cornered, trapped. †*=

HOTCHING. Walking. † (See Hotch)

HOUGHED. Derived from to hough, i.e. to cripple, to hock, to hamstring. Used also as an expletive, a meaningless profanity, an oath. +

HOUGHER. A man who houghed or houghes cattle. =

HOUP. Pegge states: "holpen, i.e. helped; from holp, the l being left out". P (See Holp)

HOUSE. To get the corn in from the fields into the barn. "We've housed all our corn". +

HOUSEL. Household, meaning household stuff or furniture. "I doan't think these here newcomers be up to much; leastways they didn't want a terr'ble big cart to fetch their housel along; they had most of it home in a wheelbar'." P+

HOUSEY. Tangled. Used to describe tangled branches of hops or two hop bines that have grown together, perhaps forming a thick canopy over the alley and difficult to disentangle to pick. *=

HOVEL1. To carry on the business of a Hoveler. +

HOVEL2. A piece of good luck; a good haul; a good turn or time of hovelling. In some of the fishing families in the past children were taught to say in their prayers "God bless father and mother and send them a good hovel tonight".

HOVELER. A coastal boatman who does odd-jobbing; goes out to the assistance of ships in distress, not sinking but generally mechanical or victualling; also carries out provisions, recovers lost anchors, chains and gear. They were first rate seamen and their vessels well built and manned. Also the name for the Hoveler's vessel. Sometimes both boatmen and their vessel was known as Hobblers or Hufflers. +*=

HOVER1. Light; puffy; raised; shivery; unwell; hunched up. Used particularly of birds if their feathers are puffed up in cold weather. +†*=

HOVER2. To throw together lightly. There was an especial use of this word with regard to hops. In East Kent and occasionally elsewhere in the county it was the custom to pick the hops, not in bins, but in large baskets that hold five or six bushels. The pickers gathered the hops into their own small baskets, boxes, baths, tubs, etc., which they then tipped into the large basket until it was full. In the past the tallyman was then called, who arrived accompanied by two other men with the greenbag or poke. One of the pickers, usually a woman, then hovered the hops. This was done by putting both hands deep into the basket as close to the bottom as possible, the woman all the time gently raising the hops with her hands. As soon as they were disturbed enough and reached the top of the basket, they were quickly shot into the greenbag or poke before the hops had time to sag or sink again. Thus very inadequate measure was obtained, as probably nearly a bushel was lost in every tally. This was partly avoided when some of the 5-bushel baskets were equipped with hovering strings that were pulled to loosen or "hover up" the hops. Hovering was nothing more than a recognised system of fraud, but not willing to lose the pickers the growers allowed it to continue, though many later used bins and a binman, a more fair method for both sides, though just prior to measuring it was still customary to hover the hops and heap them at an angle to make it easier to scoop into the bushel basket. Even today, or in recent times when hops were hand picked entirely, a measurer's popularity among pickers was gauged by whether he took a "light" or "heavy" (which see) measure when the hops were being measured out of the bin into the greenbag. (See Huvver[2])

HOVER[3]. Cold; poorly; ailing. + (See Hover[1], Huvver, Hovvery, Hovvered Up)

HOVER[4]. Light; hover ground, i.e. light ground. P (See Huvver[2])

HOVVER. As Hover[3]. †

HOVVERED-UP. Pinched up wih the cold weather; numb; cramped by the cold. † (See Pithered, Puckered Up); another meaning being tangled, as with string; in a mess; humped together. †

HOVVERY. Very shivery; numb with the cold. † (See Hovvered Up)

HOW[1]. Who. P

HOW[2]. About how, near the matter; "that's about how" meaning "that is sufficiently near to the right way of doing the thing". P

HOWSOMEDEVER, HOWSOMEEVER. Howsoever; however. "But, howsomedever, doan't ram it down tight, but hover it up a bit". P+

HUCK[1]. A corruption of hock, an ankle or foot. † (See Hucks)

HUCK[2]. A husk, pod or shell of peas, beans, but especially hazel nuts and walnuts. (See Shuck) †*=

HUCK[3]. To shell peas; to get walnuts out of their cases; to shake hazel nuts from their husks. "Are the walnuts ready to pick?" "No, sir. I tried some and they won't huck". +*=

HUCK[4]. A collar for tethering. If a dog was chained to a post with a collar but the animal set back and pulled the collar over its ears and escaped it was said to have "slipped its huck". Also applied to a horse if it pulled the strap it was tied up with, if a strap was used and not a halter. = (See Slipped Her Huck)

HUCKALONERS. Christmas nuts. =

HUCK OUT. To pull or take out something, usually from a cupboard. †

HUCKS. Ankles or feet; a corruption of hocks. the human ankles or feet. † (See Huck[1], Huxon)

HUCKY. As Ucky. Probably derived from "husky" for the outer skin, husk or shell of seeds, nuts, etc. *=

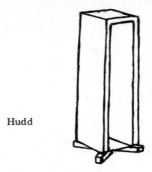

Hudd

HUDD. An upright, flat-topped wood box, six feet high, two feet wide, one side open, standing on wood crosspieces as the "feet". It was used at funerals in the 18th century when the parson wore a wig. After being carried to the graveside the parson stood inside it while he conducted the service to protect himself and his wig from the inclement weather. An example survives in St. Augustine's church, Brookland. =

HUFFKIN, HUFKIN. A kind of bun or light cake which was cut open, buttered and so eaten. +*= (See Hopkin)

HUFFLE. A merry meeting; a feast. P+ (See Hopkin, Huffkin)

HUFFLER[1]. One that carries off fresh provisions to ships. P (See Hoveler)

HUFFLER[2]. An additional hand on a sailing barge to help perform a difficult operation, particularly used of the men, often retired skippers, who assisted barges to "shoot" Rochester and Aylesford bridges. The Huffler usually took the wheel while the skipper and mate lowered the sails and mast. A highly skilled job in fast tidal races without the assistance of an engine.

HUGE, HUGY. Very. "I'm not huge well". According to Parish & Shaw; "Sometimes they make it a dissyllable, hugy. The saying hugy for huge is merely the sounding of the final e, as in the case of the name Anne, commonly pronounced. An-ni. It is not Annie". +P

HULL[1]. The shell of a pea. "After we have sheel'd them we throw the hulls away". To "hull" peas is to open the pod and remove the peas. +=

HULL[2]. To hurl; to throw. "He took and hulled a gurt libbat at me". + (See Holl, Lib, Lob)

HULL[3]. To thresh small seeds. A thresher used for White Clover threshing was always called a Clover Huller. = (See Hull[1], Hull[2])

HULVE. To gossip; stand or sit talking. = (See Elve, Chatting, Cotchering, Nabble)

HUM. To whip a top. +

HUMMOCK. A small mound. An Ammit (Ant) Hill is a Hummock. =

HUNG UP. Foiled; hindered, prevented; delayed. "He is quite hung up", i.e. so circumstanced that he is prevented from carrying out his plans. =+

HUNG UP BY THE TONGUE. Meant delayed by talking, sometimes in idle gossip, with another person. =

HUNK. A crust of bread with cheese. =* (See Chuck, Chunk, Snowl)

HURR, HURRISH. Harsh; sour; tart; astringent; crude. "These damsons be terr'ble hurrish". Fruit that dries the mouth or puts teeth on edge were described as being "a bit hurr". +*=

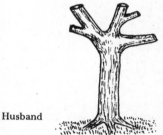

Husband

HUSBAND. A pollarded tree with branches lopped or cut back; a polled animal, ram, etc.; a stag that has shed its antlers. +=

HUSS. The Lesser Spotted Dogfish (Scyllium canicula). A good fish to eat if cooked properly. *=+ (See Robin Huss, Bull Huss, Spurfish, Sweet Williams)

HUSSLE. To wheeze; breathe roughly. "Jes listen to un how he hussles". +

HUSSLING. A wheezing; a sound of rough breathing. "He had such a hussling on his chest". +

HUSSY. To chafe or rub the hands when they are cold. +

HUSTLE. To walk briskly; to get a move on; to do a job speedily. "My! You got a hustle on with that." =*

HUTCH. The upper part of a wagon which carries the load. A wagon consists of three parts: the hutch or open box (sometimes enlarged by an addition of floats) which carries the corn or other load and is supported by the wheels; the tug, by which it is drawn; and the wheels on which it runs. P+

HUVVER[1]. Unwell; shivery; cold. "I feel all of a huvver today". = (See Hover[1], Kivver, Kivvery)

HUVVER[2]. Soil that is loose, light, nicely workable. "We can get on with planting now the earth is nicely 'uvver". Similar meaning to Hover[4]: lying lightly; ground needing to be pressed down is "too huvver"; to "huvver up" hops as Hover[2]; shake up if lying too close or dense in the oast when being dried. A moist, light wind was also "Huvver". =

HUVVERY. Very shivery; cramped with the cold. † (See Hovvery, Kivvery)

HUXON. The hocks or hams; flesh on fore or hind leg of pig immediately above foot. P+ (See Hucks)

HUY. A word used in fraying, i.e. frightening or driving hogs. From the French hue still used in the phrase "hue and cry". P

HYSTE. A call; a signal. "Just give me a hyste when tis time to go" +

I

I BE. I am. Probably the more authentic Kent usage, by the older inhabitants, whereas "I're (which see) and "I are" were most likely a later degenerate and clovenly form.

ICE. To freeze. "The pond iced over last night". +

ICE-CANDLES. Icicles. G (See Aquabob, Cobble, Cobbells, Icily, Cockbell, Cogbell".

ICILY. An unusual manner of saying icicle. +

IDDEN. Is not; isn't. "It idden in there". †

IGGET. See Nidget.

IKEY. Proud; snobbish. Not to be confused with Ikey-Mo and Piky. †*=

IKEY-MO. Possibly an abbreviation of Isaac Moses to describe a Jew, implying a person had a Jewish ancestry or background, or more commonly was a miserly, mean person. "He's a proper Ikey-Mo with his money". *=

ILES. Ails or beards of Barley. P+ (See Hoile)

ILLCONVENIENT. Inconvenient. "Twill be purty illconvenient fur me". +

INDURABLE. Durable; very durable. Endurable in general English use. P

INKLE. Strong, coarse tape, hand-made, as a single tape, on a loom. = (See Saying 82)

INKSPEWER. A Cuttlefish (Sepia officinalis) + (See Mansucker, Tortoise).

INNARDLY. Inwardly. "He says his words innardly," i.e. he mumbles. +

INNARDS1. An innings at cricket. "They bested 'em first innards". +=

INNARDS2. The entrails or intestines, either human or animal. +*=

INNOCENT. Small and pretty; applied to flowers. "I do always think they paigles looks so innocent". +

IN 'OPES. For "in hopes". Once a very common phrase, particularly in East Kent where people rarely said "I hope", but almost always "I'm in 'opes". When an enquiry was made concerning a sick person, the answer would most likely be "I'm in 'opes he's better". If a girl went to a new place "in service" her mother would remark "I'm in 'opes she'll like herself and stay." Still a frequently used expression to say "I'm living in hopes", i.e. hoping for good luck, or some change in fortune. *=

INSUNDERS. Asunder; in two halves or pieces. + (See Sinders)

INTERFERES. Annoys or hinders. "I was obliged to cut my hand t'other day, that's what interferes with me". +

INTERRUPT. To annoy; to interfere with anyone by word or deed; to assault. "He's always interrupting people". Parish & Shaw quote the instance: "A man whose companion, at cricket, kept running against him was heard to say: 'It does interrupt me to think you can't run your right side. What a thick head you must have!' "

I'RE. I are; I am. = (See I Be)

ISLAND. In East Kent "the island" meant the Isle of Thanet. "He lives up in the island some'er", i.e. he lives somewhere in Thanet. +

ITCH1. To creep; to crawl about. Variant of Hotch (which see) + (See also Ruggle-About, Utch-About)

ITCH2. To be very anxious. +

ITCHEL, ITCHELLS, ITCHULL. Used as a figure of speech for closeness, an example being the closeness of the pins forming the teeth of the hackle used to comb flax. "My little boy has got chickenpox as thick as itchells", i.e. the spots are as close together as these flax-working teeth. A mass of weeds or dense fog, etc., were also said to be "as thick as itchel". Used in Kent and Sussex. = (See Inkle in Sayings chapter).

ITCHULL. See Itchel. "I sowed some seeds and they came up as thick as itchull". =

IVY GIRL. P+ (See Holly Boys)

J

JACK.1 (See Tamsin)

JACK.2 Jack Hern (Heron); Jack and Sally Hare. =

JACK HARRY. A drag; a tool used for dragging dung out of a cart, etc., weeds out of a watery ditch, breaking down a garden. A long handled tool often made of a fork bent over at the tines, or halfway up the tines or speens. (In Sussex it is known as a Ditch-Hook-A.M.) =

JACK-IN, JACK-UP. To throw up work or a task; to give notice or give up anything from pride, impudence or bad temper. "They kep' on one wik and then they all jacked-up". "He's so poorly, he'll have to jack-in the extra work". +

JACK AND HIS WAIN. The North Pole Star and the Plough. =

JACK IN THE BOX. A reddish-purple double Polyanthus, formerly commonly grown in gardens. +

JAKES. The lavatory. =

JAUL. To throw the earth about and get the grain out of the ground when it is sown, as birds, such as Rooks, do. When they do this it is said they "jaul it" out. P+

JAWSY. Talkative; a chatterbox; referring to the jaws. P+

Jesus' Flannel

JESUS' FLANNEL. A garden plant, similar to Red Campion in shape, with whitish-grey, soft, velvet-like leaves and crimson-magenta flowers, better known as Agrostemma or Rose Campion (Lychnis coronaria) = (See Our Saviour's Flannel.) My grandmother, from Petham area of Canterbury, called it by the name of Jesus' Flannel. Known in other counties as Christ's Eye, Rose of Mary and Gardener's Delight. It is related to another Lychnis, called Jerusalem Cross.

JIMMY HEDGE MOPER. The Hedge Sparrow or Dunnock. *= (See Dicky Hedge Poker)

JOCK. To jolt; the hard form of jog. +

JOCKEY. Rough; uneven. +

JOCLET. A small manor or farm. +

JOICKS. Gipsies. =

JOIND-STOOL, JOYND-STOOL. A stool framed with joints, instead of being fashioned roughly out of a single block. +

JOKESY. Amusing; full of jokes and fun; cheerful and witty. "He's a very jokesy man". +

JOLE. A corruption of jowl, the jaw or cheek; hence the expression "Cheek by jole or jowl" — side by side. +

JOLLY1. Fit and well; in good health.†

JOLLY2. Fat; plump; sleek; in good condition; used to describe the condition of the body, not of the temperament. +

JOLLY LOOKING. Having a healthy complexion and appearance. †

JONNICK1, JONNOCK, JONNUCK. A questionable action or saying; something not fair or quite genuine; anything niggling or gouging; a cheating deed was "not quite jonnick". =

JONNICK.2 Alright; correct; in order. =

JONNIE. An adult wild rabbit. †

JOSKIN. A farm labourer, usually a driver of horses or a carter's mate, who was engaged to work the complete year for one master. +

JOSS-BLOCK, JOSSING-BLOCK, JOSTLING BLOCK. A step or several steps used in mounting a horse outside inns, stables, or by church gates. The horse block or mounting step or steps made of wood, stone, flints or bricks, to which the horse must be made to joss, i.e., come as close as possible to enable the rider to mount it. += (See Jossing-Block Custom)

Joss Block

JOSSING-BLOCK CUSTOM. There is a charity in existence at Ightham that dates back to the 16th century. When Henry Peyrse of Milton-by-Gravesend died in 1546 he decreed in his Will "that the Poor of Ightham for ever receive ye yearly sum of 6s 8d. and 2s to the churchwardens who are to distribute ye same before his mansion house door on the Friday before mid-Lent Sunday, by 2 pence a-piece as far as it will go. Payable out of his said mansion in Ightham". The latter became the "George & Dragon" Inn. Later the money was distributed from a square, stone, jossing-block, cut with three stone steps, by the side of the lych-gate at the entrance into Ightham churchyard and thus the money was called "jossing block money". "Joss-block" was Provincial English meaning a horse-block, which was used to stand on to mount a horse. For a number of years the custom was held at the "joss-block" but F.J. Bennett in "The Story of Ightham" in 1907, refers to the custom as "once more being dispensed in the shape of twopence to everyone passing by the "George & Dragon" Inn on the said Friday". The original charity left money, charged on land, to provide books for poor children to learn the catechism and bread to be distributed to the poor at Easter. = (See Joss-Block)

JOUN. Joined. "He jouned in with a party of run-o'-gate chaps and 'twasn't long afore he'd made away wid all he'd got". +=

JOUTERING. Nagging; continually arguing; grousing; grumbling. = (See Grousing)

JOY. The wild bird, the common Jay (Garrulus glandarius) =

JUDGMATICAL. With a sense of judgment. +

JULY BUG. The Cockchafer Beetle (Melolontha meloiontha). + (See Bug)

JUMPER. A device for cutting down hay and straw in a stable loft, using a foot for power. †

JUNE BUG. A species of green beetle, the Rose Chafer (Cetonia aurata), smaller than a Cockchafer or July Bug, which appeared as a pest on roses in June. But the Garden Chafer (Phyllopertha horticola), metallic bluish-green, with reddish-brown wing cases, was also known as the June Bug (See Bug) +

JUST. Very; extremely. "I was just angry with him" +

JUST SO. Very exactly; precisely; thoroughly; near perfect; in one particular way. "The mistress is not satisfied unless things are done just so". +

JUSTLY. Exactly; precisely; for certain. In other counties the word "rightly" is used for the Kentish "justly". "I cannot justly say" i.e. "I cannot say for certain". +

JUT. A pail with a long handle. +

K

KARF, KARFE. The cut made by a saw; the hole or incision made by the first strokes of an axe in felling timber or chopping wood. P+ (See Carfe)

KEAF. A calf. P

KEALS. Ninepins; skittles. +P (See Cailes, Cales, Kick Up Jenny).

KEEKLEGS. The Early Purple Orchid (Orchis mascula), occurring in Bluebell woodlands. + (See Kite's Legs, Keetlegs)

KEELER1. A cooler, being the special name given to a broad, shallow vessel of wood, wherein milk is set to cream or wort to cool. "Half a butter-tub makes as good a keeler as anything". P+

KEELER.2 An oblong wooden tub in which country housewives did their washing. Sometimes also called a Shaul, but only when mounted on trestles. † (See Shaul)

KEEN, KEYN. The Weasel (Mustela nivalis), a carnivorous wild animal. In the Bredgar area near Sittingbourne, a small weasel-type animal was known to local people as a KEAN or KEEN and thought of as a separate species similar to the larger Weasel. In Lincolnshire and East Anglia there is a rare breed of Dwarf Weasel often little larger than the mice it hunts. It is pale-coloured and known in those areas as the Mouse-Hunter. In Sussex the Weasel is known as the Cane. P= (See Kine, Puttice)

KEEP-ALL-ON. To continue; to persevere in doing something; to finish a task regardless of difficulty. +*=

KEETLEGS. (See Keeklegs, Kite's Legs). =

KEG-MEG. A newsmonger; a gossip; a rumour-monger; usually applied to women. "Doan't believe a word of Mrs Brown. She's a proper keg-meg". +

KELL. A hop kiln or other kiln. +

KELTER. Out of alignment. *†= (See Kilter)

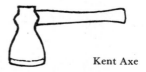

Kent Axe

KENT AXE. A general purpose axe. It was named after the county because it was first developed and used in Kent and is now the only pattern surviving out of several English axes. There are also variations of this axe, but the majority of Kent axes have a symmetrical blade with a curved cutting edge, curved shoulders, pointed lugs in front of and behind the eye and a flat poll, the side of the blade being known as the bit and the side of the axe between the lugs being the cheek. =

Kent Hoe

KENT HOE. A two-pronged hoe used by the hop "dressers" for "dressing" the hops in the gardens, sometimes used in conjunction with a Tommy Hoe (which see). = (See Clod Hoe, Clump Hoe, Corn Hoe, Half-Mattock, Axe Een Mattock, Weald Hoe, Plate Hoe, Peck, Double-Sider Hoe)

KENTISH MAN. A name given by those born and resident in the Weald to persons who lived in other parts of the county. Alternatively, those Kentish people who were born west of the Medway are Kentish Men or Women; those born east of the Medway were known as Men of Kent and still are. +*= (See Men of Kent).

KENTISH SADDLE. A simple, heavy horse saddle made in Kent and West Sussex. It comprised a tree with a well padded panel tied to the boards with leather thongs, worn without any leather housing and also without metal channels or protective plates fixed to the saddle. Instead of a back chain or Redger (which see) an iron Redger Bar or Bail Ridger (which see) was used. *=

KEPT-GOING. Active, i.e. up and out of bed; continued to work. "He's not bin well for some time, but he's kept going until Saddaday he was forced to give up". +*=

KERN. To corn; produce corn. Good cornland was said to be good kerning land. P+

KETTLEMAN. The Angler Fish or Frog-fish (Lophius piscatorius); also called the Sea Devil due to its remarkable appearance, with a large head, broader than it is long, while the body is short and tapering. It has a very wide mouth, with protruding lower jaw and two rows of sharp teeth in each jaw. +

KETTLEBENDER. A bread sop commonly eaten by poorer working folk at dinner and teatime when other food was scarce. Made by cutting a slice of bread, sometimes toasted, into a basin, salt and pepper were added and a lump of dripping if available. If latter was not Kettlebender was also still made without it. Hot water was then poured on to the bread until it was pappy and then eaten. = (See Pappy)

KEY BEER. Ale or a better sort of beer kept under lock and key. G

KEYS. Winged seeds of Ash trees, occasionally also applied to those of the Sycamore tree. Word now widely used elsewhere. Parish & Shaw state: "The Sycamore is a quick growing tree, but troublesome near a house, because the keys do get into the gutters so, and in between the stones in the stable-yard". +*=

Kibsy

KIBSY, KIPSY. A basket, with a handle over the top and having one side flat, which rests against the back and is secured around the waist by a leather belt. Used by cherry pickers and when full contains 12 lbs of cherries. *=

KICK UP JENNY. A game commonly played in public houses with ninepins, smaller than skittles, and a lead or other metal or wooden ball which was fastened to a cord suspended from the ceiling, exactly over the centre pin. When skilfully handled the ball was swung from the extreme length of the cord, so as to bring down all the pins at once. + (See Cailes, Keals)

KIDDLE. To tickle. "Stop your kiddling me". = (See Kittle)

KIDWARE. Peas, beans, etc. Pulse growing in cods or pods. The name

Kidware is also used in Hampshire where it may have originated. G+

KILK. Charlock or Wild Mustard (Brassica sinapistrum). Used in the Weald of Kent, also in other rural counties. P+*= (See Kinkle2)

KILN. The circular part of the Oast-house to one end of the building. On the ground floor are the fires, on the first floor the kiln itself, where the hops are dried. *=

KILN-BRUSH. A large kind of fagot bound with two wiffs or withies, used for heating kilns. + (See Baven, Bobbin, Fagot, Wiff)

KILLED-DEAD. Killed instantly; killed outright. Sometimes the expression still used is "killed stone dead". †

KILTER. Out of alignment. *†= (See Kelter)

KINDLY. Used in reference to land which is productive and pays for cultivation. "Some of it is kindly land, some of it ain't". +

KINE. A Weasel. = (See Keen, Keyn)

KING JOHN'S MEN. One of. A term applied to describe a short man. "He's one of King John's Men, six score to the hundred". Six score, 120, was the Old Hundred or Long Hundred. +

KINK1. A tangle; a hitch or knot in a rope, wool, etc. "Take care or you'll get it into a kink". +

KINK2. To hitch; twist; get in a tangle. Anything bent is still described as "having a kink in it". Used elsewhere. +

KINKLE1. A tangle; a confusion. Not to be confused with Kinkle for Charlock. "Now its in a proper kinkle". + (See Kink)

KINKLE2. Charlock. Used in East Kent. P+*= (See Kilk)

KINTLE. A small piece; a little corner. + (See Cantel)

KIPPERED. Chapped; spoken of the hands and lips, when the skin is cracked in cold weather. "My hands are kippered". +

KIPPER-TIME. The close season for Salmon. A.D. 1376 — "The Commons pray that no salmon be caught in the Thames between Gravesend and Henly Bridge in kippertime, i.e. between the Feast of the Invention of the Cross (14th September) and the Epiphany (6th January) and that the Wardens suffer no unlawful net

to be used therein" — Dunkin's "History of Kent". +

KISSICK. The area that is most dry, tickly or sore in a Kissicky-Throat. † (See Tissick)

KISSICKY. When the throat is dry, tickly or sore. † (See Tissicky)

KISSICKY-THROAT. A dry, tickly or sore throat. †

KITE'S LEGS. The Early Purple orchid (Orchis mascula) + (See Keek-legs, Keetlegs)

KITTENS. The baskets in which the fish were packed on the beach at Folkestone to be sent by train to London and elsewhere. +

KITTLE1. To tickle. +P

KITTLE2, KITTLISH. Ticklish; uncertain; difficult to manage; possibly variation of skittish in general use. P+ Pegge says: "So fickle and uncertain weather they call "kittle" weather".

KITTLE3. Kettle. †=*

KITTY - COME - DOWN - THE - LANE - JUMP-UP-AND-KISS-ME. The Cuckoo Pint, Wild Arum, Lords-and-Ladies, etc. (Arum maculatum)

KITTY HEARN. The Heron. + (See Hern, Hernshaw)

KITTY HEARN SHROW. The Heron. This name was used in the Chilham area where there is a famous Heronry in the grounds of the Castle. + (See Hern, Hernshaw, Kitty Hern)

Kitty Run The Street

KITTY-RUN-THE-STREET. The Wild Pansy or Heartsease (Viola tricolor).+

KIVVER1. Shiver. † (See Huvver)

KIVVER2. A Wealden corruption of cover. †

KIVVERED1. Very cold and shivery. Used in the Medway Towns area and Isle of Sheppey. † (See Kivver1)

KIVVERED2. A Wealden corruption of covered. †

KIVVERY. Shivery. Used in the Medway Towns area and Isle of Sheppey. † (See Huvvery)

KNET. To knit; as to knet stockings. P

KNOB. A round-topped hill, or a large lump; = (See Nob, Knolles)

KNOLL. A hill or bank; a small round hill; a knoll of sand, a knole; used in place names, such as Knole, Knowlton. P+ (See Nob, Knob, Knolles)

KNOLLES. Turnips. G Pegge says: "Knolls or round-headed roots, or turnips, so-called in Kent". (See Knoll)

KNOWED. Knew; known. I've knowed 'im since 'e wus a boy". +

KNUCKER. To neigh. +

KUTCHEL. Odd quantity or small amount left over of a sack of corn or meal. =

L

LACE. To flog; to beat. + (See Lamm, Lay-into, Dob, Swipe, Wallop, Lash-Out, Leather).

LADY BUG. The Ladybird beetle (see Bug, Marygold). Either the Two-spot Ladybird or Seven-spot Ladybird. In Kent it was considered unlucky to deliberately kill one because it is a useful insect and also because its name has associations with Our Lady, the Blessed Virgin Mary, as is seen by its other dialect name Marygold. +

Lady-Lords

LADY-LORDS. The Lords-and-Ladies, Cuckoo Pint, Wild Arum, etc. (Arum maculatum). + (See Kitty-Come-Down-The-Lane-Jump-Up-And-Kiss-Me, Lady Keys).

LADY KEYS. The Cowslip. (Primula veris). (See Cove Keys, Culver Keys, Paigle, Pegle, Horsebuckle). Parish & Shaw state that this dialect name was also used for the Wild Arum, Lady-Lords, Cuckoo Pint, etc. (Arum maculatum). This latter may be an error in identity or was a former local use but Lady Keys for the Cowslip was and is much more widespread in Kent. +*=

LADIES' FINGERS. The Early Purple Orchid (Orchis mascula). = (See Keeklegs, Kite's Legs)

LAID-IN. A meadow or grazing pasture is said to be laid in when stock are kept out to allow the grass to grow. Sanders gives an illustration of the use of Lay (which see). +

LAID UP. Bedridden; off work and confined to bed by ill-health or injury. A possible origin was from "laying up" of a ship for repair or breaking. =*

LAIN. A thin coat, layer or laying of snow on the ground. "There's quite a lain of snow". +

LAIRY. Odd or rough-looking. = (See Leary)

LAMM. Hit; chastise; beat; smack †*= (See Clout, Clump, Dob, Larrup, Swipe)

LANT FLOUR. Fine flour. Pegge states: "Fine flour, i.e. lawn'd or sears'd through a lawn. I think the better sort say lawn'd-flour." The verb searse means to strain. P+

LARLOES AND MEDLARS. The reply when one asked what is for sweet, or any question one does not want to answer. = (See "Air Pie", etc. in Terms and Expressions chapter).

LARRUP1. Beat; chastise; smack; clout. † (See Dob, Clump, Swipe, Lamm)

LARRUP2. Bouncing along, either walking, or said of a wheel or hoop not quite round. =

LASH-HORSE. The third horse from the plough or wagon, or horse before a pinhorse in the team. Used in East Kent. + (See Losh-horse, Rod-horse)

LASH OUT1. To be extravagent with money or goods. "He lashed out and gave his daughter a purty fine wedding"

LASH OUT2. To be in a passion or rage; to hit out; to strike. Used to describe a kick from a horse. "The old mare was fretty and lashed out with her back legs and knocked down the smith". +* (See Wallop)

LAST[1]. An ancient court in Romney Marsh held for levying rates for the preservation of the Marshes. +

LAST. Ten thousand herrings, with a hundred given in for broken fish, made a Last. +

LATCHETTY. Loose; falling to pieces; coming apart. "These old chair legs are getting latchetty". *= (See Hampery, Wee-Woeing, Wocketty)

LATH. The name for an Annual Court held in the Court House, Dymchurch, at Whitsun, where the Lords, Bailiff and Jurats took part. +

LATHE[1]. To meet. +

LATHE[2]. A division of the county of Kent, which was divided into five lathes. From the Anglo-Saxon laeth, meaning landed estate. The five lathes or administrative districts of Kent were Sutton-at-Hone, Aylesford, Scray, St. Augustine's and Shepway. P+

LATHER. Ladder. "They went up a lather to the stage" — MS Diary of Mr John Bargrave, Fellow of Peterhouse, Cambridge, 1645. Parish & Shaw state: "Mr Bargrave was nephew of the Dean of Canterbury of that name, and a Kentish man. The family were long resident at Eastry Court, in East Kent. This pronunciation is still common." +

LAVAST. Unenclosed stubble. +

LAWCUS HEART! Means "Lord Christ's Heart", an interjection or exclamation. P A similar vulgar profane exclamation used today is "For Christ's sake!" "For Christ's sake don't let them see us or we will both be in trouble". (See Lorcus Heart).

LAWK-A-MUSSEY, LAWK-A-MASSEY. Corruption of the ancient invocation to relieve an unhappy plight: "Lord Have Mercy". =

LAWYER. Long, thorny Brambles from which it is dfficult to disentangle oneself. This term is apparently in reference to belief that once a person has got in the hands of lawyers it is difficult to be free of them and the involvement of legal action. +

LAY.[1] A Kentish corruption of LEY, land untilled, a general agricultural term not confined to Kent. Sanders gives the following explanation of the use of the word Lay or Ley: "Lay, as used in the sense of Laying-in or Laid-in (which see) for hay with regards to a meadow or pasture, means that the field or fields have either been raked over with a harrow or a type of ancient harrow made from brushwood and weighted down with heavy baulks of timber or large rocks lashed into position upon the top of the brushwood harrow. The metal harrow and the brushwood harrow both serve the same purpose, which is to break up any droppings of manure, the soft tops of Mole and Ant hills, casts of worms and to brush up and scratch the ground generally and so help to clear the surface and aerate it. The brushwood harrow, a home- or farm-made affair is generally supposed to be a more effective harrow than the metal type and not so damaging. Any type of grassland worked over in this manner, be it meadow, pasture, lawn or grass poultry run, or harvested land to be left to become grassland is said to be Laid-in, if harrowed in the above way. The process is called "Laying-in". P+†

LAY[2]. Lie; Pegge: "He who will not the law obey, Here in ye Stocks must surely lay", the Stocks in this instance referred to being at Bridge. P

LAY[3]. Wager, gamble. =

LAY FORTH. To prepare for burial. Now usual to say a dead person has been "laid out".

LAY-INTO. To give a beating; to thrash. "When he comes home I'll lay-into him for breaking my window". +*

LAYSTOLE. A rubbish heap; a place where rubbish was tipped. From the Old English laystall, a place where rubbish is shot. P+

LAZY WIND. A north-east wind that blows ferociously in winter was sometimes described as "a lazy wind", because instead of blowing round you it tried to blow through you. = (See Piercing Wind)

LEACON[1]. A wet, swampy common; used in place name: Wye Leacon, Westwell Leacon, Chart Leacon, Warehorne Leacon. P+

LEACON[2]. A group of dwellings a distance from the main village. *=†

LEAD[1]. A hempen rein of a plough-horse, fixed to the halter by a chain, with which it is driven. +

LEAD². Way; manner. "Why don't you do it in this lead?" i.e. "in this way". +

LEAR. Hungry; empty. = (See Leer)

LEARY. Odd or rough-looking. = (See Lairy)

LEASE. To glean; gather up the stray ears of corn left in the corn fields. From the Anglo-Saxon lesan, to gather.

LEASE WHEAT. The corn ears picked up by the gleaners. +

LEASING. Gleaning. P+

LEASTWISE. At least; at all events; anyhow; that is to say. "Tom's gone up int' island, leastwise, he told me as how he was to go a wik come Monday". P+

LEATHER. To beat; thrash; give a good hiding. "Catched 'im among de cherries, 'e did and leathered 'im middlin' 'e did". + (See Lace, Lash-out, Lay-into, Dob, Wallop, Clout, Swipe)

LEAVENER. A snack taken at eleven o'clock; thus any light intermediate meal, eaten between main meals. + (See Elevenses)

LEER¹. Leather; tape. P+

LEER². Hungry; empty. = (See Lear)

LEERY. Uncertain; strange; doubtful. =

LEES,¹ LEAS. A common or open space of pasture ground. The Leas at Folkestone is a well known example, the name for the fine open space, once common, at the top of the cliffs. Pegge gives it as "a meadow or pasture field".

LEES² A row of trees planted to shelter a hop garden. + (See Lew)

LEETY. Slow; behind-hand; slovenly. "Purty leety sort of a farmer, I calls 'im". From Anglo-Saxon laet, late, slow, tardy. P+

LEF-SILVER. A composition paid in money by the tenants in the Weald of Kent, to their lord, for leave to plough and sow in time of pannage.

LEG-TIRED. Self-explanatory; "Are ye tired?" "No, not terribly so, only a little leg-tired". +

LERRY. The "part" which has to be learnt by a Mummer who goes round Championing (which see and Lorry) +

LET. To leak; to drip. "That tap lets the water".

LETCH. A vessel wherein they put ashes and then run water through, making lye. +

LEURY. Overcast, regarding the sky. = (See Loury)

LEW¹. A shelter. From the Anglo-Saxon hleo shelter and hleowan, to warm. A sheltered place out of the wind and cold rain. +

LEW². Sheltered. "Old Tom's place lies lew down there in the hollow". P+

LEW³. To shelter, especially to screen and protect from the wind. "Those trees will lew the house when they're upgrown", i.e. those trees will shelter the house and keep off the wind when fully grown. P+ (See Loo)

LEW⁴. A thatched hurdle, supported by sticks and set up in a meadow to screen lambs, etc., from the wind. "The lambs 'ud 'ave been froze if so be I hadn't made some lews". +

LEWING. The netting placed around a hop-garden to protect the hops and bines from wind damage, the protected end of a hop garden being known as lew. = (See Lew, Loo)

LIB. To throw; to lob; to hurl; to get walnuts from trees with libbats. + (See Libbat, Libbet, Bat, Billet, Heave, Holl, Hull)

LIBBAT. A billet of wood; a stick, sometimes out of a fagot; a thickish piece of wood or pole; a large cudgel used to knock down fruit and nuts from the trees; also used to throw at crowing cocks! Pegge states: "Libbat, Libbit, a stick to throw at anything." "I took up a libbit that lay by the sole and hove it at the hagister that was in the podder-grotten", meaning: "I took up a stick that lay by the pool and threw it at the magpie that was in the pease-stubble" P+= (See Lib, Libbet)

LIBBET. A billet of wood. G Sanders describes a different use for the word Libbet: "Here it forms a part of the materials required for a rural game called "Libbet and Daddy". The "Daddy" is a pronged stick forming a three-sided pyramid-like structure. The "Libbet" is the piece of wood placed under the three-pronged "Daddy". It is played (though rarely now) by boys. One throws a "libbet" at the "Daddy" and tries to knock it over, then, should he do so, he and also the other players make a rush to get the "Libbet" that the "Daddy" protected. Whoever succeeds in getting the "Libbet" becomes the thrower and so the game continues. The "Libbet" as mentioned in the "Kentish (Wealden) Dialect" (by Sanders, 1935), was also used at Kentish Fair coconut shies, in lieu of a ball, some 75 years ago".

LID. A coverlid or coverlet; a counterpane, the outermost covering of a bed. +

LIEF. Soon; rather; fain; gladly. "I'd as lief come tomorrow". +

LIEF-COUP. An auction of household goods. P+ (See Lit-Cop)

LIFTER CLOTH. Large sheets of sacking laid in the kiln on to which the hops are spread for drying. The dried hops are carried out of the kiln on this sacking. Hops were also spread on wire-mesh in some oast-houses and turned over with large wooden shovels or scuppets — light canvas shovels. = (See Hair)

LIGHT[1]. The whole quantity of eggs the hen lays at one laying. P+

LIGHT[2]. A bine of hops bearing few or small hop cones was called "light". = (See Slight, Heavy).

LIGHT[3]. The droppings of sheep. + (See Treddles)

LIGHT[4]. Used for the measurement of hops. A Measurer who scooped out the hops from the bin and could calculate this accurately so he did not have to touch the hops in the bushel measuring basket, or who, instead of pressing down the surplus hops, brushed them out with a hand back into the bin, was said by pickers to measure "light". = (See Heavy[2])

LIGHT UPON. To meet; a chance meeting; to fall in with any person or thing unexpectedly. "He lit on him goin' down de road". +

LIGHTLY. Mostly. P+

LIKE[1]. To be pleased with; suited for. "How do you like yourself", i.e. "how do you like your present position, circumstances and its surroundings". +

LIKE[2]. A suffix to other words, such as pleasant-like, comfortable-like, home-like. "It's too clammy-like". +

LIMB. A naughty, mischievous child; a young rascal. †*=

LIMB-OF-A-WAY. A place situated a long way off; at a considerable distance away. †

LINCH. A little strip of land to mark the boundary of the fields in open country. In other counties called landshire or landsherd to distinguish a share of land. +P

LINGER. To long after a thing or someone. "He lingers after her" +P

LINGERING. Used in the context of a protracted illness or sickness, of a consumptive character; referring to a dying person who is a long time passing away. "He's in a poor lingering way". P+

LINGY. Idle and loitering. +

LINK. To entice; beguile; seduce; mislead. "They linked him in along with a parcel of good-for-nothing runagates". +

LIRRY. An accidental or deliberate blow on the ear. + (See Larrup)

LISHY, LISHEY. Spoken of corn, plants and shrubs running up apace and thus growing tall and weak; tall and straggling, as of a plant; also sometimes outgrown its strength. Pegge states: "said of corn running high and rank, when it is growing"; also flexible, lissom. P+

LISSOM. Pliant; supple; contracted from lithesome. + (See Lither)

LISS ROAD, LIST ROAD. A by-lane, almost only a track, sometimes one along the outside of a wood; a bridle path; an unmetalled farm track. =

LIST. The condition of the atmosphere when sounds are heard easily and clearly over a large distance or area. "Its a wonderful list morning". +

LITCOP. "A sale of goods upon the breaking up of a shop; 'tis used also of household goods," Pegge stated. P (See Lief-Coup)

LITHER[1]. Limp; wilted; having a slow apathetic manner. =

LITHER[2]. Lithe; supple; pliant; gentle; limber. P+ (See Lissom)

LITHER[3]. A shady, idle, rather dishonest person, usually a man. += (See Scaddle)

LITTER. Hedge brishings; straw, grass, etc. = Now in common use.

LIT-IN. Went in. †

LIT-OUT. Went out; gone; went off. †

LIVERY. The hops which are at the bottom of the bines and so do not receive enough sun to ripen them, remaining small, weakly and greenish-white, are called white livery hops. +

LIVERY CUPBOARD. A wardrobe. = (See Court Cupboard)

LOB. To throw underhand. += (See Heave, Hull, Holl, Lib)

LOB-LOW. To fly low; birds flying just off the ground or clearing the tops of trees and hedges; another meaning is to lie low or duck down out of sight. †

LOCK. The shortest, poor quality wool from a sheep. =

LODGE¹. To lie fast or stay still without moving. "That libbat has lodged up there in the gutter and you can't get it down, leastways not without a ladder." +

LODGE². An outbuilding; a shed, such as a garden shed or a back shed. The particular use to which the lodge was put was stated, i.e. a cart-lodge, a wagon-lodge, a wood-lodge. Still used for a garden shed. Sometimes the word was used to imply the lodge was only of a temporary character. +*= (See Wood Lodge)

LODGED. Laid flat; said of corn that has been beaten down flat by wind and heavy rain. P+

LOLLOP. A casual, ungainly run or movement; used in the Darent Valley area. =*

LOLLYMAN. An itinerant salesman who visited the hop gardens daily selling his wares of sweets, buns, etc., and, where the hop pickers were living in huts, various other small necessities. (I clearly remember as a child living and "hopping" at Rainham hearing the Lollyman calling "lolly, lolly" announcing his arrival whereby all the children, who had been promised a halfpenny or penny if they "sat and picked a lot of hops for Mum", with their promised coins dashed to buy from him.—A.M.)

LOMPY. Thick; clumsy; fat; a bit awkward. +

LONESOME. Lonely. +Now in general use.

LONG DOG¹. The Greyhound. Wealden for any dog long in the body; Whippets, Dachshunds, and gipsies' and dealers' Lurchers. †

LONG DOG². "Like a long dog" meant "very quickly". Probably arose from the speed of a Greyhound or Whippet. =

'LONG-OF, 'LONG-WITH. Along of; along with. Kent dialect lazy speech. "Be you comin' 'long-of us?" : "Are you coming with us?". †

LONG TAILS¹. A nickname for the true-born inhabitants of Kent. +

Long Tails²

LONG TAILS². Wild Oats; the Oat Grass (Avena fatua), a plant pest on agricultural land. =

LONG TAILS³. The Pheasant (Phasianus colchicus). =

LOO. Sheltered. "In the loo" meant that cattle labourers, etc. were in a hollow and quite loo (sheltered) there from the wind and cold. Anything protected from the wind is "In the loo", under the lee of, sheltered. *= (See Lew³)

LOOBY. A simple, chuck-headed, slow-thinking person; a nitwit; a simpleton. Probably a variant of loony for lunatic. *= (See Chuckhead, Sawney)

LOOK'EE. Look; look here; look over there. †

LOOK'EE HERE. Look you here. †

LOOKER, LOOKERER. A kind of shepherd; considered inferior to a shepherd, a man who tended sheep and occasionally cattle grazing in the marshes. His duties were rather different from those of the shepherd who tended sheep on the uplands. A looker only worked on marshes and kept an eye on sheep and cattle to see they did not get into dykes, etc., but he could not usually deal with sickness, lambing, etc. +*=

LOOKER. To perform the work of a looker. +

LOOKERING. When the looker is checking the sheep. +

LOOK-SEE. A look at; a glance; a close scrutiny; "Let me have a look-see at it, then mebbe I can get it to work right". *= (See See)

LOOK UPON. To favour; to regard kindly. "He's bin an ole servant and so I dessay they look upon 'im." +

LOOKING-AT. Used in phrase "It

don't want no looking at", i.e., "It's plain, its obvious; clear; self-evident. +

LOPE WAY. A private footpath. P+

LORCUS-HEART. An interjection, exclamation, "O lorcus-heart" which meant "O Lord Christ's Heart". = (See Lawk-a-mussey)

LORRY. The lyric, jingling rhyme, spoken by Mummers and others when Championing. (See Championing, Lerry, Lurry)

LOSH-HORSE. The third horse of a team. + (See Lash-Horse, Rod-Horse)

LOUN. Lined; i.e., the shoes were "leather-loun". =

LOURY. Overcast, regarding the sky. = (See Leury)

LOVE. A widow. A description used in old parish registers. "Item payde for the buying of John Stokeler's love ... iiijs".

'LOW. To allow; to suppose, i.e. "I 'low he must be right". +

'LOWANCE. An allowance. Bread and cheese and ale given to the waggoners when they have brought home the load, hence any recompense for jobs of work. P+ (See Elevenses)

LOW-FRUIT. (See Stone Fruit)

LOWS. The hollows in marshland where the water stagnates. +

LUBBER HOLE. A place made in a haystack when it is three parts built, where a man may stand to reach the hay from the men in the wagon and pitch it up to those on the top of the stack. +

LUCKING MILL. A fulling mill. A place where newly made cloth went through a process of soaking, cleaning, twisting and shrinking, done by the fuller. +

LUG, SIR PETER. A person that arrived last at any meeting was called Sir Peter Lug; lug was probably a corruption of lag, which means to loister or linger behind. P+ (See Peter Grievous)

LUGS. The ears. =

LUG-SAND. The sand where the Lug-worms are found by fishermen searching for bait. +

LURRUP. To walk quickly with long strides. *=

LURRY. Nonsense; silliness; empty talk; a rambling fumble of speech; childish rhymes or talk; the lyric or jingle recited during Remembering (which see). *= (See Leery, Lorry)

LUSH. To drink. †*= (See Lushington)

LUSHINGTON. A man fond of drinking, perhaps too much so, usually beer; a drunkard. "He's a reg'lar lushington, most always drunk". += (See Lush, Rig)

LUSTY. Fat; well-grown or developed; flourishing; healthy; in good order; also applied to animals and crops, fruit and vegetables. "You've grown quite lusty sin' we seed ye last". P+

LYNCH (See Linch)

LYSTE-WAY. A green way on the edge of a field. + (See Bier-Balks)

M

MABBLED UP. Mixed up; confused. +

MAD. Enraged; furious; not crazy as used today. "I was so mad with him over it". +

MADE-A-FOOLIN'-OF. To make a fuss of a child or animal. †

MAGGOTY1. Whimsical; restless; unreliable. "He's a maggoty kind of chap". +

MAGGOTY. An apple or other fruit that has been eaten into or tunnelled by a larva of some kind, such as the Codlin moth, is said to be maggoty, although a maggot in the usual sense is the larva of a fly feeding on animal substance. *=

MAID, MAIDEN. A little frame to stand before the fire to dry small articles. +P (See Tamsin, Girl)

MALKIN. (See Mawk) =

MAMMICK. To eat untidily. † (See Mommicking)

MAN OF KENT. A term applied to those persons born east of the Medway. In days past there was keen rivalry between them and Kentish Men (which see), which dates from William I's conquest of Kent, after the Battle of Hastings. This rivalry sprang from the resistance of the Men of Kent at Swanscombe, winning themselves certain rights, and the weakness of the Kentish Men's resistance so they were easily subjugated. Afterwards the bravery of the Men of Kent made them proud while Kentish Men were thought of as weak-minded and so rivalry deepened through the latter trying to prove themselves equals. Parish & Shaw state: "A title claimed by the inhabitants of the Weald as their peculiar designation; all others they regard as Kentish Men".

MANKIE-PEAS. Common Woodlice (See Cheese Bug, Monkey Pea, Pea Bug, Pill Bug, Peasie Bug). †*=

MANNISH. Like a man; manly; applied to a forward boy, mature or intelligent beyond his age. +

MAN-SUCKER. The Cuttlefish; formerly so-called by Folkestone fishermen. + (See Inkspewer, Tortoise)

MARCH. The name of the month used in the expression "March many weathers", to describe its changeable weather. A similar expression in wide use is "February full-dyke", indicating plenty of rainfall. +*=

MARCH-MAN. A person who comes from the Marches or borderland of two counties; a borderer. = (See Below London, Foreigner, Furriner, Sheeres)

MARM. A jelly. +

MARNDER. Meander; to poke about (which see).

MARSH. In East Kent "the Marsh" means Romney Marsh, as "the Island" once meant the Isle of Thanet in East Kent or Sheppey in North Kent. + (See Mash)

MARYGOLD. The Ladybird beetle. The first part of the name refers to the Blessed Virgin Mary and the latter part, gold, to the bright orange or orange-red colour of the insect's wing cases. + (See Golding, Merrigo, Lady Bug)

MASH. A marsh. + (See Marsh, Mesh)

MATCH-ME-IF-YOU-CAN. The Striped Grass or variegated Ribbon Grass (Phalaris arundinacea), grown in gardens. Also generally known as Lady's Laces, Painted Laces, and Gardener's Garters. +

MATCH-RUNNING, MATCH-A-RUNNING. A game similar to Prisoner's Base and peculiar to Kent. + (See Stroke-Bias)

MATE. A companion; a comrade; friend; used especially by husband or wife to one another; a fellow labourer. The boy who led and tended the horses of a wagoner's or ploughman's team was called the wagoner's or ploughman's mate. + Now in general use.

MAUDRING. Mumbling. +

MAUND1, MAUN, MOAN. A large, round, open, deep wicker basket, larger at the top than bottom, with a handle on each side near the top (some had two handles, others four). Used for carrying chaff, fodder, fruit, hops etc., and for unloading coal. P+ (See Moon)

MAUND2. A haycock was called a maund of hay. +

MAUNDER. To scold; murmur; complain; also to walk in an unsteady manner; to wander about with no fixed purpose. +

MAUX. A lazy person, but not normally used of a man. It was frequently used to describe a lazy girl or young woman, plump and unwilling to share tasks in the house.; a slattern; a slipshod woman; a prostitute. To a girl of child age: "You are a bad, lazy little maux". "She'll have to be got rid of 'cause she's just a lazy maux". +=

MAWK. A slattern. An abbreviation of mawkin, malkin. = (See Maux)

MAWKSER, MAWKSIN, MAUXER. A masculine type of woman who strode about all over the place; an uncontrollable, strong-minded maiden or damsel. = (See Strommocks)

MAWKY. Sentimental. =

MAXUL +, MAXHILL +, MIXHILL G, MAXON +=†, MAXEN =, MIXON +, MIDDEN =, MISKEN +. All names for a dung heap; a dung hill; a heap of manure. Sanders describes it as "a specially built up boxlike oblong of stable or cowshed or pigsty manure; sometimes kept separately, sometimes of all three. Some of these manure heaps measure many yards in length and width and sometimes as much as six feet in height".

MAY BUG. The Cockchafer beetle. +P (See Bug, June Bug, July Bug)

MAY HILL. Used in the phrase "I don't think he'll ever get up May Hill" i.e. "I don't think he will live through the month of May. Due to the fluctuations in temperature, March, April and May especially were trying months in East Kent for infirm folk in the past, more so than today. The uncertain, trying nature of the month, owing to cold east or "out" winds is further referred to in the well-known saying: "Ne'er cast a clout, Till May is out". +

MAY-WEED. Stinking Mayweed (Anthemis cotula). Common in Kent fields and waste places. +

MAZZARD. The Wild Cherry (Prunus cerasus). + (See Gaskin)

MEACH. To creep about softly. +
(See Meecher)

MEAKERS. Mice, either House Mice
or Field Mice. † (See Meece, Mickies)

MEAL. Ground wheat or any other
grain before it is bolted. In bolt-
ing the bran is divided into two
qualities, the coarser retains the name
of bran and the finer is called pollard.
+P

MEASLY[1] Pegge states: "A measly
hog. But the distemper is more of a
dropsy. The liver is always decayed
and there are here and there in the
lean flesh, on cutting it, small white
spots or pimples which seem to be
cysts or bladders of fat. Those small
bladders, on boiling the pork, become hard, and come out of the flesh,
like so many small peas and the
spungy fat therein turns to water;
they say the neck and legs are most
infected". P

MEASLY[2]. Something poor, inadequate or mean; a "measly" helping
at a meal was a small portion. =

MEASURE-FOR-A-NEW-JACKET.
Meaning to thresh; to flog; to beat.
+ (See Lace, Lay-into, Leather).
"Now you be off or I'll measure you
for a new jacket".

MEASURER. The man who "measures" the hops in bins using a basket,
after they have been picked, usually
two or three times during the day. In
the past called the tallyman (which
see). *= A "measurer" or "land
measurer" is the rural name occasionally still used for the green
caterpillar of the Peppered moth.
*= (See Hop Dog, Measuring Bug)

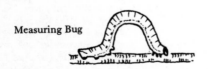

Measuring Bug

MEASURING BUG. Not a bug, but
a looper-type caterpillar, such as the
Hop Dog, that arches its body and
"measures" a leaf or twig as it progresses forward. *=+

MEDDER. Meadow. =

MEECE. Mice. P+ (See Meakers,
Mickies)

MEECHER. To creep about softly.
+ (See Meach)

MEEN. To shiver slightly. +

MEENING. A fit of the ague. Formerly heard on the Romney Marsh.
+ (See Ague)

MEGPY. The Magpie (Pica pica), a
common bird of wood, field and orchard. + (See Eckerpie)

MELT. A measure of two bushels of
coal. +

MEMBERING. Abbreviation of Remembering (which see, also Popery).

MENAGERIE. Management; a surprising and clever contrivance, i.e. "That's
a proper menagerie". +

MENDMENT. Manure. + (See Amendment, Mendments)

MENDMENTS. The name for animal
excretions; the droppings of any
animal or bird. † (See Treddles)

MENNYS. A wide tract of ground,
partly copse and partly moor; a
high common or waste piece of rising
ground. + (See Minnis)

MERCY. Used as "blessing" (which
see). "It was a mercy the house was
saved from burning down." =*

MERCIFUL. Used as "blessed" or
"mortal" are in other counties.
"They stole every merciful thing
they could find." +

MERRIGO. The Ladybird beetle. A
corruption of Marygold (which see,
also Lady Bug, Golding). +

MESH. A marsh. + (See Mash)

MESS ABOUT. To waste time. "Don't
keep all-on messing about". + (See
Act-About)

MESS OF FOOD. A large substantial
mess, a basin or plateful of hot food
in a quantity to fully satisfy the
hungriest of farm workers. †

METHER AND GEE. Waggoners'
language for the equivalent of left
and right, port and starboard. =

METT[1] A measure containing a bushel.+

METT[2], MEAUT, MEUT. Mate. =

MEWSE. An opening through the bottom of a hedge, forming a run for
game. +

MICKIES. Mice. Sanders states; "Mickie has become a generally accepted
slang term, outside of the Kentish
Weald where it originated, for the
common mouse." He then gives the
origin of the expression "To take
the mickie" as being of Weald origin
that started due to an event on Alvey
Farm, Pluckley, near Ashford, the
farm-hand who coined it being a
"Plushy" Austin, of Honey Farm,
Pluckley. †*= (See Meakers, Meece)

68

MIDDEN. A dung hill, a kitchen waste-heap was a kitchen midden. *= (See Maxul)

MIDDLEBUN. The leather thong which connected the handstaff of a flail with the swingel. +*=

MIDDLEMAS. Michaelmas. +

MIDDLING. A word with several degrees of meaning, from very much or very good to very little or very bad. The particular sense in which the word is to be taken is determined by the tone of the speaker's voice alone. "He's a middlin' tall man". +

MIDDLINGS1. An instalment of Shoe Money (which see), sometimes given to the pickers in the middle of the hop picking season. +

MIDDLINGS2. Meal fed to pigs. =

MILCH-HEARTED. Tender-hearted; kind; mild; also nervous and timid. +

MILK JUGS. The wild plant, Greater Stitchwort (Stellaria holostea). =

MILL. To melt. P+

MILLER'S EYE. An expression "to put the miller's eye out" was used when a person, making a broth, pudding, or mixing dough, poured too much water into the mixture, making it so thin that even a miller's eyes would be strained looking for the flour, the "eye" being the hole made in the middle of the flour the miller was about to mix. Then it was customarily said "I reckon you've put the miller's eye out now!" Not to be confused with Miller's Eyes (which see), a dialect name for jelly-fish.

MILLER'S-EYES. The Dover fishermen's name for a Jellyfish. + (See Sluthers, Stinger, Galls, Sea Starch, Sea Nettles, Water Galls)

MILLER'S THUMB. The freshwater fish also called the Bullhead (Cottus gobio) +P (See Cobbo, Corbeau)

MIND1. To intend; to be of a mind to a thing or purpose; to design or plan. The complete phrase spoken was "I'm a mind to do it". +P

MIND2. To remember; to recollect. "I mind" for "I remember". "Do you mind what happened that first time we went cherrying?" +P

MIND3. To feel. " 'E do mind de cold so." =

MINE. Any kind of mineral, particularly iron-stone. P+

MINNIES. Miseries; "That nipper has the minnies". =

MINNIS. As Mennys (which see). A common. There are examples commemorated in place names, such as Stelling Minnis, Roads (Rhodes) Minnis. P+

MINT. The spleen. +P

MINTY. Full of mites; used to describe cheese, meal, etc. attacked by these pests.

MINUTE1. A native of Kent would use the word to say "a little minute" or "just a minute", where in other counties it was expressed "a minute" or "just a moment". Used when someone, a customer or something, cannot be attended to immediately. P+

MINUTE2. Used in Directly-Minute meaning immediately; straight away. + (See Dreckly-Minute)

MIS, MUS. Mis is Mrs, Mus is Mr. = (See Miss, Mistus)

MISCHEEVIOUS. Mischievous. +

MISERY1. Sulking; fretty; not sorrow or distress of mind as is common in use today. Used mainly in East Kent to describe a whining, crying child. *=

MISERY2. Acute bodily pain. "He's gone in great misery for a long time".+

MISHEROON, MUSHEROON. A Mushroom. + (See Mushroon)

MISKEN. A dung hill. + (See Maxul, Mixen, Maxon, Midden).

MISS. An abbreviation of mistress; always used for Mrs., as the title of a married woman. + (See Mistus)

MIST. Very fine rain or drizzle. "Its misting outside) P+ (See Mizzle, Mizzling)

MISTUS. Mistress; the title of a married woman, a wife. (See Miss) Not the present meaning, a kept woman, prostitute, a lady-love, concubine, a paramour, nor a woman who was the head of a large household, i.e. mistress of the house. "My mistus and me's done very well and comfortable together for 'bove fifty years; not but what we've had a misword otherwhile, for she can be middlin' contrary when she likes, I can tell ye". +

MISWORD. A cross, angry or abusive word in speech. "He's never given me one misword all his life". +

MITHERWAY. A call by a waggoner to his horses, meaning "come hither away". +

MITTENS. Very large, thick leather gloves without separate fingers formerly used by hedgers to protect their hands from thorns. P+

MIXHILL. A dung hill (See Maxul) G

MIXON. A dung heap; a dung hill, but more properly one which is made of a heap of earth and dung mixed together, or, as in Thanet, of seaweed, lime and dung. From the Anglo Saxon mix, dung, and mixen, dunghill. +P (See Maxul, Maxen, Maxon, Midden, Misken)

MIZMAZE. Confusion; puzzle; stunned; dizzy. It has the same meaning in Sussex. "Time I fell off de stack, soon as ever I begun to look about a little things seemed all of a mizmaze". +

MIZZLE. A mist-like rain, falling very lightly. Word now in general use. †

MIZZLED. Misled. Another meaning: to slip away, to disappear. =

MIZZLING. A mist-like rain falling heavily; drizzling. † (See Mist)

MOAN. (See Maun) P+

MOKE. A mesh of a net. +

MOKES. The mokes of a net, i.e. the meshes. P

MOLLIE. The Hedge Sparrow or Dunnock. + (See Dicky Hedge-Poker, Jimmy Hedge Moper).

MOMMICKING. Expression used by a parent, usually a mother, to a child picking over its food leaving portions untouched. In Sussex "mommick" meant to cut up or carve awkwardly or unevenly. = (See Mammick) "Clear up your mommicks. Don't leave them round your plate".

MONEY. Used in the phrase "good money" meaning good pay, high wages. "He's getting good money I reckon." Now in general use. +

MONEY-IN-BOTH-POCKETS. The garden flower, Honesty or White Satin Flower, as it was sometimes called because of the silvery lustre of its large circular seed-cases, which, when dried, were used to dress up fireplaces in Summer and decorate chimney-mantels of cottages and village inns. Still popularly used for decorative work with dried flowers indoors. The pairs of seed cases are semi-transparent, showing the flat, disc-shaped seeds like little coins inside them, from which appearance this dialect name originated, but is now in general use. +*=

MONEY-PURSE. A purse for containing money, as opposed to a wallet for papers, a photo-wallet, etc. +

MONEY SPINNER. A small spider, usually black or brown, which if it gets upon a person's clothes or hair, etc., was supposed to foretell good luck and wealth. Better known widely elsewhere as a "Money Spider". +

MONKEY PEA. A Woodlouse. Pegge, however, is confusing on this definition. He states: "millipedes, i.e. a woodlouse. When he is rolled up he is so like a pea that one may imagine him so called from the imitation of a pea, the ape or monkey being a great imitator." Then Pegge revokes this opinion and states "Monkepee, a woodlouse; a corruption of millipes or multipes". A millipede is an entirely different creature. Parish & Shaw also add: "The Ligia oceanica (Sea-Slater), which resembles the Woodlouse and lives in the holes made in the stone by the Pholades (Piddocks)". Ligia more usually occurs under seaweed and stones, in cracks in harbour walls and similar. P+*= (See Mankie Pea, Pea Bug)

MONT. Month. P+

MOOCH. To dawdle; creep; slouch; idle time away; to move in a slovenly or flat-footed manner. "Don't mooch about so". Later in universal use. += (See Doddle)

MOON. A large measuring basket. = (See Maun, Maund, Moan)

MOOR. Swampy and wet pieces of ground. P+

MOORNEN. The Moorhen (Gallinula chloropus)

Moot

MOOT. The root or stump of a tree, which, when felled, is divided into three parts: 1. the moot, 2. the stem, 3. the branches. +

MORE. Used of size and dimensions; "as big more" meaning "as big again". +P

MORE-NIGH. Close to, near by. =*

MORT. Many; abundance; a multitude; a large quantity; plenty; a lot.

Used in "a mort of money" — apples, birds, men, etc. P+G

MORTACIOUS. Very. "The old sow's on her last legs surelye. She's so mortacious bad". G (See Mortal, Mortally)

MORTAL, MORTALLY. Meaning very; also used to mean wholesome. "A mortal good doctor." "My apple crop is mortally (mortal) poor this year". G (See Mortacious)

MOSES. A young Frog. Used in East Kent. +

MOST-TIMES. Generally; usually. +=

MOSTEST. Farthest; greatest distance. "The mostest she's bin is five miles from home". +

MOT. Abundance. PG+ (See Mort)

MOTHER OF THOUSANDS. The wild plant, Ivy-leaved Toadflax (Linaria cymbalaria). + Used in other counties.

MOTHERY. Out of condition; muddy; thick; when applied to food, with a scum or mould on it. "The beer's got pretty mothery, seeminly". + (See Abited, Ampery, Mowl, Bythe, Bythy)

MOUTH-ALMIGHTY. Rowdy; cheeky; mouthy; loud-mouthed. Used elsewhere. *=

MOVE. An action; plan; scheme. "That's a clever move if it comes off." + Used generally now.

MOWL. Mould. + (See Abited, Ampery, Fenny, Mothery)

MOWN. As Moon (which see). =

MUCH1. To fondle; caress; soothe; pet. To much a child was to fondle it when it was peevish, according to Pegge. "However did you manage to tame those wild sheep?". "Well, I muched 'em, ye see". P+

MUCH2. Used with regard to the state of the health. "How are ye today?" "Not much, thank ye". +*=

MUCH AS EVER. Hardly; scarcely; only just; with difficulty. "Shall you get done (i.e. finish your job) today?". "Much as ever". It was also occasionally used to mean that things, a scene, life, had hardly changed. "The village is much as ever it was". +*+

MUCH AS HARDLY. Not quite; nearly; almost. =

MUCH OF A MUCHNESS. Very much alike; similar; as like as two peas. "Tom and Will are very much of a muchness."

MUCK1. A busy person; the one in charge; the supervision of a task. "The squire was the head muck over the Jubilee celebrations", or "The squire was quite head muck over this Jubilee job". +*=

MUCK2. To dirty; to work over-hard; to spoil. + (See Mucked Up)

MUCK3. To carry, to hump something with difficulty. = (See Muck2).

MUCK ABOUT. To work hard; to toil. "He's most times mucking about somewheres or another." Also to fool about. + (See Mucking About)

MUCKING ABOUT. As Muck About; also to mean playing the fool; skylarking about; messing about or fooling around with something; wasting time.

MUCK UP. To lift up; also to spoil, ruin. †*= (See Mucked Up)

MUCKED UP. All in confusion and disorder; spoilt; ruined; broken; damaged. "He's certainly mucked up all my plans." "I lay you never see such a place as what master's study is; 'tis quite entirely mucked up with books". = +

MUDDIE. A man who dug up mud from the mudflats to build up the seawall on the North Kent coastline, or loaded such mud into barges at low tide for transporting at high tide back to the works for cement manufacture. (One of my grandfathers was a muddie early in his working life - A.M.) *= (See Skevalmen)

MUDDLE ABOUT. To do a little work. "As long as I can muddle about I don't mind". A comparable phrase today is "to potter about". +*=

MUGGY. Close; hot steamy weather. =

MULLOCK. To damp the heat of an oven, was to mullock an oven. P+

MUMPING. Seeking alms during the "Hooden Horse" custom. = (See Hoodening)

MUNG. To cadge. "I'm on the mung": "I'm cadging". =

MUNTON. The mullion of a window. This is nearer to the medieval form "munnion". +

MUS, MUSS. Abbreviation of muster, (which see), i.e. master. "I're taking a bottle of cider to Mus Smiff (Smith)". += (See Muster)

MUSHROON. A Mushroom. From French moucheron (mousseron). P (See Misheroon, Musheroon)

71

MUSTER. Master; Mister; Mr. The title given to an employer and often contracted into Mus or Muss (which see). The labourer's title was Master contracted into Mass, but there was considerable levity over the use of this by one person to another or employer to employee. "Where be you goin', Mass Tompsett?" "Well, I be goin' 'cross to Muss Chickses". + (See Mistus)

MYSTOLE. Possibly a variation of Playstool (which see), common land used as a public recreation ground. An example is Mystole Green, lying in front of Mystole House, 1½ miles south-west of Chartham, near Canterbury, formerly an area where the public flocked in great numbers to attend country revels, fairs, and bull-baiting. (My maternal grandmother who lived in a cottage, Underdown, opposite the area, as a child, remembered it being used as a common for cattle, the tethering of bulls, and, when the grass was cut, as a source of hay. Now it is in private ownership. —A.M.) *=

N

NABBLE. To gossip; to chat; talk idly, an irrelevant chatter. "My nabble!" was an expletive for the noun nabbler (which see) = (See Chat, Hulve)

NABBLER. An argumentative, captious person; a gossip; a mischief-maker or rumour-monger. + (See Nabble, Chat). Someone who drinks too much at an inn or gathering, then creates a disturbance by arguing.

NABBLERIG. Derived from Nabbler, an argumentative person and Rig, an excessive drinker. = (See Lush)

NAG-NARROWING. Nagging; a nagger. A nagging woman or a fault-finder was referred to as a "nag-narrowing old besom." = (See Besom)

NAIL. A weight of eight pounds. P+

NAILBOURNE. An intermittent stream. Two well-known Kent nail-bournes which course through the countryside periodically, usually after a wet winter when the underground springs in the chalk become overfull, are those at Petham and Elham. In other counties they are called Winterbournes. +*= (See Eylebourne)

NARL. A knot in wood. Corruption of gnarled. Narl is also a corruption of Nail. †

NARLIE. Much knotted in the wood so it is poor timber. †

NARLIE WOOD. As Narlie. †

Natches

NATCHES; applied to the battlement-like castellations on a church tower. +

NATE. Naught; nothing; bad. +

NATIVE. Native place; birthplace; place of origin. "Timblestun (Tilmanstone) is my native, but I've lived in Eastry nearly forty years come Michaelmas". +

NATURE. Way; manner. "In this nature", on this manner, this way. "Doan't take no notice of 'im. Its just 'is nature to be like that". P+*=

NAWN STEERS. Small steers. From the French nain, dwarf. P+

NEAT. To make neat and clean; to tidy. "She neats about", i.e. "She goes about the house making things neat and clean". P+

NEB. A peg used to fasten the pole of an ox plough to the yoke. + (See Dyster)

NECESSARY HOUSE. A convenience; a lavatory; a wash-house. + (See Dover House.)

NE'ER A ONCE. Never once; not once. "Ne'er a once have I seen him in church". +

NEIGHBOUR. To associate with. "Though we live next door we don't neighbour". +

NEIGHBOURY. A corruption of neighbourly. =

NESS. A promontory, cape or headland. Used in placenames such as Sheerness, Dungeness, Shellness, Foreness Point. From French Nez. So the English sailors used to call Blanc Nez, opposite Dover, Blankness or Black-ness. +P

NET. A knitted woollen scarf. +

NETTLE-FRIG. A fidget; a restless person; generally applied to a child. Sanders states this term derives from the fidgetings of a person or child stung on the legs by Stinging Nettles. "Sit still! You're a proper nettle-frig". †

72

NEWLAND. Land newly broken up or ploughed. Ancient grazing pasture ploughed for corn or other crops. P+=

NICKOPIT. A bog; a quagmire; a deep hole in a dyke. +

NIDGET, NIDYATT, NIGGETT. A horse-drawn, heavy wood frame, usually oak, with nine or ten iron tines, used for cleaning the ground between the rows of beans, hops, etc., the dead weight of the implement forcing the tines into the ground. Sometimes spoken as Igget. +*= (See Shim)

NIGGLING. Trifling; petty; troublesome because the task was small and awkward. "There, I tell ye, I ain't got no time for no such niggling jobs". +

Nimble Dick (Gad Fly)

NIMBLE DICK. The Horse Fly or Gad Fly. +*= (See Brimp)

NIP1. Walk quickly; hurry; now in universal use. To nip along. *=

NIP2. A nap; a short period of sleep. =

NIPPER. A nickname given to the smallest or youngest member of a family. +*=

NISY. A ninny; a nincompoop; a simpleton. +

NIZG'D. The smallest pig in a litter. Spelling phonetic as original, spelling uncertain. = (See Anthony Pig, Daniel, Runt, Runtlet)

NOB. A hill; large exposed mound. =* (See Knoll)

NOD. The nape of the neck. With this are connected Noddle, Noddy, as in the nursery rhyme "Little Tom Noddy, All head and no body". +*=

NODDLE. The head and neck. "Did you bump your little noddle? Never mind, let me kiss it better. " +=*

NODDY. (See Nod)

NOHOW. In no way; not at all; not practical. "I don't see as how I can do it, not nohow". +

NONCE. The phrase "For the nonce" means "for the once"; for that particular occasion only; hence, on purpose with design or intent. P+

NONE. Neither. "None of them both", i.e. "neither of them". P+

NONE-SO-PRETTY. The garden plant London Pride.

NOOKIT. A nook. + (See Nucket)

NOON-DRINK. (See Nuncheon) =

NOONY1. Uncharacteristic behaviour. An ailing chicken that acted strangely was said to be "noony". (See Cluck1)

NOONY2. A fretty, ailing child was said to be "noony". Possibly variant of common moony, i.e. listless. =

NO OUGHT. Ought not. "The doctor said I no ought to go out". +

NO PRINCIPLE. No scruples. This expression was applied only in Kent to people who did not pay their debts. "She walks about in her finery and has no principle about owing for it all these last six months". +

NO RABBITS CAUGHT. Nothing done; nothing seemingly achieved. †

NORATION. A fuss; a bother; a row; a set-out or disturbance, either in language or action. +

NOR YET. Nor. P

NO SENSE. Nothing to speak of; of little account or importance; not much. Of a man hard of hearing; " 'E doan't 'ear no sense". "It don't rain, leastways, not no sense". +

NOSE HOLES. The nostrils =*

NOTCH. To reckon; to count; to score; "to notch up" referred to an old method of reckoning at cricket, where it was the practise to take a stick and cut a notch (a nick or slit) in it for every run that was made. The term may also have had its origin in Kent from a similar method used in the hop gardens, of cutting a notch in a talley stick for every bushel picked and measured. P+*= (See Tallyman)

NOT FORCE PUT. Under no pressure; not obliged. =

NOYES. Noisome; noxious; dangerous; bad to travel on. +

NUBBY. Rough ground, lumpy coal, etc., was said to be nubby. Probably a variant of knobby or knobs of coal. =

NUCKET. A recess; a space between bushes. = (See Nookit)

NUNCHEON, NUNCHION. A mid-day or afternoon meal or draught. The original meaning was a noon-drink from the Middle English nonechenche; none ME for noon. Pegge states "In Kent, a noonchion or nunchion of bread, or any edible, is a great piece, enough to serve for

73

the nooning, or dinner of any common eater". P+

NURITY. The goodness, vitality or strength of a plant. Used in West Kent. "The bruts run away with all the nurity of the potatoes". + (See Bruts)

NUT WANDS. Long new growths of Cob-Nut or Hazel cut every autumn, which were dried and hardened and tied in bundles, which, after sharpening one end and being trimmed were used for staking plants, prior to Bamboo canes. Superior to Wands (which see)

NUTHER. Neither; giving an emphatic termination to a sentence. "And I'm not going to it, nuther", i.e. "I am not going to do it, you may be sure!" +

O

OARE. Seaweed; sea wrack. The name of a parish, Oare, near Faversham, North Kent, bordered on the north side by the river Swale, where in the past large quantities of seaweek collected or grew and possibly gave the name to the parish. " ... To forbid and restrain the burning or taking up of any sea oare within the Isle of Thanet" — Rev. J. Lewis, "History and Antiquities etc. of the Isle of Tenet in Kent", 1736. + (See Waur, Waure)

OAST. A kiln for drying hops or malt, but anciently used for any kind of kiln, lime-kiln, brick-kiln, etc. Pegge states "A kill for drying hops. Brykhost, i.e. brick kiln — Old Parish Book of Wye, 34 Henry VIII." Probably from the Dutch eest, a drying-kiln. Rev. W. Skeat was indebted to Rev. Canon W.A. Scott Robertson for the interesting note (which Parish & Shaw also quote): "This name for a kiln was used, in Kent, long before hops were introduced. In a deed, dated 28 Edward I, we find Roger de Faukham granting to William de Wykewane and Sarah his wife, 3 acres of land which 'jacent apud le Lymoste in parochia de Faukham.' During Wat Tyler's insurrection some of the insurgents 'went to a place called Lymost, in Preston next Faversham, on the 5th of June, 1381, and ejected . . . goods and chattels of

Philip Bode found there, to wit, lime, sacks, etc. (Arch. Cantiana, iii, 90). In a lease, dated 1445, and granted by the Churchwardens of Dartford to John Grey and John Vynor, we read = 'the tenants to build a new lime oast that shall burn eight quarters of lime at once' — Landale's "Documents of Dartford", page 8. Limehouse, a suburb of London, seems to have been named from a lym-oste; it was not formed into a parish until the 18th century. In a valuation of the town of Dartford 29 Edward I, we find mention of John Ost, William Ost and Walter Ost" — W.A.S.R."

Oast-House

OAST-HOUSE. In the hop oast-house, where the hops are dried, pressed and pocketed, there are two floors. The lower being a store for the pocketed hops and for coal, and having the fires. The upper floor is where the hops are taken to be dried and pressed. Although applied now to drying hops, in the past it seems that oast or host was synonymous with kiln. The oast was any kind of kiln, for drying malt, bricks, lime, etc., e.g. bryk-host, brick-kiln. =* (See Oast, Oastus)

OASTUS. Oasthouse. = (See Oast House)

OBEDIENCE. An obeisance; a bow or curtsey; an acknowledgment of a greeting. "Now, Polly, make your obedience to the gentleman, there's a good girl". +

OCKARD. Awkward. *=

'OD RABBIT IT. A profane expression, meaning "May God subvert it". From the French "rabattre". +

OF. Used for with. "I have no acquaintaince of him", i.e. "I have no acquaintance with him". P+

OFFER. To lift up; to hold up anything for the purpose of displaying it to the best advantage. An example is that of a master paperhanger telling his assistant, when a customer was inspecting some samples of wallpapers: "Just offer up this paper for the lady to see." Occasionally still used in this context. +*=

OFF FROM. To avoid; prevent. "I couldn't be off from going, he made such a point of it". +

OLD. This was and still is constantly applied to anything or anybody without it meaning their or its age. The use of old as a derogatory word is characteristically Kentish. "They had a fine old set-to before the argument ended". "The wind's a tidy old blow", i.e. very strong. +*=

OLD LIP. Cheek; sauciness; backchat; impulsiveness. Usually employed with reference to a cheeky girl or woman. Now used elsewhere. "Now don't you give me none of your old lip". After the final sets of hops had been cleared at the end of hop picking it was the custom to choose who was thought to be the cheekiest and sauciest girl or woman and put her in a bin or the large baskets sometimes used, then to cover her with hops until she pleaded for "mercy" to atone for all her "old lip" to everyone throughout the "hopping" season. *= (See Polt, Hopping)

OLD MAN. Southernwood (Artemisia abrotarium), a herb with odorous leaves formerly used for making a tea. Sometimes also used for the Common Tansy (Tanacetum vulgare)

OLD WOMAN'S ORCHID. The Lady or Dark-winged Orchid (Orchis purpurea), confined almost entirely to Kent. =

OLT. Hold. "Now den git olt uv it". =

ON THE GAMMOCK. Gadding about.=

ONE-EYED. Inconvenient; a general expression of disapproval; an unpromising sight or place. "That's a middlin' one-eyed place".

ONE YOKE, TWO YOKE. A method of early meal times. When work on the farm was done with horses and the job was too far from the stable to go home to dinner at 12 o'clock and return at 1 o'clock, the labourers, waggoners, etc., used to lunch at 10 to 10.30 and work through until 3 p.m. This was called "One Yoke", as opposed to the usual times called "Two Yoke". Until the horses got used to the change of meal times they were difficult to get to work after 12 o'clock. Custom slightly varied in West Kent. = (See Bait, Yoke)

OO. Used in speech, such as "I feel all of an oo", i.e. "I feel ill", or "That's all of an oo", i.e. "That is all in confusion" +

OO BE DAT DEN? A villager to another on seeing a stranger nearby would ask this, i.e. "Who is that person?" =

OOD. Seaweed; also used for wood. +

ORATION. (See Noration)

ORDER. To be "in order" was a common expression for being in a passion or rage. "When the old chap knows them cows have been out in the clover he'll be in middlin' order. He'll begin to storm and no mistake". +

ORNARY, ORNERY. A corruption of ordinary; common; poor, inferior, bad; also means irritable and bad-tempered and was used as an unfriendly expression or disparaging term concerning anything or persons. "Them wuts be terr'ble ornary". +=

ORTS. Scraps of food; leavings, fragments; odds and ends. Sometimes called Erts. "Nobody will want to eat your orts". "Come on, clear up your erts". = (See Mommicking)

OTHERSOME. Some others. +

OTHERWHERE-ELSE. Elsewhere +

OTHERWHILE. Occasionally. In speech "Every otherwhile a little" meant "a little now and then". +P

OUR SAVIOUR'S FLANNEL. In some areas, such as Bridge, near Canterbury, this was the name given to Viper's Bugloss (Echium vulgare), a wild plant. In other areas, particularly Faversham and elsewhere in North Kent, the name was applied to the Great Mullein (Verbascum thapsus), also a wild plant and was supposedly so-named due to the Mullein having soft, velvety-smooth leaves. + (See Jesus' Flannel)

OURN. Ours. =+ (See Hern, Yourn, Theirn, Hisn)

OUST. Oast. G (See Oast)

OUT. Applied to a north, north-east or east wind. "The wind is out today" i.e. it is in the east, north-east or north. P+ (See Downward, Upward)

OUT-ASKED. Used of couples whose banns have been "asked", called or published three times and who have come out of that stage unchallenged.+

OUTFACE. To withstand; resist face to face; brazen it out; not to shirk. *=+ (See Outstand)

OUT OF DOORS. Out of fashion. "I played de clarrynet, time we had a band in church and used to sing de psalms, but 'tis all upset now; dere's nothing goos down but a harmonium and a passel o'squallin' children, and dese here new-fangled hymns. As for poor old David, he's quite entirely put out o' doors". +

OUTROOPE. An auction of household goods. +

OUTRUNNINGS. A straggling wood beyond a hedgerow, not measured in with the part to be cut. + (See Cant2)

OUTSTAND. To oppose; to stand out against, either in making a bargain or an assertion. "He outstood me that he hadn't seen him among the currants". P+

OUT OF KILTER. Out of alignment; out of order when applied to implements. *= (See Kelter, Kilter, Hamper, Tilter)

OVEN. To "go to oven" is to bake. P+ (See also Forge)

OVER. To. "I'm going over Tom's cottage", i.e. "I'm going to Tom's cottage". +

OVERLAID. Overslept; slept later than intended. Used elsewhere. *=

OVER-RUN. To overtake and pass. +

OX-BIRD. The wading shore-bird, Dunlin (Calidris alpina schinzii). Name now in general use. Also called Oxybird on the Isle of Sheppey. +*=

P

PAAL. A pole. =

PACK. A litter of puppies or kittens. †

PADDOCK. A Toad. + (See Puddock, Tooad)

PADDY1. Worm-eaten. P+

PADDY2. In a temper; angry; tantrums. "Missus is in a proper paddy today". Still used *= (See Pucker)

PADDY DISH WASHER. The Pied Wagtail. = (See Peggy, Peggy Dish Washer, Peggy Wash Dish)

PAIGLE. The Cowslip (Primula veris) +*= (See Pegle, Cove Keys, Culver Keys, Horsebuckle)

PAILED. Piled; especially in northeast Kent around the Chatham-Rochester district according to Sanders. "We pailed they potatoes in a great heap". =†

PALM TREE. A Yew tree (Taxus baccata). It was formerly the custom in Kent on Palm Sunday to dress the church with Yew branches, which is curious for two reasons. First the Yew was usually considered a funereal tree, tree of death, wherein resided the spirits of the dead in the churchyard. Secondly, in other counties then and even today, as in Kent, it is customary to gather sprays of "Palm", the Sallow Willow, to decorate the church. Possibly in the absence of "Palm" Sallow, boughs of Yew were carried instead in procession on Palm Sunday, unless Yew was formerly used as a symbol of immortality until ousted for some reason by "Palm" Sallow. Pegge states: "And what is strange, they will sometimes on Palm Sunday dress a church with yew branches; which I think very strange, because this was always esteemed a funereal tree; but after they once called it the palm tree, the other mistake followed as it were on course". This definition was particularly used in East Kent. At Woodnesborough there is a public-house called The Palm Tree, which formerly had an inn sign depicting a Yew tree P+

PALTER. To wreck or pilfer stranded vessels and ill-use shipwrecked sailors. + (See Guile-Shares)

PANDLE. A Shrimp. +

PAPPY. Soft; mashy. Bread that is soggy through becoming wet is said to be pappy. *= (See Kettlebender)

PARCEL. A portion; a quantity. "He took a good parcel of bread and cheese for bait". + (See Passel)

PARGE. To put on an ordinary coat of mortar or plaster next to brickwork and tiling. P+ (See Parget)

PARGET. Mortar; plaster surface on a wall, sometimes decorated with patterns, in half-timbered houses. +*=

PARISH OVEN. The mouth. When administering medicine a mother would say to the child: "Come on, open your parish oven". =

PARKY. Chilly cold. Used elsewhere. *=

PARNCH. Paunch; only used to speak of the stomach of a rabbit, hare or sheep † (See Pauncher, Parnch-Bag)

PARNCH-BAG. A rabbit's stomach. A Wealden word. † (See Parnch, Pauncher)

PARNEY. Rain or water. Used when it rained. "Look out. Here comes the parney". =

PAROCK. A meeting to take an account of rents and pannage in the Weald of Kent, held by the bailiff or beadle of the lord, squire or landowner. +

PART. This word was frequently used redundantly, especially after "back", i.e., "You'll be glad to see the back part of me", meaning "to see my back", "for me to depart", "to get me gone." +

PARTIAL. Fond of. "I be very partial to pandles". +

PASS THE TIME O' DAY. To greet those met in the street, shopping, etc., with "Good morning", "Good Afternoon", "Good Evening", according to the time of the day at that moment. "I don't know the man, except just to pass the time of day". +

PASSEL. A parcel; a number. "There was a passel of boys hulling stones". +

PATTERN. To imitate. "I shouldn't think of patterning my mistress". +

PAUNCHER. Wealden dialect for a very poor shot; an almost useless type of gun sportsman. Sometimes called a Parncher † or prefixed by Rabbit: a Rabbit-Pauncher, † to describe a shot so bad that the sportsman can only manage to hit a running rabbit, at very close range and then to aim so low as to blow off the underparts or paunch of the rabbit. The words Rabbit-Pauncher is not considered an insult, only a term of disparagement, by gamekeepers and beaters towards such guns as previously described. † (See Parnch, Parnch-Bag)

PAWL. A pole; stake; prop or strut, placed against a Lodge or other building to support it. +

PAY-GATE. A turnpike gate, toll gate, where a fee was paid to use the road. +

PEA BINE. (See Bine, Hop Bine)

PEA BUG. A Woodlouse, found under tree bark, stones, refuse, which when touched rolls itself into a ball about pea size. (See Monkey Pea, Mankie Pea, Pill Bug, Peasie Bug, Cheese Bug)

Pea Bug, Pill Bug, Etc.

PEA HOOK. An implement used in conjunction with a Hink for cutting peas. It was like a Ripping Hook, but mounted on a longer handle. + (See Hink, Bagging Hook, Sickle, Swap Hook)

PEA HUCKERS. Pea pickers. † (See Home Peasies, Furrin Peasies)

PEA HUCKING. Pea picking, also pea shelling, opening the hucks, shells or pods for the peas. †

PEAL, PEEL. A long-handled broad wooden shovel used for putting bread into and retrieving from the oven. =+

PEART. Lively; energetic; brisk. + (See Brish[1])

PEASIES. Peas. † Also Pea Pickers (See Home Peasies, Furrin Peasies)

PEASIE-BUG. The Wood Louse. † (See Pea Bug)

PECK[1]. A knife used by fishermen for heading fish. +

PECK[2]. A pick; a pick-axe. =

PECK[3]. Similar to Weald Hoe, but longer in the blade and heavier than a Plate Hoe. The Peck is often referred to as a Half-Mattock. Pecks were used in hop gardens, in place of the lighter Plate Hoe, to hack out the tough weeds growing around the hop "hills". *= (See Pecker, Clod Hoe, Kent Hoe, Tommy Hoe, Canterbury Hoe, Corn Hoe, Half-Mattock, Axe Een Mattock, Weald Hoe, Plate Hoe, Double-sider Hoe)

PECK[4]. To chop with a hoe, i.e. to peck up weeds. =

PECKER. A half-mattock used as a hoe on clay soil; a long, narrow-bladed tool used to peck out thistles. = (See Thistle-Packer, Thistle-Pecker)

PEDDLER. (See Hop Peddler)

PEDIGREE. A long story; a rigmarole. "He made a middlin' pedigree over it". †

PEDLAR, PEDLER. A small, narrow tool used in a garden to draw out seed drills. = (See Hop Peddler).

PEEK. To stare, to gape; look at; commonly, to peep, take a peek at something, such as food glanced at while cooking in the oven. Used universally. +*=

PEEKED UP. Feeling queer; unwell; ill. †

PEEKINGS. Gleanings of fruit trees after main crops have been picked. +

PEEKY. Looking ill or poorly; often used of children when out of sorts and fretty. "He's peart enough agin' today, but he was terrible peeky yesterday." +*=

PEEL, PEAL. A long-handled, broad, wooden shovel used for putting bread into the oven and retrieving it when baked. +=

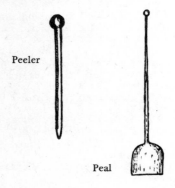

Peeler

Peal

PEELER. A heavy, pointed, round iron bar, used for making the holes into which hop poles, fence posts or wattles are placed. +*= (See Fold-Pitcher, Hop Pitcher, Hop Peeler)

PEEPERS. The eyes. *= (See Weekers)

PEGGY. A Pied Wagtail. (See Paddy Dish Washer, Peggy Dish Washer). +

PEGGY DISH WASHER, PEGGY WASH DISH. The Pied Wagtail. (See Peggy, Paddy Dish Washer) +*=

PEGLE. The Cowslip. "As yellow as a pegle". +*= (See Paigle, Lady Keys, Culver Keys, Horsebuckle)

PELL. A deep place or hole in a river. +

PELT. Refuse; rubbish; rags. Still used. P+*= (See Culch, Reffidge, Sculch, Scutchell)

PELT MAN. A rag and bone man or refuse collector, dustman. =

PENNER. A catch or fastening, often home-made from wood, with a screw in the middle and swivelled across the door edge to keep it shut. =* (See Pinner)

PENT. A slope or inclination. In the parish of Postling there is a place called "The Pent" on a hillside. From the French pente, a slope or declivity. +

PERK. To fidget about restlessly; to be all of a dither. "How that cat does keep perking about". +

PESTER-UP. To bother; to hamper; to crowd. +

PET. A pit of any kind. +

PETER-GRIEVOUS. Fretful; whining; complaining; possibly had its origin by being used sarcastically of ecclesiastics. + (See Creeping Jesus, that has a similar origin, also Sir Peter Lug)

PETH. To pith; to sever the spinal cord or marrow of an animal. +

PETT. A clump of trees. =

PETTY-COAT. A man's or boy's waistcoat. P+

PHARISEES. Fairies. +P (See Fairisees, Fairisies)

PICK THE BIN. Remove leaves from the hops in the bin before "measuring" them, as few leaves as possible being required. =

PICK UPON. To tease; annoy; aggravate; make a butt of. Still used. "Don't you keep picking on him. Let him be." +*=

PICK-LICKING. If children helped themselves from the food table before the family was seated for a meal they would be told to "stop pick-licking". =

PIERCING WIND. A very bitter cold wind that chills the face and hands and seems to find its way through the thickest clothes and makes the person shiver and feel cold inwardly. "Tis a piercing wind that blows right through you". *= (See Bitter-Cold)

PIG GATE. A six-barred gate formerly often used for pig pounds (which see) or sties. †

PIG-HEADED. Obstinate; awkward; deliberately argumentative. =* (See Hog-headed)

PIG-POUND. A pig sty. Used elsewhere = (See Pig Gate)

PIKEY, PIKY, PYKIE. A turnpike traveller; a gipsy; a vagabond; also used to describe a scruffy, badly-dressed person; a low fellow; low type of person. A saying was "eat like a pikey", i.e. in a bad-mannered fashion. When girls refused to have their hair brushed it was said by their mother to them "Alright, go like a piky then". Not to be confused with Ikey. +*=

PILCH. A triangular piece of flannel worn by babies and infants. Probably a type of napkin. +

PILL BUG. The Woodlouse. This dialect name originates from the time when it was the custom to eat a rolled-up Pill Bug, with honey, as a country remedy for various ailments. *= (See Pea Bug, Mankie-Pea, Monkey Pea, Cheese Bug)

PILLOW-BERE. A pillow case. +

PILLOW-COOTS. Pillow coats; pillow cases. + (See Pillow-Bere)

PIMP. A small bundle of cleft wood used for lighting fires; a bundle of brushwood twigs bound together with tarred string and used as kindling wood. The method of cutting pimps was: The woodman, wearing a heavy leather apron covering his body from neck to knees, would bend the withies across his chest and cut off the twigs with a small bill or bill-hook against his leather apron. The larger pieces of wood were chopped and split into kindling size with a billhook on top of a large tree stump. The pimps were stacked, in bundles of twenty-five, in pimp sheds in the woodlands ready for carting. The Hon. Mrs Maurice Lubbock told me that this method of cutting firewood continued at High Elms, Farnborough, Kent, where the Lubbocks have lived since 1802, certainly until the outbreak of the Second World War. They have references requesting the supply of pimps from High Elms to their town house in London, in a "Day-book", sent regularly to and from their High Elms estate bailiff, dating back at least to 1816. += (See Baven, Bobbin, Kilnbrush, Wiff)

PINCH. A short, steep hill. =

PINCHERWIG. The Common Earwig, (Forficula auricularia), so-named because of the pair of forcep-like callipers on the rear body used to defend itself against attack by siezing and holding on (pinching) an enemy or prey. *=

PINCHYWIG. As Pincherwig. *=

PIN-HORSE. The second horse of a team, next in front of the Rod-Horse. + (See Lash-Horse, Rod-Horse)

PINIES. Peonies, the garden flowers, Paeonia. +

PINNER. The little button or fastening of a cupboard door; a swivel door fastener. +=

PINNOCK. A Wooden drain or conduit beneath a gateway. + (See Thurrock)

PIP. To have the "pip" means feeling depressed, disagreeable or annoyed. *=

PIPPY. Looking off-colour. As Peeky. =

PITCHER. A much shorter Peeler (which see). *=

PITHER. To search for; to seek; to find out. = (See Pithering, Pitter)

PITHERED. Pinched with the cold; shivery; puckered up. = (See Hovered, Pitter, Puckered Up)

PITHERING. Dithery; dithering sporadically from one thing to another or one task to another: messing about; not doing anything of importance or necessity; also meant something unimportant. *= (See Pitter, Spuddle)

PITTER. To loosen the earth or throw it up lightly; to throw it up gently. Also used in the expression "to pitter about" meaning to go about fussing or fidgeting. Parish & Shaw state "sometimes miswritten pither". + (See Pither)

PITTERING IRON. A poker. P+

PLACE1. A manor house. P

PLACE2. A barton; a courtyard. + (See Barton)

PLAGUED. Pestered by; annoyed by. =

PLAGUESOME. Troublesome. "My corns are terrible plaguesome" +

PLAGUEY DEATH. Extremely deaf. =

PLANETS. Used in the expression "It rains by planets" meaning when showers fall in a small area, as opposed to general rainfall. +

PLASH. To repair a live hedge, by cutting half through some of the stems near the ground and then bending the upper parts down and training them into the hedge to form a thick laid growth. Sometimes kept in place by means of hooked sticks driven into the bank. +*= (See Splash)

PLASHING. Pegge states "pleaching a hedge". Action as Plash (which see) P*=

PLAT, PLATT. A grassy lane; small area, patch or plot of ground; an area of cultivated land, often referring to fruit growing, an apple orchard of small trees; a filbert or Kent cob nut plantation. *=

PLATE HOE. Similar to a Weald Hoe, but narrow at the eye broadening in a curve to the cutting or tilling edge and a much lighter tool for general hoeing. There are modern variations. = (See Corn Hoe, Peck, Weald Hoe, Canterbury Hoe, Kent Hoe, Tommy Hoe, Half-Mattock, Axe Een Mattock, Double-sider Hoe)

PLATES. Horse Brasses. =

PLATTY. Scattered; uncertain; here and there; uneven; fastidious. Used to describe a thin crop of corn or of a child who is sickly and dainty over food. P+

PLATTY-LIKE. In and out. Probably derived from plaiting. "The mouse ran platty-like amongst the furniture until the old cat caught it." =

PLAY UPON. To dwell upon; to work; to worry. Still used. "It plays upon her mind". +*=

PLAYSTOOL. An old word which described common land used as a recreation ground for local folk. The word is still commonly known in Kent as the name of a field which was once parish property. Playstool is a corruption of playstall, a play place. The plestor at Selborne referred to by Gilbert White is the same word and meaning. Plaistow is another version. += (See Mystole)

PLAY THE BAND. It was frequent to hear country folk say "They are going to play the band", treating it almost as a machine and not men and musical instruments, instead of saying, as we do now, "The band is going to play". +

PLEXICLE. Apoplexy. "All of a sudden he falls down in a plexicle fit". =

PLOG1. To clog; to hamper; to retard; to be a drawback or disadvantage. "I reckon it must plog him terribly to be forced to goo about wid a wooden leg".

PLOG2. The block of wood at the end of a halter, to prevent it slipping through the ring of the manger. An intermediate form between plug and block. Elsewhere called a clog. +

PLOT. A plan; a design; drawing; sketch. +

PLUM1. Very; plum pleasant, very pleasant. G

PLUM2. Quite; Plum wrong was quite or directly wrong; anything standing plum was standing fast. P

PLUMP. Dry; hard. The lanes and ways are plump means that the earth is hard; a plump Whiting was a dried Whiting. When paths after rain are almost dry they are said to be plump, i.e. the earth is just moist enough to fill up all the crevices. P+

PLY-GOLDING. A Ladybird beetle. = (See Golding, Marygold)

POACH, POCH. To tread the ground into holes as cattle do in wet weather or around a drinking trough. P+ (See Putch)

POACHY, POCHY. Description of the earth that has been trampled into mud by the feet of cattle. Land or a lane full of puddles. P+ (See Putch, Stodgy, Stotch).

POAD MILK. The first meals of milk that come from a cow lately calved. + (See Beasts, Biskins, Bismilk)

POCKET. A measure of hops about 168 lbs. The long sack of tough material into which the dry hops are pressed. It is suspended through a hole in the floor of the first floor of the oast into the ground floor below; held in place by a metal ring. +*=

POD. A large stomach or paunch. Someone who is obese with a drooping, flabby stomach was said to have a large pod. *= (See Parnch, Podded)

PODDED. A rabbit that had eaten too much of the wrong food, such as wet greenstuff, and caused its stomach to swell tight was said to be podded. *= (See Parnch)

PODDER. A name given to beans, peas, tares, vetches and any such plants or vegetables which have pods. Derivation is doubtful. P+ (See Podware, Codware, Kidware)

PODDER GRATTEN, PODDER GROTTEN. Podder stubble; the stubble of beans, peas, etc. P+ (See Gratten, Grotten, Ersh, Eddish)

PODGE. A hole; a pit; a cesspool. +

PODWARE. Pulse growing in cods or pods. Pegge states: "Beans, peas, tares or vetches or such ware as has pods". Skeat doubts this derivation. P (See Codware, Kidware, Podder)

POINTING POST. A sign post, finger post, direction post. Still in common use standing at junction where two or more roads meet and pointing the way travellers should take to reach their destination. + (See Bishop's Finger, Throws, Went)

POKE1. A cesspool; a puddle of liquid draining from dung, stable manure, forming a manure pit. P (See Putch)

POKE2. A sack, from which the common phrase "To buy a pig in a poke" arose, i.e. to buy your pig, goods, etc., without seeing it or them and thus make a bad bargain. +*=

POKE3. Another name for the "green-bag" in which hops are conveyed from the hop garden to the oasthouse. The large green or yellow sack into which 10 bushels of hops are put after measuring from the bins for easy conveyance. Not to be confused with a Pocket (which see). +*= (See Measurer, Green-Bag)

POKE ABOUT. To just look at anything and everything; walk about slowly and do nothing around a house or garden; to look at or into things in a shed and replace without doing anything with them. =

POLDER. An area of boggy soil; a marsh. This name is still used in Holland for a tract of reclaimed land lying below sea level. In Eastry a place now called Felder land was anciently called Polder land. +*=

POLEWORK. An old method of training hops involving no wires; the hops were trained up thin poles, one at each "hill". Now obsolete in Kent hop growing areas. = (See Hop Dog, Hop Jack)

POLE-PULLER. Also known as the Bin-man. In the past the man in charge of several rows of hops or bins, who pulled up the poles. He used a Hop Dog for the purpose (which see). Now, as poles are no longer used (See Polework) as the training support for the hop bines, the Pole-Puller, in gardens which are still hand picked, now just has the task of using a Hop Goad or Hop-Hook (which see) to retrieve the "heads" of hops left on the wires after the bines have been pulled and carry them to the pickers in the row, but the old name survives. Another task of his in the past was to collect their kettles from the women and light a fire to boil them and take back to their owners so that the latter could make a pot of tea at dinnertime. Vacuum flasks ended this task, too. *=

POLP. Pulp. A name given to cattle food comprising roots, grains, chaff, fodder, etc., all mashed, cut up small and mixed together. +

POLRUMPTIOUS. Rude; obstreperous; restive; unruly. PG+ (See Boldrumptious)

POLT1. A kind of rat trap, that falls down. P+

POLT2. Saucy; audacious; cheeky. + (See Old Lip)

POLT3. To knock; to beat; to strike. GP+ (See Clobber, Clout; Lamm, Dob, Clump, Wallop, Pounce)

PONGELLOW. G said as a J. When years ago hop washing or tree washing was done against pest and disease by horsedrawn sprayers, men, usually boys though, had to carry the mixed wash into the hop garden or orchard in pails on yokes and if the washer ran out of wash he would shout "pongellow" indicating more was needed. =

PONGER. The large Edible Crab (Cancer pagurus) was best known by this name in North Kent, the name "crab" being restricted to use for the Common Shore or Green Crab (Carcinus maenas). + (See Heaver, Pung)

POOCH OUT, POOCH. To protrude; to pout; mostly used in reference to the lips or cheeks. "Don't keep pooching out your face like that" was used when a child puffed up its cheeks with air for cheekiness. Also used for an expression of dismay or not being in agreement with anything, a suggestion or action, in which the "face falls" with pooched lips. "When I axed him to raise my wages I see his lip pooched out purty much and didn't like it much he didn't". +*= (See Pook2)

POOCHY. A bathe; a paddle in shallow water. "Let's go and have a poochy". +

POOK1. Peak; the poke or peak of a boy's or man's cap. +*=

POOK2. To glare and to push out the lips at another person in an angry, defiant manner; usually by a child not allowed to have its way. *= (See Pooch Out)

POOR. Bad; as in "Tis terrible poor land", "poor weather", "a poor thing", "a poor day". Not meaning poverty stricken or without money or property as today. P+

POOT BIRD. The Spotted Flycatcher (Muscicapa striata). = (See Post Bird)

POPEING. To go "popeing" was to go round with a Guy Fawkes dummy on the 5th November, as children do now and several weeks beforehand. Firework Night, 5th November, was also called the "Popey Night" Presumably only dates from the time of the Popery implications of the Gunpowder Plot. "Please, sir, remember the old Pope" was formerly said by children, now its "A penny for the guy". (See Remembering)

POPY. A Poppy, the o being marked as long. P+

POPEY. A piece of road or lane allowed to become derelict, overgrown and unused, or land used as a road or lane but not surfaced. There is an example between Tufton Road and Webster Road, Rainham, where formerly children played. =

PORED MILK. (See Biskins) P

POST BIRD. The Spotted Flycatcher (Muscicapa striata); the name being given for its habit of perching on some post or position from which it makes a short flight to gain insects, then returns to the post or position. + (See Poot Bird)

POST HOLES1. Holes dug in the ground for the insertion of a gate or fencing posts. +

POST HOLES2. Used as comic words to mean nothing. "What have ye got in the cart there?" "Oh, only a load of post holes". +

POTHER-HOOK. A hook used for cutting a hedge. Pegge called it a "sickle". P+ (See Hook, Brishing Hook, Bagging Hook, Pea Hook, Ripping Hook)

POTHERY1. A disease which affects sheep and pigs, causing them to go round and round, till they fall exhausted. + (See Addle Pated)

POTHERY2. In a muddled state. †

POTHERY3. Rotten; decayed; as applied to vegetables and fruit. =

POTHERED. Upset and mentally muddled; confused. †

POTHER-HEADED. Absent-minded; forgetful. †

POTTLE. A small basket. = (See Punnet)

POUNCE. A punch or blow with a stick or the closed fist. + (See Clout, Dob, Polt, Clobber, Lash Out, Swipe, Wallop)

POUT1. Used in the phrase "plays old pout" which was probably similar to "plays old Harry" or "plays merry hell". Possibly a variant of "pouk" which in Middle English meant "the devil". "I've been out of work these three days and that plays old pout with you when you've got a family" +

POUT2. POWT. G A small round stack, of hay or straw. In the fields hay was put up into smaller heaps called cocks, or larger ones called pouts or powts. When carted it was built into a stack. A hay powt, a hay cock. PG+*=

POUTERS. Whiting-Pouts (Gadus merlangus). So-called at Folkestone. + (See Stink-Alive)

PREHAPS. Perhaps. +

PRENSEL. Presently. =

PRESENT. Presently; at present; now. P+

PRETTY BETTY or BETSY. The wild plant, Red Spur Valerian (Kentranthus ruber).

PRETTY NIGH. Very nearly. "Tis purty nigh time you was gone home". +

PRICK UP THE EARS. A proverbial saying is "You prick up your ears like an old sow in beans". People who overhear conversation or learn a secret they are not supposed to "prick up their ears" when listening to it. +

PRICKLE1. A basket used at Whitstable, containing about ten gallons, for measuring the Oysters. Two prickles equalled one London bushel. One prickle equalled two wash, for Whelks. The prickle was not exact enough to be used for very accurate measuring. + (See Strike, Wash)

PRICKLE2. A basket for gathering vegetables; the same basket as a Kibsy but with different handles. =

PRICKYBAT. A freshwater fish, the Sticklebat, either of the species. + (See Crowfish, Tittlebat)

PRIM. The shrub Privet (Ligustrum vulgare)

PRINT. Bright; clear; of starlight or moonlight, that is light enough to read by. "The night is very print", "The moon looks print tonight", "The moonlight is very print". GP+

PRINT STAR, PRINT MOONLIGHT. A bright clear star or clear moonlight. G (See Print)

PRITCHEL. An iron share fixed on a thick staff for making holes in the ground. +

PRODIGAL. Proud. "Ah! He's a proper prodigal old chap he is". P+

PROGGER. Food taken as a mid-morning lunch; a refreshment; sometimes wrapped in a spotted handkerchief tied at each corner; a snack; a carried cold meal similar to Bait. In some areas it was taken about 10.30 a.m. and consisted usually of a cup of tea and a bun or hunk of home-made cake. "Got your progger?" †=* (See Bait, Tommy)

PROLE. Not the usual sense but a stroll, a pleasurable short walk; used for a short walk a convalescent person would take; to wander. "He manages to get a little prole most days when 'tis fine". +

PROLL,PROWL. As Prole. †

PRONGS. Small pitchforks as used for stacking corn, hay, etc. =

PROPER. Thorough; capital; excellent; beautiful; peculiarly good or fitting. +

PROPERLY. Thoroughly. "We went over last wik and played de Feversham party. Our party belted em properly, fancy we did!" +

Prule

PRULE. A gaff-hook. So-called by the Folkestone fishermen. + (See Heaf)

PUCKER. A state of excitement or temper. + (See Paddy)

PUCKERED UP. Pinched or pithered with the cold; almost overcome and numb; shivery. = (See Pithered, Pucker)

PUDDING-PIE. A flat tart, made like a cheese-cake, sometimes twelve inches in diameter or more, with a raised crust to hold a quantity of custard, or ground rice and milk that had currants sprinkled on it. These "cakes" were eaten at Easter, but also at other times of the year and were considered a delicacy. A variation, "Lent Pie", contains milk, ground rice, egg mixture in a pastry shell with currants on top or in the ground rice mixture. =†*

PUDDOCK. A large Frog. + (See Paddock, Puttock)

PUG1. A Ferret. =

PUG2. Hidden away. =

PUG3. Soft ground; slack earth; clayey soil; brick-earth ready for moulding. +=*

PUGGY. Wet, as soil after heavy rain. = (See Pug).

PULL. To pull up before the magistrates; to debilitate. "If he knocks me about again I shall pull him". "The ague's properly pulled him this time." Pegge states: "To pull down, weaken." "It has pulled him sadly". P+

PULL-BACK. A hindrance; a drawback; a relapse after convalescence or recovering from an illness. +

PUMPIN. A Pumpkin. +

PUNG. As Ponger. (which see) +

PUNGER. As Ponger (which see). Punger was used in the Deal, Dover, Folkestone areas for large Crabs. Pegge states: "By a punger they mean the largest crabs; for the small ones they call crabs". P+ (See Heaver)

PUNNET. A small basket in which chiefly strawberries and occasionally other soft fruit are sold. Also known as a Pottle (which see). Punnet still used commonly elsewhere as well as Kent. +=*

PURTY NIGH. (See Pretty Nigh). =

PURTY TIGHT. Pretty well; very fairly. + (See Pretty Nigh)

PUTCH. A puddle; a water-filled pit or hole; a putch of water. P+ (See Poke1, Poachy)

PUTT. Pronunciation of to put. =

PUTTICE, PUTTAS. A Weasel or Stoat. When a rabbit screams and is killed by a Weasel it was said to be "putticed". + (See Keen)

PUTTOCK. A Kite. Parish & Shaw state: "So Puttock's-Down, a place in the ancient parish of Eastry, now in Worth parish, means kite's-down." +

PUTTOCK-CANDLE. The smallest candle in a quantity, put in to make up the weight, in the days when candles were made by hand by dipping or in moulds. +

PUT UPON. To worry and bother a person selfishly by giving him an unfair amount of work or exacting from him time, strength or money, for matters which are not properly within his province. "He's so easy, ye see, he let his-self be put upon by anybody". +*=

Q

QUANT[1]. A walking stick, a stick for driving cattle. +

QUANT[2]. A long pole used by bargemen. +

QUANT[3]. A young Oak sapling. + (See Tiller)

QUARRELS. Quarries or panes of glass. +

QUEEN HOPS. Hops which are unusually large and have small leaves growing from them. Some varieties of hops are more prone to this than others. Superstitiously believed by pickers that these freaks are lucky to find. Also called French Hops. =*

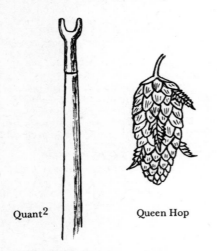

Quant[2]   Queen Hop

QUEENIE, QUEENY. A truculent child that required reprimanding. =

QUEER. To make or cause to feel queer; to puzzle; to halt someone or something from being done. "It queers me how it ever got there". Now in universal use. +*=

QUEER STREET. An awkward position; great or poor straits; serious difficulties; debt, trouble or disrepute. Anyone who has lost money or investments and bankrupted themselves was said to be in Queer Street. Possibly originated as a corruption of Carey Street, the site of the Bankruptcy Court in London. "But for that I should have been in Queer Street". +*=

QUERN. A handmill for grinding grain or seed. In general use. +*

QUICK. The Hawthorn (Crataegus monogyna). A "quick" hedge was applied to a Hawthorn hedge because it soon makes plenty of growth. +*= (See Arzy-Garzeys, Haazes, Harves)

QUICKEN. The Mountain Ash or Rowan (Sorbus aucuparia). +

QUID. The cud. In Kent it was common to hear it said cows were chewing the quid. Possibly an origin of chewing tobacco being called quid, as this is still known. Pegge refers to "quid tobacco" and "a quid of tobacco". P+*=

QUIDDY. Brisk. P+

QUILLER, QUOILER. Shaft harness, worn by the horse in shafts. = (See Coiler-Harness, Vill-Horse)

QUILLIES. To cut some quillies was to get up to some antics, usually unintentionally as when a man or other person couldn't get the hang of how a job should be done and made a mess of trying. = (See Quilly).

QUILLY. A prank; a caper; a freak. +

QUITTEE FOR QUOTTEE. An equivalent; quid pro quo; tit for tat. = (See Quitter For Quatter, Whicket for Whacket)

QUITTER FOR QUATTER. One thing in return for another; tit for tat; quid pro quo. P+ (See Quittee For Quottee, Whicket For Whacket)

QUOT. Cloyed; glutted. P+

R

RABBIT'S MOUTH, BUNNY MOUTH. The garden flower, Antirrhinum or Snapdragon. +*=

RACE MEASURE. Even measure; as distinguished from Full Measure, which is 21 to the score, as of corn, coal, etc., while Race Measure is 20. Full in this instance refers to the manner of measurement. When the bushel is heaped up it is Full; when struck with a Strickle and made even it is Race Measure, i.e., Razed Measure. P+

RACKSENED, RACKSINED. Overrun with; given up to; also for poor, exhausted soil, such soil being called "tillered out". +

84

RAD. A rod; a perch; a measure, 16½ feet. The ancient rod was 20 feet in length; a rod of brickwork was 16½ feet square. P+

RADDIS-CHIMNEY. A chimney made of rods, lathes or raddles and covered with loam or lime. P+

RADDLE-HEDGE. A hedge made with raddles. P+ (See Rattlegate, Teen, Backstay).

RADDLE. A green stick, such as wattle-hurdles are made of. Raddle is the diminutive of rad, i.e. rod. P+ (See Ruddle-Wattle)

RADE. Coming before the usual time; early. P+ (See Raid)

RADICAL. A wild, ungovernable, impudent, troublesome fellow. "He's a rammed young radical." +

RAFE. Rush; hurry; to rush about. †

RAFF. Spoil; plunder. +

RAFT. A rabble; a crowd of people. "There was such a raft of people there argifyin' ". +

RAFTER, ROUGHTER. A rasp file for woodworking. =

RAGGED JACK. The wild flower Ragged Robin (Lychnis flos-cuculi). In the past also called the "Cuckoo Flower" which is correctly applied to Ladies Smock. +

RAID. To rise early; soon. G (See Rade)

RAIN BUG. A term applied to certain black beetles, usually the Ground Beetle family, found under debris and stones during the day. It was commonly believed that if one was accidentally or deliberately trodden on or otherwise killed it would cause much rain to fall. =*

RAMMED. Parish & Shaw state "A substitute for a worse word". Damned ? — A.M. Pegge states "excessive hard; "rammed dear", dearer than ordinary". P+

RAN. A Folkestone herring net, which is about 30 yards long, is made four rans deep, and there are 60 meshes to a ran. +

RANGERS. The bars with which the Herring-Hangs were fitted. Upon these rangers were placed the spits upon which the Herrings were hung up. + (See Herring-Hang)

RAPID. Violent; severe; as applied to pain. A sciatic or chronic rheumatic pain was said to be a rapid pain. +

RASTY, REASTY. Rank; rancid; bad; spoken of butter or bacon. "Don't eat that butter it tastes rasty" + (See Gone Off)

RATTLEGATE. A wattle-hurdle. + (See Raddle-Hedge)

RATTY. Bad tempered; irritable. †=* (See Rousey)

RAVEL-BREAD. Pegge says: "A middling sort of bread, neither white nor brown, but mixed". P+

RAW. Angry; "I feel mighty raw for what he did". +

RAYER. Mid-Kent pronunciation of Rare. † (See Rear)

REACH. A creek; a level uninterrupted stretch of water on a river. In general use. *=+

REAR. Pronounced rare. Meaning early; soon. Meat under-roasted, boiled or broiled was said to be rear or rare (as it still is), from being taken too soon or early off the fire. "Why do you up so rear?" i.e. "Why do you rise so early?"

REASTY. Rusty; rank; rancid. + (See Rasty)

REC. An abbreviated name for a recreation ground, sometimes a football ground. At Rainham the recreation ground adjoining Wakeley Road is still known as "the rec". In the Borough Green area "rec" is the expression for a football ground, much to the confusion of players arriving from elsewhere. =*

RECKON. To consider; to give an opinion. "I reckon" is an expression still used to strengthen opinions and observations. "I reckon it'll stay dry today". +*=

Red Bottle

RED BOTTLE. The wild red Corn Poppy, any of the species. = (See Red Petticoat, Blue Bottle, Yellow Bottle)

RED BUTCHERS. The Early Purple orchid (Orchis mascula) = (See Keeklegs, Kite's Legs)

RED PETTICOAT. The wild, common Scarlet Poppy (Papaver rhoeas); also applied to the three other native members of the Poppy family — the Round Rough-headed, Long Prickly-headed, Long Smooth-headed. It was also sometimes known as Redweed. + (See Red Bottle)

REDGER, RIDGER. A chain which passes over the saddle on the horse's back to support the shafts or rods; a ridge band. =*+ (See Bail Ridger)

REDGER BAR. As Bail Ridger (which see). Used on the Kentish Saddle (which see) that had no housing. *=

REDGERS. (See Yorks) =

REDGUM. A sore; a rash to which very young infants were subject. P

REECE. A piece of wood fixed to the side of the chap, i.e. the part of a plough on which the share was placed, + (See Wreest)

REEMER. Very good or excellent. =+

REEMING. Very good; superior. =+

REEVE, REVE. A bailiff. 1596 — "In auncient time almost every manor had his reve, whose authoritie was not only to levie the lord's rents, to set to worke his servants and to husband his demeasnes to his best profit and commoditie, but also to governe his tenants in peace and to leade them foorth to war, when necessitie so required". Lambarde's "Perambulation". + (See Wood Reeve)

REFFIDGE. Refuse; worthless items; also good for nothing. "I have never seen so many reffidge taturs about as what there is this yer". + (See Culch, Pelt, Scutchell, Refuge)

REFUGE. The worst of a flock, crop, etc.; also refuse, rubbish, waste. + (See Reffidge)

REMEMBERING. The custom of children to go around with a Guy Fawkes effigy on 5th November to collect money was called "Remembering" or " 'memberin' ". Probably arose from the jingle formerly commonly related "Remember, remember the 5th of November, Gunpowder, Treason and Plot, etc." "George and me went round remembering and got pretty nigh fower and threepence." + (See Popeing, Lurry, Membering)

RENAG. To renege; used in games, cards, draughts, to break the rules of what is being played. =

RENTS. Cottages or houses being rented. "The Rents" sometimes applied to a complete street of dwelling houses, and also the name of the owner was applied in description or in the address, e.g. Naylor's Rents, Fullwood's Rents. +=

REXEN, REXON, RIXON, WRAXEN, WREXON. To infect, as with the small-pox, itch or any other infectious disorder; to taint with disease. GP+

REZON. A wall plate; a piece of timber placed horizontally in or on a wall, to support the ends of the girders or joists. Pegge states; "A raising, reason, rezon, rezen or reson means a raising plate, i.e. a longitudinal timber on which the roof stands or is raised". P+

RIB. A stick the thickness of a raddle and about five feet long. Ribs were bound into bundles, with two wiffs and were used for lighting fires and making raddle-fences. P+ (See Bob-bin, Fagot, Kiln-Brush, Raddle, Pimp, Wiff)

RIBSPARE. The spare rib of meat. A cut of pork consisting of the upper part of a row of ribs with the meat adhering to them. Ribspare roasted or broiled was considered a delicacy. Also known as Spear-Rib. P+ (See Cost)

RICE. Small wood; twigs; a branch. P+ (See Roist)

RID. Rode. "I rid the mare first time this morning since her leg played up". +

RIDE1. To collect; to ride tithe was to ride about for the purpose of collecting it. P+

RIDE2. An iron hinge on which a gate is hung and by which it swings and rides. + (See Charnail)

RIDE3. To ride upon the stomach; cause indigestion; indigestible food sometimes rises on the stomach. "I can't ne'er eat dese ere radishes, not with no comfort, as they do ride so". P+

RIDER. A saddle-horse. "He kips several riders". +

RIDDLE-WALL. A wall made up with split sticks woven across each other. =

RIG1. The Tope (Galeus vulgaris), a small Shark. Still caught and sold in East Kent fishmongers under the name of Rig. +*= (See Bull-Huss, Huss, Robin-Huss)

RIG2. An excessive drinker. = (See Lushington)

RIGHT. The phrase "To have a right to do anything" meant it was right that such a thing should be done. Not in the meaning "correct" or "accurate" or a "direction", as opposed to left hand or left side. Used universally now. The word was also used added into speech when an incident was being described: "He was right bad-tempered when he came to work". +*= Also used elsewhere.

RIGHTS. To go to rights; to go the nearest or shortest way. To do anything to rights is also to do it thoroughly. P+ (See Droits)

RING. A row + (See Ringe1)

RINGE1. Wood when it is felled lies in ringes before it is made up into fagots, etc. P+

RINGE2. A large tub containing 14 or 16 gallons, with which two servants fetched water from a distant place. The tub had two iron ears, a pole being passed through the ears or rings, the pole lying on the shoulders of the bearers. P+

RINGE3. A long heap in which mangolds are kept for the winter. + (See Clamp, Clump)

RINGE4. RINGEING. To put potatoes, mangolds, etc. into a ringe. "I reckon tomorrow I shall be ringeing the wurzels". +

RINGLE1. A ring put through a hog's snout; name for any ring, such as the ring of a scythe. +

RINGLE2. To put a ring through a hog's snout. +

RINGLE3. An iron ring which forms the bit of a horse at plough. +

RIP1. To reap. P+. (See Ripping Hook)

RIP2. To cover a roof with lathes, tiles, etc. To unrip the roof of a building is to take off the tiles, slates, etc. To rip it or new rip it is to put on new lathes and replace the tiles.

RIP3. A pannier or basket, used in pairs and slung on each side of a horse, for carrying loads, such as sand, salt, fish, etc. + (See Ripper1)

RIPE. A bank; the sea shore, as Lydd Ripe. Parish & Shaw state: "In East Kent the village of Ripple derives its name from the Latin word ripa'".

RIPPER1. A man who carried fish for sale in a rip or basket; a fish-pedlar. P+

RIPPER2. A long three-pronged instrument used by wreckers to tear off copper from wrecked ships. =

Reaping Hook

RIPPING HOOK, REAPING HOOK. A hook for cutting and reaping (ripping) corn. Unlike the Sickle (which see) the Ripping Hook had no teeth in the serrated cutting edge. In Sussex it was also known by these names and Reaphook and Riphook. + (See Bagging Hook, Brishing Hook, Fagging Hook, Pea Hook, Sickle, Wheat Hook)

RISH, RISHES. A Rush; Rushes. "There be lots o' rishes in them there mayshes". +

RIT. To dry hemp or flax. +

RITS. The ears of Oats are so-called and if there is a good crop and the ears are full and large they were said to be well ritted. +

RIVANCE. Last place of abode. Short for Arrivance (which see). "I don't justly know where his rivance is". i.e. where he came from or where he lived last. +

ROAD BAT. A bat or piece of wood that guided the coulter of a plough. + (See Bat, Spread-Bat)

ROAD PROUD. Crops which appear well and healthy from the road, but are not so good as they look are said to be road-proud. +

ROBIN HUSS. The Lesser Spotted Dogfish (Scyllium canicula). + (See Huss, Bull Huss, Rig)

ROBIN-ROOK. The garden bird, the Robin or Redbreast (Erithacus rubecula melophilus. +P (See Ruddock)

RODFALL. Sometimes in a woodland there was a belt of wood, about a rod, 16½ feet deep, not belonging to the same owner as the bulk of the timber and was felled at a different time. +

ROD-HORSE. A horse in the shafts or rods. The four horses of a team were called: 1. The Rod-Horse; 2. The Pin-Horse; 3. The Losh-Horse; 4. The Fore-Horse. +

RODS. The shafts of a cart or wagon. P+

ROIL. To make a disturbance; to romp in a rough and indecent manner; to stir up. Variation of Rile. Both in universal use now. +*= (See Roister)

ROIST. A switch for a cane; brushwood before it is made up into fagots. P+ (See Rice, Baven, Kilnbrush, Wiff, Pimp)

ROISTER, ROYSTER. To play about roughly and noisily. "That there old tom cat has been a-roysterin' all over the place, same as though he was a kitten. I reckon we shall have some weather afore long". =

ROMANCE. To play in a foolish manner; to tell exaggerated stories; to use too much imagination. In this context the word has no connection with love or courtship. +

ROMNEY MARSH. In the past, before the railway and motor car made it easily accessible, the Marsh was considered to be an area completely by itself. A saying of Kent and East Sussex described the world as divided into five parts — Europe, Asia, Africa, America and Romney Marsh. +*=

ROOKERY. A dispute accompanied with many words; a general altercation or argument, sometimes among several people. Presumably derived from the actions of Rooks in their rookery. +

ROOK STARVING. Scaring Rooks from crops. Usually done by a lad, who would hide himself in cover, such as a hedge bottom, until the Rooks landed in a field, then by jumping out scared them away again with a wooden clapper or other instrument that made a suitable loud noise. This was sometimes the first task a boy had on being employed on a farm. + (See Bo-boy)

ROOK-TOLL. A Rookery. = (See Toll)

ROOMS. An abbreviation of Mushrooms; used as "grass" for Asparagus. +

ROOTLE. To root up. Pigs rootle for plant roots and tubers. +

ROUGH1. A small woodland; any rough, woody scrubby place. +P

ROUGH2. Cross; peevish; not well; of uncertain temper; difficult to please. "I lay you'll find him pretty rough today". "I feel a bit rough". Still in use. +*= (See Tatter)

ROUGHET +, ROUGHIT +, RUFFET †, RUFFIT †. A small wood, containing little or no large timber, comprising chiefly Hazel or Ash saplings, or both, with a thick Bramble undergrowth; small woodland that has been neglected. (See Rough1, Frith)

ROUGHINGS. The grass after mowing. P (See Ersh, Aftermeath)

ROUNDLE. Anything round in shape. For example, the part of the hop oast where the fires are made, which is usually circular. +

ROUND-TILTH. The system of sowing of land continuously without lying in fallow. +

ROUSEY. Bad-tempered. †

ROWENS1. The aftermath; events after a disaster or catastrophe. =

ROWENS2. The second crop of grass following haymaking; the third cut of clover was so-called in East Kent. Also used for stubble. + (See Ersh, Aftermeath, Roughings, Gratten)

ROZZ. To tighten; to firm down. =

RUBBER. A whetstone for sharpening sickles, scythes, bagging hooks, etc., with a rubbing action. The mowers of grass, corn, always carried one in a leather loop attached to the back of their trouser belts. +*= (See Bat, Sharper)

RUBBIDGE. Rubbish; weeds; refuse; pelt. + (See Culch, Pelt)

RUBBLE. Corruption of Rabble. Sanders states this was also used at Chatham and Luton nearby to describe a noisy crowd of people, a noisy herd of cattle or other group of animals or birds, often being used to describe an ordinary town crowd of people or a group of shoppers or visitors. † (See Rubble-of-Noise)

RUBBLE-OF-NOISE. Sanders states this was used in Chatham and Luton nearby to mean the confusion of noise made by a talking, moving crowd. † (See Rubble)

RUCK1. An uneven, irregular heap or lump; a wrinkle, creases or uneven fold in cloth, linen, silk, etc. "Look at your skirt, child, its all rucked up". (See Smirk) +*=

RUCK2. Temper; anger; annoyance. If a person was angry it used to be said "they had their ruck up". +

RUCKLE. A struggle. P+

RUDDLE. To make a fence of split sticks plaited across one another. + (See Raddle)

RUDDLE-WATTLE. A hurdle made of small Hazel rods interwoven. +P (See Raddles)

RUDDOCK. The garden bird, the Robin. P+ (See Robin-Rook)

RUDE HEART. By heart; learnt off pat. "She read the psalms down, but lor! She didn't want no book. She knowed 'em all rude heart." +

RUDY. Rude; of children according to Pegge. P+

RUGGLE-ABOUT. A term used by elderly people and invalids to express walking or moving about with difficulty. "I'm troubled to ruggle-about much". + (See Hotch, Itch, Utch-About)

RUINS. Remains of a joint of meat or of poultry. =

RUMBALL FEAST. (See Rumball Whitings)

RUMBALL WHITINGS. Whitings sold for the Rumbal Feast. Pegge quotes from Harris' "History of Kent" (from which Parish & Shaw also quoted the same): "The present Minister, Mr Sacket, acquainted me with an odd custom used by the fishermen of Folkestone to this day. They chuse eight of the largest and best whitings out of every boat, when they come home from that fishery, and sell them apart from the rest; and out of this separate money is a feast made every Christmas Eve, which they call rumball. The master of each boat provides this feast for his own company, so that there are as many different entertainments as there are boats. These whitings they call also rumball whitings. He conjectures, probably enough, that this word is a corruption from Rumwold; and they were anciently designed as an offering for St. Rumwold, to whom a chapel, he saith, was once dedicated and which stood between Folkestone and Hythe, but is long since demolished". To this Pegge added at a later date "A rumbal of whitings, a certain quantity". P+

RUMBOLD WHITINGS. As Rumball

Whitings; also alluding to the Whiting being best in season about St. Rumbold's Day. =

RUNAGATE. A wild, reckless, dissolute young man; a good-for-nothing person; a tearaway. +

RUN AGIN. To run against, i.e. to meet. "I'm glad I run agin ye. I bin wanting to see ye". +

RUN A HEAD. To be delirious. "He was running a head all night long". +

RUNNER. The decorated strap holding a metal ring through which the reins are passed. =

RUNNET, RENNET. A herb, the Yellow Ladies Bedstraw (Galium verum), found on dry banks and Kent Downland. P+

RUNNING. (See Stroke-Bias). P+

RUNT, RUNTLET, RUNTLING, RUTLING. A small pig; the smallest, weakest piglet in a litter; also a diminutive or undersized person. + (See Anthony Pig, Daniel)

RUSH. The rash or spotted fever; any blood disorder affecting the skin. +P

RUSTLE UP. To gather together; to get; to fetch. "Wait awhile an' I'll rustle up something to eat". =*

RUSTY. Crabbed; out of temper. +

RUT. To be meddling and doing mischief. +

RUTTLE, RUTTLING. To rattle; to rustle; referring to the death rattle; also chestiness; a looseness of phlegm in the throat or lungs, caused by hard coughing or heavy, laboured breathing. "I doan't like to hear him ruttle so in his throat o'nights. I am most afeared he won't be here much longer". +

S

SAFE-SOWN. Self-sown; said of corn or other seeds, vegetables, such as potatoes, which grow again from the previous year's crop. +

SAG. Pronounced sag, saig, seg. To sink; bend; give way; to be depressed by weight. The wind sags, i.e. falls. Still in universal use. P+*=

SAGE. The garden herb. Parish & Shaw state: "They have a saying round Appledore that when a plant of sage blooms or flowers then misfortune is nigh. It rarely flowers, because household requirements generally keep it well cut. My informant told me of a man who saw the sage in his garden in bloom; he was horrified and told his daughter to cut off all the blossoms, but before she could do so, he met with an accident, by which he was killed". +

SAIME, SEAM. Lard; hog's lard. + (See Seam)

SAINT'S-ALIVE. An exclamatory utterance. = (See Dear Hearts-Alive)

SAINT'S-BELL. The small bell which was rung just before a service began. The saint's-bell is the old sanctus-bell formerly rung at the elevation of the Host during the Mass, to remind those inside and outside the church building of the solemn moment at the altar. +P

SALLY BATT. A willow or sallow pole. = (See Bat).

SALTERNS. Marshy places near the sea which are covered by the tide. + (See Salts, Saltings)

SALTINGS. Salt marshes on the sea side of the sea walls; a meadow or pasture close to the sea, rich in salt and thus excellent pasture for cattle. In some examples saltings are rich land, but too much intersected by grips to be of much use for cattle grazing. +*= (See Grip)

SALTS. As Salterns (which see). +

SALVEY. Soapy; close; spoken to describe potatoes which are not floury when cooked. +

SAND-RATE. The Thornback Ray (Raja clavata), so-called at Folkestone. +

SAP. To catch Eels with worms threaded on worsted. Elsewhere this is called Bobbing. +

SARE1. Tender; worn; faded; rotten. "My coat is old and very sare". P+ (See Sere)

SARE2. Dry, of wood; opposed to green wood which won't burn. P (See Sere)

SARCE. Sauce; cheek. = (See Old Lip, Tongue)

SARTIN. Stern; severe; steadfast. +

SAUCE. For sauciness. "I don't want none of your sauce". + (See Sarce, Old Lip)

SAWNEY. A nit-wit; a simpleton; simple-minded. = (See Looby)

SAY1. To try; to essay. "When a hog has once say'd a garden, you'll be troubled to keep him out". P+

SAY2. "Give us something to say" means "give us a toast". +

SAY SWEAR. A term of annoyance.

Used in the phrases "Take care or I shall say swear," i.e., "don't exasperate me too much."; or, "If you go on, I shall say swear," i.e., "I shall be thoroughly put out and use any amount of bad language". +

SCAD, SKAD. Pegge states; "Black bullace or a bastard damasin growing in the hedges". Parish & Shaw state; "A small black plum, between a damson and a sloe; a bastard damson which grows wild in the hedges. The taste of it is so very harsh that few, except children, can eat it raw, nor even when boiled up with sugar". The former is most likely the Bullace or Wild Plum (Prunus insititia). In most places where it grows it is an escape from cultivation. P+=

SCADDLE, SCEDDLE. Wild; mischievous; thievish; rapacious. Dogs that worried sheep or were apt to steal or snatch anything that came their way were said to be scaddle. It was also applied to a cat that poached, a cow that broke fences or a boy that was generally thievish, inclined to pilfer, be troublesome and mischievous. P+G

SCADDLY. Thieving; light-fingered. = (See Scaddle).

SCAGS, SKEGS. Wild Damsons. = (See Scad)

SCALLION. A name given to the poor and weakly plants in an onion bed, which are thinned out to make room for the development of the stronger plants. +

SCARCEY. Scarce. +P

SCAREFUL. Frightful; frightening; that which tends to scare. P+

SCARIFY, SCURIFY. To tear the ground apart with a large cultivator, such as a steam tackle. =

SCARLINGS. Scorched peas. Possibly a version of the Northern dialect word Carlings for peas. =

SCEDDLE. (See Scaddle) +

SCHOAT. A kneading trough. +P (See Scout, Shoat)

SCIMMINGER. A piece of counterfeit money. +

SCITHERS. Scissors. +

SCITTLE. Skittish. +

SCOASE, SCORSE. To exchange. "I'll scoase horses with you". +P

SCOFF, SCORF. To gobble; to eat greedily. "Don't scorf your food so". +*= (See Bolt, Gollop, Guzzle, Yaffle)

SCOON, SCOONING. To peer after; look round for; search closely; to pry about. =

SCOPPEL. A broad wooden shovel used by threshers. P+ (See Scubbit, Scuppet)

SCORE. In East Kent oxen and pigs were sold by the score; sheep and calves by the stone of 8 lbs. Score was probably a cut, hence twenty was denoted by a long cut on a notched stick. P+

SCORF. (See Scoff)

SCORSE. P (See Scoase)

SCOTCHEN. A badge; shortened from Escutcheon. +

SCOURGE. To sweep with a besom. "I must scourge those leaves off the lawn". +

SCOUT. A kneading trough. P+ (See Schoat)

SCRABBLE[1]. To scramble with difficulty, to climb over a loose surface, up a bank, over a hedge. †

SCRABBLE[2]. To poke or probe about in loose refuse, etc.; to pull things about. †

SCRABBLE[3]. To struggle with an animal or person; to scratch. †

SCRAN. A snack of food; the refreshment that labourers take with them into the fields. "What scran have ye got?" + (See Bait, Beaver, Elevenses)

SCRAP. To fight; word usually for the encounters between children. +*=

SCRAPS. Herrings which, being broken, cannot be hung up by their heads to dry. Also called Tie-Tails. +

SCRATCH[1]. To do anything in a hurried, hasty, scrambling way. "I scratched out of bed purty quick when I saw it was light". +*=

SCRATCH[2]. A rough, pronged prop, used to support a clothes line; a pole with a natural fork at the end of it. An older form of the word Crutch. + (See Stilt)

SCRATCH ALONG. To pull through hard times. "Times is bad but I just manage to scratch along". +

SCRATCHIT. An expression. If two men working in a field saw another person in the distance coming towards them, perhaps with a message, they didn't use the distant person's name, but one would say to the other "Here comes old scratchit". =

SCRATCHING. Picking hops from the bine as fast as possible by the picker. *=

SCRAWNCH. Crunch; crush with the teeth when eating. =

SCREECH OWL. The Summer bird visitor, the Swift (Apus apus), referring to its shrieking call or noise made in flight. In the remainder of Britain this name is used for the Barn Owl. +

SCROOCH. To make a dull scraping noise, such as when pushing back a chair along a floor or when children drag their feet deliberately. +=* (See Slooch)

SCROOGE, SCROUGE. To squeeze, crowd, push past or force through. =+

SCROOP. Similar to Scrooch (which see) but also means to creak or squeak, such as a squeaky wheel or a gate swinging on a rusty, squeaking hinge.=

SCROW. A cross, peevish, ill-natured person. + (See Frail, Tatter)

SCRUMP. A stunted, badly developed apple; a withered undersized, shrivelled person. +*= (See Scrumps, Scrumping)

SCRUMPS. Small, withered fruit left hanging on the trees; little apples. *= (See Scrump). "This orchard isn't worth much, one sieve out of every four 'ull be scrumps".

SCRUMPING. Stealing any ripe fruit in orchards during the picking season. Possibly an earlier origin was the word was used for the task of going over the trees, after first picking, to gather any good sound fruit still hanging among the scrumps (which see). "Let's go scrumping in the orchard, but better not be caught or the farmer will have us in court". =*

SCRUNCH, SCRONCH. To crunch or crush; to squash; to bite. To bite an apple noisily is to scronch it. +*=

SCRY. A large standing sieve, against which, when it is set up at an angle on the barn floor, the corn is thrown with a scubbit (which see) to clean and sift it. It was also used for sifting coal and ashes. +

Scry

Scubbit, Scuppet, Scuppit

SCUBBIT. A wooden shovel; a type used by maltsters and hop driers had a short handle; a scubbit used by farmers for moving corn on the barn floor, prior to the introduction of the threshing machine, had a long handle. + (See Scoppel, Scuppet)

SCUDGER. Well-knit; bonded; close friends were said to be "pretty scudger". =

SCUDGERING. Scratching. A horse rubbing an itchy back against a tree or fence post was scudgering itself. =

SCUFFLE. As Scarify. =

SCUFFLING. A scuffling apron was one to do hard or dirty work in. +

SCULCH, SCULTCH. Rubbish; trash. Variously used with reference to the unwholesome things children delight in eating. A variant of Culch (which see, also Pelt, Reffidge, Scutchell)

SCULL. A corruption of Cull, used in the sense of weeding vegetable and flower plants. †

SCULLED. A corruption of Culled used also in the sense of weeding with a hoe using it here and there in a garden instead of one particular row of plants. †

SCULLING. Not used in the boating sense, but meaning to move about, in a restricted area, such as a garden, small meadow, in a kitchen; also meaning a mode of walking about in a restricted area and continually getting in the way of others. †*=

SCULLING ABOUT. To loiter about and inclining to inquisitiveness; peer about; to hang about. †*=

SCULLING AROUND. As Sculling About (which see) †*=

SCUPPER. A scoop or scooper. +

SCUPPET, SCUPPIT. A large wooden shovel used in the hop oasts; a shovel consisting of a wooden frame covered with canvas used for scuppeting the hops. = (See Scuppeting)

SCUPPETING. To move the hops across the cooling floor with a scuppet during drying in the oasthouse. = (See Scuppeting In)

SCUPPETING IN. The action of shovelling the hops with the broad wood shovels into the press in an oasthouse after the hops have been dried. = (See Scoppel, Scuppit, Scubbit)

SCURF. To handle roughly. =

SCUT. The tail of a rabbit or hare, especially the white underpart of the rabbit's tail that shows as it moves about. Called a Scat in Somerset. +=

SCUTCHELL. Lumber; rubbish; a mound of sawdust, wood chips and bark accumulating around a wood craftsman's chopping block, such as that of a chestnut fencing maker; waste from a pile of thatching straw; light litter as swept up by a road-sweeper. += (See Scultch, Sculch, Culch, Pelt, Reffidge)

SEA COB. A Seagull. +

SEA-GRAPES. The eggs of the Cuttle-fish. Used elsewhere. + (See Ink-spewer, Man-sucker)

SEA KITTY. A Seagull. + (See Sea Cob)

SEA NETTLES. Jellyfish, on account of the unpleasant stings they inflict. + (See Stinger)

SEA SNAIL. The Periwinkle. Used elsewhere. +

SEA STARCH. Jellyfish. + (See Sluthers, Stinger, Galls, Water Galls)

SEAM[1]. Hog's lard. P+

SEAM[2]. Eight bushels was called a Seam because that quantity formed a horse-load, which is the proper and original meaning of seam. From the Anglo-Saxon seam meaning eight bushels or a horseload. Jno. Godfrey in his Will, 1572, gives his wife: "two seames of wheat, half a seame of oats, two seams of malt". P+ (See Seme)

SEARSE. To strain or shift, as through a sieve or strainer. +

SEASON. To sow corn; also said of the condition of land for sowing, the tilth. "The Dover fil's nice and plump now after the rain. I shall be able to go wheat seasoning today". + (See Seasoning)

SEASONING. Barley seasoning, Wheat seasoning, was seed sowing. = (See Season)

SEA-WAUR. The Wrack, Oare or Sea Weed used formerly largely in the Isle of Thanet and elsewhere, for making Maxhills (which see) (See also Waur) +

SECONDS. The second course of a meal; the pudding course. = (See Afters)

SECOND MAN. In the past there used to be a gradation of ranks among farm workers. The First Man was the waggoner, the highest rank attained, who had charge of the first team and was assisted by his "mate". The Second Man had charge of a second team and was assisted by his "mate" and so on. There was also a Yard Man, whose task it was to look after the stock in the yard. An Odd Man or Allworks (which see) did his variable tasks. There was also an order for moving along a road if together. The First Man would lead with his team, the Second Man next, etc., each one walking with his own horses. +

SEE, SEED. Saw. "I see him at Canterbury yesterday". Still used. P+*= (See Sen, Look See)

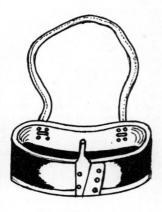

Seed Cord

SEED-CORD, SEED-KOD. A box or basket used by the sower for holding the seed and suspended from his neck by a strap or cord. It was an instrument of husbandry in common use before the invention of the seed drill and generally contained some five or six gallons of seed. It was superceded by the seed-fiddle with a thonged bow and the broadcaster with its ingenious cog-wheel system. +*= (See Seed-Lip)

SEED-LIP. A box of thin wood, kidney-shaped to fit against the body, in which the sower carried the seed. += (See Seed-Cord)

SEEMING, SEEMINGLY. Apparently. Still used elsewhere. +

SEEN. A cow's teat. +

SELYNGE. A toll; a tribute; custom; taken from boats that came in to anchor in the mouth of rivers. Lewis in his "History and Antiquities of the Isle of Tenet in Kent," 1736, records "The Prior of Christ Church, Canterbury, used to take in the stream of the water or river Stoure, before the mouth of the said Flete, a certain custom which was called Selynge, of every little boat which came to an anchor before the mouth of the said Flete". + (See Sess)

SEME. As Seam. Lewis says: "Seme, a quarter of corn or eight bushels, a horseload". P+

SEN. Seen; used in the past tense of "to see". In some cases used as bad speech. "Have you sen that child of ours anywheres?" +=

SENGREEN. The House Leek (Sempervivum tectorum) From the Anglo-Saxon singrene, evergreen, the Anglo-Saxon prefix sin meaing ever. A relative of the Stonecrops it is frequently found on the roofs of old houses where it was formerly deliberately planted to hold the slates and tiles together. Now name is in general use. +

SENSE. Used with the negative to mean "Nothing to signify"; anything inadequately or faultily done. "It don't rain but no sense", i.e. "there is no rain in any quantity to speak of" + (See No Sense)

SEP. The secretion which gathers in the corners of the eyes during sleep, particularly in elderly people. +

SERE. Dry, as distinct from green, sappy wood; not withered; was usually applied to firewood; wood fit for the fire was sere. += (See Sare)

SERVER. In parts of the county where there were no wells, formerly in the Weald of Kent, to obtain fresh water, the pond that served the house was called the server to distinguish it from the horse-pond. P+

SESS, SESSE. A levy; a tax; a rate; an assessment. + (See Selynge)

SESSIONS. A disturbance or fuss. "There's going to be middlin' sessions over this, seemingly". +

SET1. To sit. "I was just setting in my chair". +P

SET2. Firm; fixed in purpose; obstinate; in a rut. "He's terrible set in his ways, there ain't no turning an' 'im". +*=

SET3. A division in a hop garden for picking, containing 24 hills, or a group of bins in a drift in the charge of one Pole-Puller. +*=

SETTING1. As Set3 (which see) =

SETTING2. A heavy setting of fruit, such as cherries, is when each branch and twig is heavily loaded with sound fruit. =*

SETTING3. The placing of a ladder in a tree for fruit gathering. Some trees have many suitable settings for a ladder to rest against safely, while other trees are all twiggy, with weak branches and have few good settings. *=

SET-OUT. A great fuss; a row; a bother; a disturbance; also an event causing excitement and talk; a grand display. "There was a grand set-out at Mary's wedding". "Oh, the set-out we had when Jim got drunk". +*= (See Noration, Start, Bobbery, Ceremony)

SET UP. A word expressing movement or actions of several kinds; a man "sets up" a trap or snare for a rabbit, where he would normally be said to set a trap. A horse "sets up", i.e. jibs and rears. A direction to a coachman: "Set up a little" meant that he was to drive on a yard or two then stop. +=*

SEVEN WHISTLERS. When heard at night inshore fishermen called the call note of the Curlew (Numerius arquata), found on sandy and muddy coastlines, the Seven-Whistlers. They considered it a warning of foreboding and disaster and being superstitious usually returned to shore. Probably if the Curlews were flying inland and calling, it was a sign of rough, wet weather being on the way and they were calling so as to keep together in flight. The Whistler is also another local name for either the Golden-eye Duck, Golden Plover or Wigeon, heard by fishermen when these birds are on migration. + (See Whistlers)

SEW1. Dry. "To go sew", i.e. to go dry, spoken of a cow. +P

SEW2. To dry; to drain; as "to sew a pond", i.e. to drain it and make it dry. P+

SEWELLS. Feathers tied on a string which was stretched across a part of a park to prevent the deer from passing and straying. +

SEWER. A drainage channel under a marsh, boggy land or similar. =

SHACKELLS, SHACKLES. Similar to Kettlebender (which see). An onion was cut up into slices and boiled, then both hot liquid and onion were poured into a basin containing bread and cheese, all being liberally sprinkled with salt and pepper. A basin of this when eaten hot just before retiring to bed was said to be a good cure for or helpful in relieving a cold. A hot pot. A variant also called Shack-ells was a bowl of soup containing a mixture of bones and vegetables of all kinds in it as supper and alternatively sometimes as a bowl of broth with bread and cheese in it with boiling water poured over and a liberal sprinkling of salt and pepper for a winter morning breakfast. *=

SHACKLER. A horse that does odd light work, mostly an older animal. =

SHADDER. To be afraid of. +

SHAGGED. Fatigued; fagged; exhausted; tired out. "We'll have to rest the horse, he's nigh shagged out". +=

SHAKE-A-DONNIE. To shake or wave a hand, on departure, to another person or persons. It was said chiefly to children to do, usually those very young. †

SHALE. The mesh of a fishing net. + (See Ran)

SHALINGS, SHALES'S. Tenements to which no land belongs. +

SHARPED. Sharpened; to sharpen. "These knives ought to be sharped". =

SHARPER. A stone used for sharpening knives; a whetstone for Scythes, Bagging Hooks, etc. = (See Bat, Rubber)

SHATTER1. To scatter; blow about; sprinkle. +

SHATTER2. Flowers, when they drop their petals, were said to shatter. "The roses are beginning to shatter". =*

SHATTER3. When hops are too dry and brittle and break to pieces they are said to be shatter or shattery. *= (See Cream)

SHATTER4. To be afraid of. + (See Shadder)

SHATTER5. To rain slightly. +

SHATTER6. A scattering or sprinkling of rain. "We've had quite a nice shatter of rain". +

SHAUL, SHALL. Shallow; shole-water, i.e. a shoal. P+

SHAUL, SHAWL, SHOWLE. A wooden tub with sloping sides. There were two types: (a) the kneading showle used for kneading bread, generally made of oak and standing on four legs, and (b) the laundry washing shaul or shawl, made of a common wood as an oblong wooden tub without legs, mounted on trestles. Not to be confused with Shoul +P (See Keeler)

SHAVE. A corruption of Shaw (which see), a wood encompassing a close or spinney; a copse or small woodland by the side of a field; a coppice or little wood by the laneside. PG+=* (See Shaw, Carvet, Toll, Pett)

SHAVER. A small child; a nipper. A little nipper is a little shaver. =

SHAW. A small copse or hanging wood or narrow plantation of trees dividing two fields; a wood that encompasses a close; a clump of trees. GP+=* (See Shave, Toll, Pett)

SHAY1. Pale; faint-coloured. P+

SHAY2. A shadow; a dim or faint resemblance, a faint glimpse of something; a general likeness of resemblance. "I caught a shay of 'im as 'e was running out the orchard and dunno as shaan't taak to 'im next time I gets alongside an 'im". +P (See Bly, Favour)

SHE. Used in the phrase "A regular old she"; a term of contempt for anything that is poor, bad, or worthless; often applied to a very bad ball at cricket. +

SHEAD. A rough pole of wood. +

SHEAL1, SHEEL. To peel; to scale off; used of the scales or flakes of skin peeling off a person who has been ill with measles, scarlet fever, etc. +

SHEAL2. To shell; before being put in a press walnuts were first shealed, shelled, then dried in the sun. +

SHEAR. A spear; a three-pronged fork. + (See Eel-Shear, Spean)

SHEAT, SHEET. A young hog of the first year. P+ (See Shoot)

'SHEEN. An abbreviated form of Machine. +

SHEENY, GREENY. A Shrove Tuesday custom in which children took part. They would gather any early wild Spring flowers, such as Coltsfoot, and make them into small garlands or posies. Then they would call at houses and cottages to recite the rhyme:
"Flowers, flowers, high-do,
Sheeny, greeny, rino,
Sheeny, greeny, sheeny, greeny,
Rum, tum, fra."

Sheep Gate

SHEEP-GATE. A hurdle with bars. +

SHEEP'S TREDDLES. Sheep's droppings; excreta. +

SHEER. Bright, pure, clear, bare. Used to describe the appearance of stars, or the bright glossy appearance of the skin which forms over a wound. P+ (See Weather, Print)

SHEERES. Shires. All parts of the world except Kent, Sussex, and Surrey. A person coming into Kent from any county beyond London was said to "Come out of the sheeres", or if a person is spoken of as living in any other part of England, they said "He's living down in the sheeres somewheres. + (See Below London, Foreigner, Furriner, Marchman.)

SHEER-MOUSE. Probably a variation of Shrew-Mouse, to describe a member of the Shrews or Mice. A field or garden mouse. P+

SHEER-WAY. A bridle path or way through grounds or land otherwise private, separate and divided from the common road or public highway. P+

SHELL. To split open pea pods, hucks or shucks to obtain the peas inside. =* (See Huck, Shuck.)

SHELL-FIRE. The phosphorescence from decayed wood, straw, touch-wood, etc., sometimes seen in farm-yards and woods. P+ (See Composant, Fairy Sparks)

SHENT, SHUNT. To chide; reproach; reprove. P+ (See Shreap)

SHEPPEY. Sheep Island, once famous for the numbers of sheep bred on it and surrounding marshes. Situated at the mouth of the Thames the island-ers called themselves "Sons of Shep-pey" and when rowed across the Swale onto the mainland talked of "going into England". Those who lived in the marshes called the higher parts of Sheppey, "the Island", as it was once, being one of the three isles of Sheppey. A very early name for the island was Shipay. +

SHET-KNIFE, SHUT-KNIFE. A fold-ing bladed clasp knife, jack-knife or better known as a pen-knife; a knife with one or more blades that can be opened then shut by folding each into its own compartment in the handle. Thus named to distinguish it from Stick-knife (which see). A farming expression of years ago was "A waggoner should have a shilling and a shet knife." †*=

SHIDE, SHYDE. A long slip of wood; a plank; a thin board. +

SHIFT1. A fritter. P

SHIFT2. A division of land; to divide. Pegge states "To shift land", i.e. to divide it into two or more equal parts". P+

SHIM. A horse-hoe, used for lightly tilling the earth between the rows of peas, beans, hops, etc. The horse-drawn hop shim consisted of an iron-frame with tines, adjustable to the width of the alleys, its weight forcing the tines into the ground. (See Nidget). Still used; in a recent farm imple-ment sale catalogue were listed; "strawberry harrow and shim" and a "shim hoe". Also sometimes known as a Shove-Shim. P+*=

SHINGLE. A piece of seasoned oak about 12 inches long by 3 inches wide, ¼ inch in thickness, used in covering buildings and especially for church spires in many parts of the country where wood was plentiful as in the Weald. Used elsewhere. +*= (See Shingler)

SHINGLER. A wood tiler; a man who puts on shingles (which see). +*=

SHINING STICK. A thin, peeled stick, carried by farm labourers at statute fairs October 11th, to show that they sought employment for the coming year. October 11th, Michael-mas Day, Middlemas, year's end of the annual hiring of servants, labour-ers, etc. Various emblems were carried by the servants, maids, etc. to show they were seeking employment and a "Shining Stick" is one example. At this time an expression used was "Stop again or how?". Two farm labourers meeting would say "Stop again or how?" i.e. "Staying or are you looking for another job?" +=

SHINING BUG, SHINEY BUG. The Glow-worm Beetle (Lampyris nocti-luca) + (See Bug)

SHIP. Sheep. The word sheep must have been pronounced in this way in Shakespeare's lifetime, as can be seen from the following: "Twenty to one, then, he is shipp'd already, And I have played the sheep (pro-nounced ship) in loving him" — "Two Gentlemen of Verona", Act 1, Sc. 1. P+=

SHIP GATE. A sheep gate (which see) or moveable hurdle in a fence. +

SHIRE WAY. A bridle way. + (See Sheer-Way)

SHOAL-IN. To pick sides at cricket or any game with a team. +

SHOAT. A kneading trough. P+ (See Schoat, Scout)

SHOAVE. A tool like a fork used to gather up Oats when cut. +

SHOCK. A stook of corn sheaves, which was up to twelve sheaves of corn, placed standing upright together in the field in such a way that they supported each other to dry and mat-ure before carting. "To shock" meant to arrange sheaves of corn in shocks. Parish & Shaw incorrectly state a shock is a single sheaf of corn. (See Stook, Cop) +=*

SHOCKLED, SHROCKLED. A shock-led or shrockled apple was a shrivel-led apple. P

SHOE MONEY. When strangers passed through or visited a hop garden where picking was taking place their shoes were wiped with a bundle of hop bine and they were expected to pay their footing, or suffer the penal-ty of being put into the basket or bin. The money collected was called "Shoe-money" and spent on bread, cheese and ale, which were consumed in the hop garden by pickers during or at the end of the last day of the hopping season. The custom of wiping the shoes of visitors or passers-by was also practised in some of the cherry growing districts of North Kent. += (See Old Lip)

SHOOLER. A beggar. +P (See Shooling)

SHOOLING. Begging. "To go a-shooling" P+

SHOOT. A young pig of the first year. + (See Sheat, Sheet, Runt)

SHOP GOODS. Goods purchased at a shop, especially groceries, as opposed to goods purchased from a stall, market, or travelling merchant. +

SHORE1. A prop; a strut; a support. It is still used in expression to "shore up" a house, a tree, etc., i.e. support it. P+*=

SHORE2. The sides of ditches that had a slope on both sides going to the bottom were said to have "plenty of shore". If a ditch had an upright side and near-upright slope on the other side opposite the sides would eventually slip. =

SHORN BUG, SHARN BUG. The Stag Beetle (Lucanus cervus). + (See Bug, May Bug, July Bug, June Bug, Shining Bug)

SHORT-WORK. Work in odd corners of fields which does not come in long straight furrows. +

SHOT. A handful of hemp. +

SHOT-FARE. The Mackerel fishing season. It was commonly commenced about the beginning of May, when the sowing of Barley was ended. +

SHOT-NET. A Mackerel net.

SHOT OF. Rid of. +*= (See Shut of)

SHOTOVER. Mackerel. = (See Shotver-Men)

SHOTTEN. Fish, usually Mackerel, without roes. At the beginning of the season it was said that all the fish have roes; towards the end of the season they are all shotten, i.e. that have no roes. +

SHOTVER-MEN. The Mackerel fishermen of Dover, whose nets are called shot-nets (which see). P+ There was an old saying: "A north-east wind in May, Makes the shotver-men a prey". The north-east wind being considered favourable for Mackerel fishing. (See variant, in Terms, Expression, etc. chapter)

SHOUL. A shovel. Not to be confused with Shaul. +

SHOUN. Shone. "And glory shoun around". +

SHOWS FOR. It looks like. "It shows for rain". +

SHOY. Weakly; shy of bearing; giving poor crops; used mainly for plants and trees. "That plum tree is terrible shoy". +

SHRAPE. To scold, to chide. + (See Shreap)

SHREAP, SHRIP. To chide, to scold. P+ (See Shent, Shunt)

SHRIVE. To remove, saw off, the small branches from the trunk of a tree. +

SHROCKLED. Shrunk; shrivelled; wrinkled; puckered up. +P (See Shockled)

SHRUGGLE. To shrug the shoulders. +

SHUCK1. A husk or shell, of nuts, vegetables; bean shucks, i.e. bean shells. P+*= (See Huck, Shell)

SHUCK2. To shell peas, beans, nuts; shucks, being empty bean shells, pea pods. +*=

SHUCK3. An expression of contempt for a shifty person. "A regular old shuck". +

SHUCK4. To do things in a restless, hurried way as, e.g. to shuck about. + (See Shuckle)

SHUCKING. Shelling peas =

SHUCKISH. Unreliable, uncertain, changeable; when applied to the weather. "Looks as though we be going to have a lot of this shuckish weather"; also means shifty, tricky, when applied to people. +*= (See Shuck3, Shucky, Shuckle, Gagey)

SHUCKLE. To shuffle along or slink along in walking. + (See Shuck4)

SHUCKY. Changeable when applied to the weather; a shucky person was shiftless, unreliable. A "shucky time" was an unsettled rainy period in summer. =* (See Shuck3, Shuckish, Gagey)

SHUNNEL. Undersized; a runt; a smallish man or boy was "a little short shunnel". =

SHUT1. A young pig that has finished sucking and is weaned. + (See Sheat, Shoot).

SHUT2. To do; to manage. +

SHUT-FISTED. Brave; a courageous deed. =

SHUT OF. To rid oneself; to drive away. + (See Shot of)

SHUT-OUT. Exceedingly cold; feeling the effect of cold and exposure; very cold for various reasons. "You look quite shut-out" + (See Pithered)

SHUTT. A hill or gentler slope. Shutt rhymes with foot. =

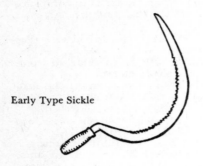

Early Type Sickle

SICKLE. A curved hook for cutting corn. The original Sickle or Wheat Hook had a serrated edge, was light and small, 12 to 18 inches across the crescent-shaped blade, with an angled handle for balance, blade either on same plane as handle or cranked to clear ground when in use. Its use was too slow so larger examples were introduced weighing about a pound with a 16 to 20 inch cutting edge and 300 or more serrations, with the serrations pointing backwards towards the 6 inch long handle. The intention was that the serrations would make the blade less likely to slip in damp straw, grass, hay, etc. The snag was that the teeth wore away quickly or broke off so the Reaping or Ripping Hook, again larger, with a plain cutting edge and the blade cranked to clear ground superceded the Sickle for this task. This in turn gave way to the larger, heavier hook known as the Bagging Hook, by the mid-19th century, with a weight of around 4 lbs, its balance concentrated on the end and not the handle. Sickle has become a general name for this type of hook with a plain-edge blade and Bagging Hooks are now made in many sizes and angles of curve, with a square or rounded end, and different shaped handles, all of which causes much confusion in identity. The Reaping Hook was itself superceded by the Scythe for reaping corn, having the advantage of the reaper

being able to stand almost upright. There were various parts of the Scythe. One was the shaft known as the sneath, sneeth, snaith or snead (which see). The shaft used in rural southern counties was usually nearly straight with a bend at the bottom to give the blade a set. There were also shafts with an S-shape curve, known as the American sneath, which, instead of being cut from naturally curved wood, were manufactured being bent by steaming. The two handles called doles, dolls or dollies, were on iron rings loosely circling the sneath, fixed tight by wedging, and were adjustable by the scythe user so they were correctly positioned in relation to the blade. The iron ring around the bottom of the sneath into which the hook end of the blade fitted and was wedged was called the cray ring (which see). There were various lengths of scythe blades, over 3 feet long, depending on their use. A very short thick one was called a litter scythe and used to cut bracken, rushes, etc., for cattle litter. The larger blades had a strut from the blade to a point up the sneath. This had two uses, one, to give some rigidity and support the blade and, two, it stopped grass, etc., from clogging the heel end of the scythe. Usually it was a piece of thick wire stapled on to the sneath and pushed through a hole in the end of the blade. There was also a cradle or creet (which see), if a bow (which see) was not used, this having several wood prongs or fingers, braced to the shaft and parallel with the blade to catch the corn as it was cut and deposit it at the end of each swing. About five swings, according to the thickness of the crop, would be a sheaf when using a cradle. (When we cut corn by scythe it was mostly to cut or open a road round a field to allow a binder to go around the first time without running down the corn. When we cut the road we mostly swung the scythe towards the standing corn. This meant going lefthanded around the field and left the corn propped against the standing corn to be taken out with a Brish Hook and tied into sheaves. To tie these we used a bond made of straws of corn (See Wimble). To set up a new or a different scythe for use the first time a man used his arms as a guide to measure, the full length from armpit to tips of fingers from bottom sneath to first doll and from elbow to top of clenched fist between dolls. The blade was then fixed on and by holding the dolls as if to swing the scythe he would just be able to touch the top of the blade with his toe, leg outstretched, this giving a reasonable set, being adjusted slightly for a good set — R.B.) +*=

SIESIN. Yeast; barm. +P (See Barm, God's Good, Sizzing)

SIEVE. A measure of cherries, containing a bushel, 56 lbs. In West Kent Sieve and Half-Sieve were equivalent to a bushel and half-bushel. Half-sieve baskets were lined with blue paper for protection, with crossed Hazel twigs acting as retainers to keep the destination label and cherries in position securely. Now largely replaced by the Chip Basket. + (See Sive)

SIFTER. A fire shovel. +

SIG. Urine. Pegge gives it as "old urine". P+

SIGHT. A great number or quantity. "There was a sight of apples laying on the ground". +

SIMPLE. Silly; foolish; stupid; person who is unable to mentally understand or comprehend. "Poor Billy will never be no good. He's too simple". +

SIMSON. The Common Groundsel, (Senecio vulgaris), a weed plant. +

SIN1. Since. "Its a long time sin I heard uv 'im". +

SIN2. Seen. "I haven't sin him for a long while". *=

SINDER. To separate or settle the lees or dregs of liquor. Said when a liquor clears with standing. P+

SINDERS. Asunders. + (See In Sunders)

SIPID. Insipid. "I calls this 'ere claret wine terr'ble sipid stuff".

SIR PETER LUG. A person that arrived late or last at a meeting was called Sir Peter Lug; lug is possibly a corruption of lag or laggard. = (See Peter Grievous)

SISSLE. To hiss or splutter; applied mostly to food cooking, such as bacon frying. Still used as sizzling. "De old kettle sissles, 'twunt be long afore 'tis teatime I reckond". +=

SISSLING (See Sissle) +

SIVE. Pegge says "A sive of cherries, 52 lbs; two sives make one bushel". P (See Sieve)

SIVER. A boatload of Whitings, so-called at Folkestone. +

SIZING. A game with cards, called "Jack Running for Sizing". +

SIZZING. Yeast; barm; so-called from the sound made by beer or ale in working. +P (See Siesin, Barm, God's Good)

SKARMISH. A skirmish; a fight; a row; a bit of horseplay and tomfoolery. +

SKEER'D. Scared; frightened. +

SKEETED. Squirted. =

SKENT. Look askance; regard with doubt or suspicion; to scowl. +

SKEVALMEN. Used in the Faversham area to describe the men who cleaned out the local creeks. From scuffle, a shovel. + (See Muddie)

SKID. Stop; halt; show. Waggoners and anyone working with a cart or similar laden vehicle used to skid a wheel, to drag it, so as to prevent it turning when going down a steep hill, by placing a wood block under the wheel, or applying a wooden handbrake against it, to act as a brake. Pegge says "to skid a wheel with an iron hook fastened to the axis to keep it from turning round upon the descent of a steep hill". PG*= Now in general use.

SKILLET. A stewpan or pipkin. +

SKIMMY. Scheme; plan. =

Skip Jack

SKIP-JACK. The Sand-hopper (Talitrus saltator), as used in the Folkestone area. This name is used generally for the Click Beetle. +=*

SKIVER. A skewer. It was the practice in winter for men to go round the hedgerows, cut the long sharp thorns from the "thorn" (Hawthorn or Blackthorn) bushes, then peel, bleach and dry them and sell them to butchers, the latter using them in fixing tickets to their meat. +P

SKRIMSHANKER. An idle layabout;

a workshy person. Not to be confused with the pastime of skrimshanking aboard ship by crewmen, making items to sell or take home in the 19th century. =

SKUT. To crouch down. "We skut down by the hedge to avoid the wind". +

SKYANCED. Puzzled. †

SKYANCER. A person gaining a living from small dealing and trading, mostly from waste materials. Sanders states only used in the Medway Towns. †

SKYANCING. To earn one's living in one of the petty dealer trades, such as rag dealing, bones, rabbits skins and left off clothing, secondhand furniture; to use one's wits to get a living from basically waste products. Sanders states only used in the Medway Towns. †

SKYMAROOTING. Hunting around; seeking something; searching among items; also dodging, rambling; expectant at what might lie around the next corner or what was over the other side of the next hedge. =*

SLAB. A rough plank; the outside cut of a tree when sawn up. +

SLABBY. Wet, slippery, greasy, dirty, sticky. = (See Slappy, Barvel)

SLACK. Underdone; underdressed; insufficiently cooked; applied to meat not cooked enough or bread insufficiently baked. + (See Slack Dried)

SLACK DRIED. Applied to hops not sufficiently dried. = (See Gone Back, Slack)

SLAGGER. To slacken speed; to slow down; to walk lame; to limp. +

SLANK. A slope or incline. +

SLANT, SLAINT. To miscarry; to give premature birth to; to slip or drop a calf before the proper time. +P

SLANTED. Aborted; a cow that slanted her calf miscarried or aborted her calf. = (See Slant)

SLAP CABBAGE. A term used for a slattern; an untidy woman. = (See Draggletail, Slommucky, Slummocks)

SLAPPY. Slippery through being wet. P+ (See Slabby, Sloppy, Slick)

SLASHER, SLASHING HOOK. A sharp-bladed, long-handled tool, similar to a long billhook or handbill but less curved; fairly weighty the long handle is intended so it can be swung with force when used for clearing woody undergrowth, cutting back high branches of hedge trees, foliage from watercourses, etc. There are modern, different-named variations. = * (See Hedge Slasher)

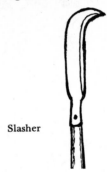

Slasher

SLATER. = (See Cheese Bug, Monkey Pea, Pill Bug, Pea Bug)

SLATS. Thin; flat; unfilled pea pods. +*=

SLAY-WATTLE. A hurdle made of narrow boards. +P

SLAY-WORM, SLOY-WORM. A corruption of Slow-Worm, the legless lizard (Anguis fragilis) †+ (See Slorry)

SLICK. Slippery + (See Slappy)

SLIGHT. Few hops on a bine or a small light crop throughout the garden were said to be slight. =* (See Light, Heavy)

SLIMMUCKS. A slinking fellow. +

SLIP. An alleyway, as in a hop garden. =

SLIPHUCKS. A person incompetent to do anything correctly or properly, either performing it clumsily or breaking the object. = (See Slipped Her Huck)

SLIPPED HER HUCK. This expression meant that an animal had broken loose after being tethered. This was particularly used on farms when the occasion arose. If a dog had been tied up with a collar and chain and it then set back and pulled the collar over its ears, or if a horse had pulled the strap or broken a rope to escape each had "slipped its huck". = (See Huck, Sliphucks)

SLIPPER[1]. According to Parish & Shaw = "A curious Eel-like fish, with an ugly pert-looking head and frill down the back (like the frill of an old beau's dining-out shirt) and a spotted and exceedingly slimy body. So-called at Herne Bay because it slips from the hand so easily". This is probably the small fish, the Spotted

Gunnel or Butterfish, usually found in rock pools, growing to a length of six inches. — A.M.

SLIPPER[2]. According to Parish & Shaw the "Small Sole", so-called at Folkestone, but this may have been a local name for either one of the four species of the Sole or the Solenette (Solea lutea), the latter being caught in shrimpers' nets but too small to be marketable. +=

SLITHER. A sliver; a small splinter that enters the skin. = (See Sliver, Smithers)

SLIVER[1]. A thin piece of split wood; a slice; a splinter; a stiff shaving. +* (See Stud, Bodge, Trug)

SLIVER[2]. To slice; to cut off a thin portion. *= (See Slither, Smithers)

SLOBBED. Slopped; spilt. +

SLOMMUCK. Sprawl or lounge about; slink about; also a lazy, untidy woman. =† (See Slummocks, Draggletail, Slap Cabbage, Strommocks, Sprollucks)

SLOOCH. To slouch; to sprawl; to drag one's feet when walking. *= (See Scrooch, Strooch)

SLOOP. To walk aimlessly; to meander. =

SLOP.[1] A short, round type of smock frock made of coarse material, put on over the head and worn by men to protect their other clothes. + (See Gaberdine)

SLOP[2]. A blue drill jacket worn for working in. =

SLOPE. To disappear from the scene. "John's sloped off somewhere". =

SLOPPY. Wet but not slippery. = (See Slick, Slappy)

SLORRY. The Slow-Worm or Blindworm (Anguis fragilis). P+ (See Slay-Worm, Sloy-Worm)

SLOSH, SLUSH. Dirty water; a muddy wash; liquid mud. Both formed from the sound and each used distinctively. Slosh represents more a muddy wash which makes the louder noise when splashed about and Slush, liquid mud, which makes a duller sound. +

SLUB. Liquid mud; a slimy wash; semi-liquid manure. Used to describe coastal land which is slowly increased by the action of the sea casting it up with sand. + (See Slosh, Slurry)

SLUGGERED UP. Slowed down. =

SLUMMOCKS, SLUMMOCKY. A slattern, a lazy dishevelled woman (See Slommuck, Slap Cabbage, Draggletail.)

SLURRY. Wet mud; watery mud that slops in dollops. + (See Slosh, Slub)

SLUTHERS, SLUTTERS. Jellyfish. + (See Miller's-eyes, Sea Starch, Stinger, Water Galls)

SMAAMER. A knock. +

SMACK-SMOOTH. Flat; smooth; level with the ground. P+

SMARMED. Smeared with mud or other sticky substance. =

SMART. Considerable; a large sum. Still used. "I reckon it'll cost him a smart penny before he's done". +

SMARTY. Something done well; pleased with oneself; outcome very satisfactory; got something to be cunning over; a "clever dick" attitude. Still used generally. *=

SMICKERY. Uneven; said of a thread when it is spun. +P

SMIGGY. Descriptive of little, inferior apples. = (See Chats, Shrockled)

SMIRK. To get the creases out of linen, that it may be more easily folded up. "Oh give it a smirking and you'll get it smooth". + (See Ruck)

SMITHERS. Slivers; splinters. + (See Slither, Sliver)

SMOULT. Hot; sultry. +

SMUG. To steal. +

SNAG. To entangle something; to become hooked up, such as in Brambles; to tear. "Look out. You'll snag yourself on that wire". =*

Snag

SNAG,[2] SNAIG, SNEG. A dialect name applied to all common species of Snails, usually in the garden, particularly Helix aspersa, the Garden Snail. In West Kent the word was applied to Slugs, Snails being called Shell-Snags. From the Anglo-Saxon snaegel. Children who found a Snail would sing: "Sneg, sneg, put out your horn, And then I'll give you a barley-corn." +*=†P (See Dodman, Hodman-Dod)

SNAGGLE[1]. To hack; to carve badly; commonly applied to meat; to nibble; peck at. +

SNAGGLE[2]. Long, pointed teeth. =

SNAGGLETOOTH. As Snaggle[2]. =

SNATAGOG. A Yew berry. +

SNAZZUMS. Hiccups. =

SNEAD. The long handle or bat of a scythe. + (See Sneath, Cray Ring, also Sickle)

SNEATH. As Snead. +*=

SNIGGER. To cut roughly; unevenly. +

SNIRK. To dry; to wither. "You had better carry your hay or it will get all snirked up, sure as you're alive". +

SNIRKING. Anything withered or dry. As dry as a snirking". +

SNOB. A cobbler; shoe repairer; a travelling shoemaker. Not used in this sense to mean snootiness or contempt. However, in areas of Sussex it was considered a derogatory description to say of a stranger that he is "a broken-down snob from Kent." "Yu'd better take these shoes to the snobs". +*= (See Snobbing)

SNOBBING. Cobbling; shoe repairing. +*= (See Snob)

SNODGOG. A Snodberry or Yew Berry; similar to the Goosegog which is a Gooseberry. += (See Snatagog)

SNOODS. Fishing lines. The lines laid for Dungeness Conger Eels are 75 fathoms long and on each line are attached, at right angles, other small lines called the snoods —twenty-three snoods to each line, each snood being nine feet long. +

SNORK. Snort. A child with a cold would snork to clear their nose. =

SNOUT, SNOWT. A part of a cake or loaf shaped like a snout. =

SNOWL. A large lump of cake or bread. = (See Chuck, Hunk)

SNUFFLICATED. Suffocated. =

SNURK. Burn; to overdry. "He snurked the hops on the last load". =

SNYING. Bent; twisted; curved; and usually applied to timber thus affected. P+

SO. Used as a correction or assent to an action. As a correction "Open the door, the window so," i.e. "Open the door, I mean the window". As an assent: "Would you like some drink?" "I would so". Used in other counties. P+

SOB. To soak or wet through thoroughly. +

SOBBED. Soaked. = (See Drean)

SOCK[1]. A shy child that clings to its nurse and loves to be fondled; a pet animal reared by hand (See Sock Lamb). Sock also means spoiled. A child or animal treated too well, granted every whim and thus the character sometimes was "spoiled". An elderly man at Mongeham talking about his terrier said she was "proper sock", i.e. spoiled. P+*=

SOCK[2]. To shroud or wrap a corpse in grave clothes; to sew a body in its winding sheet. +

SOCK-LAMB, SUCKLE-LAMB. A lamb, usually orphaned, bottle-fed and reared by hand; a pet lamb. Sock lambs often became very tame through being spoiled. P+=* (See Hob Lamb)

SOCKLE. To suckle, as a calf. P+ (See Sock)

SOIL[1]. To scour or purge. The use of greenmeat as a purge for animals gave rise to the old East Kent saying: "King Grin (i.e. green), Better than all medcin". P+

SOIL[2]. Refuse, dirt, and filth in corn; has the seeds of several kinds of weeds and suchlike mixed in with it. +P

SOLE. A pond or pool or water; standing dirty water. Latter is its probable original meaning, being derived from the Anglo-Saxon sol, meaning mud, mire. Lewis also says "soal, a dirty pond of standing water". Used in part of the names of places where such ponds existed, Barnsole, Buttsole, Maidensole, Sole Street. P+*=

SOME'RS. Somewheres; for somewhere. "Directly ye be back-turned he'll be off some'rs or 'nother". +

SPOMER-LAND. (See Summer-land) =

SOME-ONE-TIME. Now and then. "I rarely goes to that place, except some-one-time when I be forced to it". +

SONNIE. A kindly appellative for a boy. Now in common use. +*=

SOODLE. Saunter. =

SOSHELL, SOSHULL. To move about; to fidget. A post loose in a hole or a horse that fidgets his feet is said to be soshull. =

SOSS[1]. A mess. If a person caused a place to be wet and dirty it was said "They've made a soss". +=

SOSS[2], SOSSEL. To mix several slops or pour tea backwards and forwards between cup and saucer to cool it; sometimes used of children playing with their food at mealtime. +

SOSSING. To toy with food or drink, particularly of children playing with their food at mealtimes. = (See Soss[2])

SOSSLE. To drink noisily. = (See Soss[2])

SOTLY. Softly. P+

SOW BREAD. The Common Sow Thistle (Sonchus oleraceus), found in fields and waste places. +

SOWSE-TUB. A tub for pickling meat. +

SPADDLE. To make dirt or litter; for children to play in mud and wet and become in "a pickle"; to traipse dirt, wet and mud indoors; also to shuffle in walking. +

SPADDLING. Walking in mud and wet conditions. = (See Spannel, Stock)

SPADGERS. House Sparrows. =

SPALT. Heedless; impudent. P+

Spalter

SPALTER. To split and break away, as the underside of a branch when it is partially cut through or sawn through and then allowed to come down by its own weight. + (See Spolt)

SPAN. To fetter a horse. +

SPANDLE. To leave marks of wet feet, or shoes, on a floor, like a dog does with its footprints. In Sussex the word is Spannel. + (See Spannel, Spaddle)

SPANISH. Liquid liquorice. Now applied to any liquorice confection. "I took some Spanish but my cough is still terr'ble bad". +

SPANNER. A wrench; a screw nut. Now in universal use. "Have ye sin my spanner anywheres about?" +

SPANNEL. Children often like to spannel out in the wet or rain or tread through puddles or mud; occasionally used on the West Kent border area with Sussex. = (See Spandle, Spaddle, Stoch)

SPANNELING. (See Spaddling) =

SPARR. For the House Sparrow, as arr for arrow, barr for barrow. +

SPARROWGRASS, GRASS. Asparagus. = (See Rooms)

SPARTICLES. A curious corruption of Spectacles, eye-glasses. †

SPAT. A knock; a blow; a clout; a smack in reprimand. + (See Clout, Clump)

SPATTER. The first drops of rain before a heavy downfall. "Let's go home. It's beginning to spatter." *= (See Spattering)

SPATTERING. The first drops of rain before it falls more heavily. *= (See Spatter)

SPEAKS THE TRUTH. Is accurate. Two carpenters may be discussing the merits of two spirit levels: "No, that ain't no good. Doesn't speak the truth. That's the one that speaks the truth". =

SPEAN, SPEEN. The teat of an animal, or the tooth or spike of a fork or prong. P+ (See Speens, Eelshear, Shear, Deals)

SPEAR[1]. A blade of grass, fresh young shoot, or sprout of any vegetation. +

SPEAR[2]. To sprout. + (See Brut)

SPEAR[3]. To remove the growing shoots of potatoes. + (See Brut, Brutting)

SPEAR-RIB. (See Ribspare)

SPECKS. The iron tips or toes on the undersole or heel of workmen's or labourer's boots; heel and toe caps placed on shoes and boots to save wear. Now in universal use. +

SPEEN HOE. A hoe with three tines or speens. Another name for the Canterbury Hoe. =

SPEENS. The teats of an animal, particularly the cow. P+ (See Deals)

SPEER-WORTY. The liver of a dead, rotten sheep when it is full of white knots is said to be speer-worty. Pegge states the herbs Greater Spearwort (Speerwort) and Lesser Spearwort are supposed to produce this disorder of the liver and from this fact they got their names. The former is now rare and the latter rather uncommon. P+

SPIKE. The workhouse. Used elsewhere. =

SPINDLE. The piece of iron which supports the wreest or rest of a turnwreest plough. + (See Underspindled)

SPILLED. Spoilt. P+

SPILT. Spoilt. +

SPIT[1]. The depth of soil turned up by a spade or other tool in digging. Used elsewhere. +*=

SPIT[2]. A likeness to; a resemblance; a double or counterpart. "He's the very spit of his brother". + (See Bly, Favour)

SPIT[3]. Long, narrow point of land or sandbank extending into the sea. An example is the Pollard Spit in Whitstable Bay. =

SPITS. Name for the pieces of wood, usually pine, about the length and the thickness of a walking stick, on which the Herrings were dried. + (See Herring-hang, Tie-Tails)

SPLASH. To make a hedge by nearly severing the live wood at the bottom and then interweaving it between the stakes. It shoots out in Springtime and makes a thick hedge. + (See Plash, Splisher)

SPLISHER. To splisher, when a hedge is being laid, is to cut part of the way through the piece being paid. = (See Plash, Splash).

SPLUT. Split. "It was splut when I seed it". +*=

SPLUTHER. To sputter; to splutter; make a jabbering noise or speech; to stutter. +*=

SPOLT. To break. + (See Spalter)

SPONG. To sew; to mend; to repair. "Come here and let me spong that tear in your gaberdin". + (See Sponging)

SPONGING. Sewing. Pronounced spong-ing, not spunj-ing. Now used to describe an action, as spunjing, different to this, i.e. borrowing. = (See Spong)

SPONSIBLE. Responsible; reliable. +

SPOON-MEAT. (See Dish-Meat) =

SPOTTY. Here and there in places; uneven; scattered; uncertain; variable; used to describe a thin crop. "The beans look middlin' spotty this year". +

SPRAT-LOON. The Red-throated Diver (Colymbus stellatus). Once common on the salt waters and coastline of North Kent, now probably only a winter visitor, but still breeds in Scotland. +

SPREAD-BAT. The bat or stick used for keeping the traces of a ploughhorse apart. + (See Stretch Stick)

SPRIG[1]. A thick twig or thin branch of a tree. = (See Spring, Sprog, Strig)

SPRIG[2]. A staple for fencing wire. =

SPRING. The undergrowth of growing timber two to four years old; a young wood. + (See Spring-Shaw)

SPRING-SHAW. A strip of young undergrowth of wood, from two to three rods wide. + (See Sprig, Spring, Shaw, Shave)

SPROCKET. A projecting piece often put on at the bottom or foot of a rafter to throw the water off. +

SPROG. The forked sprig, twig or lesser branch of a tree or shrub. + (See Sprig[1])

SPROLLUCKS. One who sprawls out his feet. + (See Slommuck, Strommocks)

SPRONKY. A plant or tree having many roots; anything spread out in all directions; forked. +=

SPRY[1]. Smart; brisk; quick; lively; energetic.

SPRY[2]. A broom for sweeping the barn floor; also used in the threshing of corn. + (See Frail, Scubbit, Toff-Sieve)

SPRY-FOOT, SPRAY-FOOT. Splayfoot. +

SPRY-WOOD, SPRAY-WOOD. Small wood. +

Spud

SPUD[1]. A garden tool for getting up weeds; a fork for digging out ditches. +*= (See Dodger)

SPUD[2]. To get up weeds with a spud. Potatoes that become stabbed on to the prongs of the fork when digging them up are said to be "spudded". +*=

SPUDDER. A large, widely spaced three-tined fork for use in earthing up potatoes. The same tool was used in the hop gardens as a Hop Spud. *=

SPUDDING. Picking up potatoes in the fields and pecking out thistles with a Spud; both actions were known as spudding. *=

SPUDDLE[1]. To spuddle was to loosen earth around plants with a Spud. +

SPUDDLE[2]. Pithering about in the soil; almost aimlessly to potter about in the garden. = (See Pithering)

SPUDS. Potatoes. =

SPUN OUT. Penniless; short of something. "Can't finish the job, the rope's spun out". =

SPUR-FISH. The Piked or Picked Dog-fish (Acanthias vulgaris), so-named because it has a spine in front of each of its dorsal fins. + (See Rig, Robin Huss, Bull Huss, Huss)

SQUAB[1]. An unfledged sparrow or pigeon. +*=

SQUAB[2]. A pillow; a cushion; especially the long under-cushion of a sofa. +

SQUASHLE. To squelch; to make a splashing noise. "It was so wet my feet squashled in my shoes". +

SQUAT[1]. To make flat; to squash; also to put a piece of stone or wood under a carriage wheel to prevent it moving on a slope.

Squat[2]

SQUAT[2]. The wedge placed under a carriage wheel to act as a brake. +

SQUATTED. Splashed with mire or dirt or puddle water from a passing vehicle. G+

SQUAYER. Square. †

SQUENCH. Quench, as for fire or thirst. =

SQUIB[1]. A syringe; a squirt. "He stood back of the tree and skeeted water at me caterwise with a squib". +

SQUIB[2]. A Cuttlefish; so called because it squirts sepia as part of its defence. + (See Squib[1])

SQUIRREL HUNTING. A kind of sport in which people from the surrounding districts used to assemble on 30th November, St. Andrew's Day, to beat the woodlands and hunt squirrels. Under the pretence of doing so it gave the less honest participants an opportunity to indulge in poaching. Presumably it was a sort of practice, as Pigeon shooting or Otter hunting and Fox hunting are now, the prey being Red Squirrels. It is unlikely Grey Squirrels were the prey as these had only just been introduced at this time from North America. +

STAB. A Rabbit's nest in a burrow or hutch; a short burrow. =

STADLE, STADEL. The step of a ladder. += (See Stale, Stath)

Staddle

STADDLE. The support of a stack of corn; a building of timber standing on legs or steddles, to raise it out of the mud. These poor dwelling places were once common in small fishing towns, such as Queenborough, along the Kentish coast. Barns were often built on Staddle Stones, mushroom-shaped stones specially made for the purpose, as the shape of the latter made it difficult for rats to climb them to enter the barn for grain, fruit, etc. +*= (See Steddle)

STALDER. A stillen or frame to put barrels on. P+

STALE. To put stales, stiles or rungs into a ladder. + (See Stadel, Stath)

STALES. The stiles, staves or risings of a ladder, or the staves of a rack in a stable. From the Anglo-Saxon stael, stela, a stalk, stem or handle. Allied to Still and Stall; the Stale being that by which the foot is kept firm. P+ (See Stale)

STALKER. A Crab pot or trap made of hoops and nets. +

STAN' 'ARD. A waggoner's call "Stand Hard", to his mate on the load on the wagon when he is about to get up himself; also when about to move off over a field when carting corn the waggoner shouted "Stand Hard". =

STAND. To stop; be hindered; one famous usage was highwaymen ordering "Stand and deliver!" "We don't stand for this weather", i.e. "We keep working regardless of the weather". +

STANMEL, STAMMEL. The name given to a kind of woollen cloth of a red colour, for making petticoats and other clothing. +

STARF TAKE YOU. An imprecation to call down evil used in Kent, from the Anglo-Saxon "steorfa" (a plague). Instead of saying "The plague take you" as a curse, malediction or phrase of annoyance used in other counties, in Kent this was "The starf take you". Another use of the same word was "What a starf be ye got at now?" +

STARGOG. The Starling (Sturnus vulgaris) †

START. A proceeding; a business; a set-out; a poor beginning to a project. "This is a rum start, I reckon". +*=

STARVE NAKED. Stark naked; nude. Starved in Kent also sometimes meant extremely cold, as well as extremely hungry. +

STATH. A step of a ladder. + (See Stadel, Stale)

STAYER, STAYERS. Stair; stairs. †

STAUNCH. To walk clumsily and heavily. +

STEADY. Slow; taking it easy; such as after an accident or illness. "I get along middlin' well if I go steady". +

STEAN, STEENE. To line or pave with bricks or stones. On churchyard graves, usually table tombs, it is some-times possible to read "In this steened grave rest the mortal remains of etc." Pegge says "To stean a wall, to build the sides with stones. P+

Steddle

STEDDLE. A wooden framework placed on Staddle Stones for supporting corn stacks; a framework on which to stand something, i.e. a bed-steddle, a bedstead; + (See Bedsteddle, Staddle)

STEEP. To make anything slope; to steep a stack was to make the sides smooth and even and to slope it up to the point of the roof. P+

STEEVERS. Beer. =

STENT. Used by the North Kent Oyster dredgers to denote the amount or number of Oysters, fixed by the rules of their Association, that they may dredge in one day. This quantity or total is much smaller than it would in fact be possible to get up. Possibly Stent is derived from stint, meaning a restriction, a limitation. +

STEW POND. A stew was a pool to preserve fish in specially for the table. P

STICK KNIFE. A knife with a single blade rigidly fixed in the handle,

such as a dagger-type knife; a sharp-pointed carving knife; a knife used by pig killers in the past for "sticking" or killing pigs and sometimes called a "pig sticker". † (See Shet Knife, Shut Knife)

STILLEN. A stand for a cask, barrel or washing tub. + (See Stalder)

STILT. A crutch. +P

STINGER. Jellyfish, so-called at Dover. + (See Miller's Eyes, Sea Starch, Sea Nettles, Sluthers, Water Galls)

STINK-ALIVE. The Whiting-Pout. Given this name because it soon becomes unfit to eat after being caught unless quickly cooked or frozen. + (See Pouters)

STIPERS. The four poles at the sides of a Bobbin-Tug, which stand up two on each side and keep the bobbins in their places. + (See Bobbin-Tug, Pimps)

STIVER. To flutter; to stagger; to struggle along; also means broke, penniless, coinless. "Haven't got a stiver". +=

STOACH, STOCH. To tread or work in the mud and dirt; said of cattle treading the ground when it is wet and making puddles. †P+*= (See Stodge, Spandle, Stodgy, Stotch, Spaddle, Stodging)

STOCK1. The udder of a cow. Now also used for cattle of all kinds, in general use.

STOCK2. A trough; a stoup; usually in composition, i.e. as a holy water-stock, a brine-stock, a pig-stock. P+

STOCK3. The back of a fireplace. Because this is generally black with soot the phrase "Black as the stock" was once commonly used, modern usage being "black as soot", "black as ink", etc. P+

STOCK-BOW. A Crossbow. +

STOCK-LOG. The larger piece of wood which is laid behind the rest on a wood fire to form a backing for it. P+

STODGER. A sturdy fellow able to get about in all sorts of weather. +

STODGY. Muddy earth; something thick, glutinous. + (See Stoach, Stoch, Stotch)

STOKE. Disturb the fire with a poker; raise the embers. "You'd better stoke the fore or it will go out". =

STOLDRED. Stealth. +

STOLT. Brisk and hearty; stout; sturdy. A stolty person was a strong, sturdy person. P+

STOMP. To stamp about; walk heavily around. Deep litter is pressed down where the stock have been stomping. "Don't keep stomping on the floor in them heavy boots". =*

STONE. A weight of eight pounds. P+

STONE-FRUIT. Explanatory to describe fruit with "stones", plums, cherries, peaches, greengages, etc., as opposed to "Hard-Fruit", apples, pears, and "Low-Fruit", currants, raspberries, gooseberries, etc. +

STONE HORSE. A horse that has not been castrated. = (See Stones)

STONE-REACH. A section of a stony field where the stones for a considerable distance lie very much thicker than in any other part. The stones in a Stone-Reach were gathered off the fields for use in road laying and repairs. So great was the demand in former times such stones became scarce and commanded high prices, but eventually other means of road making and repair replaced them. P+

STONES. The testes of a horse. = (See Stone Horse)

STOOK. A group of sheaves set up in a field. "To stook" meant to arrange the sheaves in a stook. =* (See Cop, Shock)

STORTER. A trestle or stand as used by carpenters, or as used in public houses in the past to stand beer barrels upon. =

STOTCH, STODGE. To tread wet land into holes. + (See Stock, Poach, Stodgy)

STOUNDED. Astounded; astonished. +

STOVE. To dry in an oven. +P

STOW. As Stove. P+

STOW-BOATING. To go dredging up stones at sea for making Roman cement. +

STRAIGHT. Grave; serious; solemn; shocked; used in phrase "To look straight", i.e. "To look grave or shocked". In general use. +

STRAMMERLY. Awkwardly; ungainly. +

STRANDS. The dry bents of grass run to seed. +

STRANGERS. The name in Kent used for the people from east London who annually came to Kent for hop picking. In East Farleigh churchyard, near Maidstone, in a hop growing district, there is a wooden memorial cross with the wording "In memory of 43 Strangers who died of cholera, September 1849. R.I.P." The date month is significant being during the hop picking season. = (See Foreigners, March-men, Sheeres)

STRAY. A winding creek or stream flowing into the sea and affected by tides. An example exists at Lower Halstow, near Sittingbourne, where in my childhood days it was called "The Stray" — A.M.

STRETCH STICK. The piece of harness between the trace chains to keep them apart and free of the horse's flanks. = (See Spread Bat)

STRICKLE[1]. A striker; a smooth, straight, flat-edged piece of wood, with which the heaped-up measure of loose corn lying above the level of the rim of the vessel was struck off and made even. The measure thus evened by the strickle was called Race Measure, i.e, razed measure. + (See Race Measure)

STRICKLE[2]. A type of sharpening implement. A length of square-sectioned wood with grooves across it. It was smeared with grease or animal fat and covered with sand. The grooves held the grease and sand mixture so it could be used like a file on the blade edge of a scythe, etc., to sharpen it. =

STRIG[1]. The stalk of a flower or fruit, such as the strigs of strawberries, cherries, currants. "Now don't 'ee put the cherry strig in yer mouth". P+*=

STRIG[2]. To take the fruit from off the stalk or strig; as to strig cherries, currants, strawberries, etc. "Will you help me strig these currants?" +*=

STRIG[3]. The string of a button. +

STRIKE[1]. To "strike a bucket" was to draw a full bucket towards the side of the wall as it hung by the chain of the windlass and land it safely on the well-side. +

STRIKE[2]. To melt down; to re-cast and so make smooth, as of wax. One sense of strike was to stroke, to make smooth. +

STRIKE[3]. As Strickle[1] (which see)

STRIKE[4]. A measure of four bushels. = (See Prickle, Wash)

STRIKE-BAULK. To plough one furrow and leave another. P+

STRIKING PLOUGH. A kind of plough used in some parts of Kent. =

STRINGY. If Runner Beans are cooked when late in season and the outer case is still tough to eat they are said to be stringy. = (See Hucky, Ucky)

STRIPING. The description of a heavy defeat at football particularly used by the farm workers in the Sutton-at-Hone area. =*

STRIP-SHIRT. In shirt sleeves. A man was said to be working strip-shirt when he had his coat and waistcoat off. Still used. +*=

STROD. The fork of a tree; a catapult is strod shaped. =

STRODDLE. Straddle. =

STROKE-BIAS. An old sport that was, according to Parish & Shaw, peculiar to Kent, especially the eastern part of the county. It consisted of trials of speed between members of two or more villages and from the description of it given in Brome's "Travels over England", 1700, it appears to have borne some resemblance to Prisoners' Base and was also called a Running. However, Shakespeare knew it as Country-Base, in Cymbeline v. 3. 20. P+ (See Match Running)

STROMMOCKS, STROMMUCKS. A person or animal awkward with its feet. Applied to an old mare "unhandy" with her feet which sprawls about and treads on her work; also applied to an ungainly wench, striding and sprawling about. = (See Slommuck, Sprollucks, Unhandy, Mawkser, Unthrum, Goyster)

STROOCH. To drag the feet along the ground. + (See Scrooch, Slooch)

STUB¹. The stump of a tree or plant, such as the stalk of a Brussells Sprout, when the sprouts have been removed; the stumps of trees in a wood after being felled. +

STUB². To grub up; to remove; used of taking up the stubble from a field; of getting up the roots of a tree from the ground; or clearing hop bines to replant the area with a different crop. + (See Grubbed Up, Grubbed Out)

STUD¹. A support; a prop; a stop. The feet on which a Trug-basket stands are called studs. +

STUD². The name given to a row of small trees cut off about two feet from the ground and left to sprout so as to form a boundary line. + (See Dole)

STULPE. A post, particularly a short, stout post put in to mark a boundary; also spelt stoop and stolpe. +

STUNT. Sullen; dogged; obstinate. +

Stuppin, Stuppnet

STUPPIN, STUPEN. A stew pan or skillet. P+

STUPPNET. A stew pan or skillet. + (See Stuppin)

STURM. Stern; morose. +

STURT. A Stoat. P

SUCK HER JOLE. To kiss her. =

SULING, SULLING, SOLIN. A Domesday measure of land which occurs only that part of the Domesday Record which relates to Kent. It is supposed to contain the same quantity of land as a carucate. This is as much land as may be tilled and laboured with one plough and the beasts belonging thereto, in a year; having meadow, pasture and houses for the householders and cattle belonging to it. The hide was the measure of land in the reign of Edward the Confessor; the carucate, that to which it was reduced in William the Conqueror's new standard. From Anglo-Saxon sulh, a plough. P+ (See Swilling Land). Pegge states "a ploughland".

SULLAGE, SUILLAGE. Muck; dung; sewage; dirty water and suchlike. P+

SUM. To reckon; to count; to cast up accounts; to learn arithmetic. From the French sommer. P+

SUMMER LAND. Ground that lies fallow all the summer. P+ (See Somer Land)

SUMMUT. Something. "As soon as I seed him coming along the road I knew summut was wrong". +

SUMP. A muddy shallow, as is typical along the North Kent coast in and on the mouth of a creek, where barges and fishing vessels could anchor; a small cove as an anchorage. +

SUNDAYS AND WORKY-DAYS. i.e. all one's time; altogether. A phrase that was used when a man's whole time was taken up by any necessary duties. "Sundays and worky-days

(Work days, weekdays) is all one to him". +

SUN-DOG. A halo around the sun, seen when the air is very moist and generally supposed to forecast the approach of rain or rough weather within a day or two. The same meaning for Sun-Hound. Sometimes used for a bright, shiny rainbow-like spot on a cloud during the same climatic conditions and presaging rain. +*= (See Sun-Hound)

SUN-HOUND. Same as for Sun-Dog (which see). +

SUPM. Something. +

SURELYE. Surely. "Well, that ain't you, is it?" Surelye, tis!" +=

SWAB. To swab peas, to reap them. P (See Swap)

SWALLOWS. Places where a stream enters the earth and runs underground for some distance before reappearing. Formerly so-called in Bishopsbourne area.

SWAP1. To reap with a Swap Hook. + (See Swab, Swap2, Swop)

SWAP2, SWAP HOOK. An implement used for reaping peas and beans, consisting of part of a scythe blade, about 18 inches long, fastened to the end of a pole handle about 3 feet long. Some examples had a loop of leather on the top of the handle to put an arm through. Also sometimes a Bagging Hook was called a Swap. +*= (See Pea Hook, Bagging Hook, Sickle)

SWARF. The line or row of cut grass as left by the mowing machine. = (See Swath, Swarth).

SWARMING. Sauntering aimlessly. =

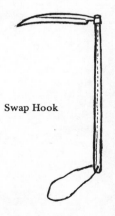

Swap Hook

SWART, SWARTH. Of a dark colour; swarthy. "The sky looks very swarth all of a sudden". Pegge states "a dark green." "The wheat looks very swarth". P+

SWARVE. To be choked with sediment; to fill up. When the channel of a river, creek or ditch becomes choked and blocked with sediment deposited by the water flowing into it, it was said to swarve up. +

SWATCH1. A wand; a flexible twig or rod. + (See Swatchel)

SWATCH2. A channel or water passage such as between rocks, mudbanks and sands, a famous example being the swatch dividing the Goodwin Sands. +

SWATCHEL. To beat with a swatch or wand. + (See Swatch1)

SWATH, SWARTH, SWEATH. A row of grass or corn as it is laid on the ground by the mowers. Swath is in general use now. + (See Swarf)

SWAY. To carry some sway was to excel in anything or to have considerable influence; to be the best man; the most skilled. "No matter what 'twas, mowin', or rippin' or crickut, or anything 'twas all the same, I always carried the sway when I was a young chap". +

SWEAL. To singe a pig. +

SWEEPS, SWIPS. The sails of a windmill. In general use. + (See Swifts)

SWEET-LIQUOR. The wort or malt extract; a mixture of crushed malt (grist) and liquor, to which is added hops and sugar, then yeast to cause the process of fermentation and turn the sweet insipid wort into beer. P+

SWEET WILLIAMS. The Lesser Spotted Dogfish (Scyllium canicula), the name also being applied to other members of the Dogfish family. (See Huss, Bull Huss, Robin Huss, Rig) =

SWEET-WORT. (See Sweet-Liquor) +

SWELKED. Overcome by excessive heat. + (See Sweltry)

SWELTRY. Sultry; hot and close; probably corruption of swelter or sweltering. + (See Smoult)

SWIFTS. The arms or sails of a windmill. + (See Sweeps, Swips)

SWIG. To take a drink, as from a bottle. =

SWILLICK. A drink. =

SWILLING-LAND. A ploughland. + (See Suling)

SWIMY, SWIMMY, SWIMMY-HEAD-ED, SWYMMEE. Giddy; dizzy; faint. From Anglo-Saxon swima, a swoon, swimming in the head. +*=

SWINGEL. The upper part of a Flail which swings to and fro and beats the corn out of the ears. Anglo-Saxon swingel, a beater. +

SWIPE. Hit; clout; smack. Now universally used. =* (See Dob, Clump, Clout)

SWIPPER. A sweeper; a besom; a broom. =

SWISH ALONG. To move with great speed. Still used. "She swished by me so I was nearly knocked over". +*=

SWOP. To cut down, such as nettles with a Bagging Hook † (See Swab, Swap)

SWOP-FOOTED. Left-footed. = (See Cack-Handed)

SWOT. Soot. P+

T

TAANT. Usually applied to the masts of a ship, by seamen, when very high or tall or out of proportion. +P

TACK. An unpleasant taste. + (See Twang, Tackle)

TACKLE. Used in describing something that is of poor quality, damaged, or inferior. "This soup is some poor old tackle". *=

TAFFETY. Squeamish; dainty; particular and fussy about food. Used in East Kent. =

TAG, TAGGE. A Sheep of the first year. P+*=

TAILS. The long thin lateral stems on the lower part of the hop bine, each with only about two leaves and two hops at each node. =* (See Heads)

TAKE AND. Go; do; to go ahead and do something; used in the expression "He'd better by half take and get married" or "You take and wash them dishes now". +

TALLY. A stick, 9 inches long by 1½ inches wide, on which the number of bushels picked by the hop picker was reckoned and noted, there being some mark or means of identifying the picker on it. The tally stick was sawn into two pieces. The longer piece with a hole in it, so it could be hung on a string over his shoulder with all the others of other pickers, was kept by the Tallyman, the picker retaining the shorter piece. After hops had been measured the two pieces were put together and notches made across them with a triangular file to denote the total of bushels picked, the small piece then being handed back to the picker. In most gardens a single notch was cut for every 5 bushels picked. Tally sticks were replaced by hop growers having their own stamped metal tallies or tokens, similar to trade tokens, of different measure values, which were given to the picker at each measuring and redeemed at the end of the season. += (See Measurer, Tallyman)

TALLYMAN. The man who took the tallies, notched them and so kept account of the number of bushels picked by the hop pickers. Replaced by the Measurer and Clerk. +=

TAMSIN. A little clothes horse or frame to stand before a fire to warm a shirt or a shift or a child's linen. Tamsen, Thomasine, Thomasin, were formerly popular female Christian names and they were used more as a nickname for the "horse" that did the work of the maidservant of that particular name. For the same reason it was also called a Maid or Maiden. As well as Tamsen, Thomasine, this "Horse" was also called any other girl's Christian or maiden name, Jenny, Molly, etc. A very small clothes-horse was called a Girl. +P

TAN. The bark of a young Oak tree, i.e. that which tans as oak bark does. P+

TANDY. Football. Nippers or children in rural areas played tandy or football. =

TANKS. Large iron troughs for watering sheep and cattle. = (See Bat)

TANTED1. Fainted. "She came over swimy and tanted away in my arms".=

TANTED2. Applied to a child or person being obstreperous or feigning an illness to get their own way. = (See Tants)

TANTS. Childish tantrums; stubbornness; naughtiness; bad-tempered. =*

TAR GRASS. The Tufted Vetch (Vicia cracca), a wild plant in hedges and bushy places, so-named due to its association, according to Pegge, with "tares and vetches and having something of the tare in it". P+

TARNAL, TARNEL. A strong expletive; really "eternal", used to denote something very good or very bad, generally the latter. +

TARSE, TAS. A mow of corn. In Early English taas was any sort of heap. +

TART. A sweetheart, not meant with malice as now for a heavily made-up, gaudy, overdressed, prostitute-type girl or woman. =

TASS CUTTER. An implement used to cut hay in the stack. P+

TATTER, TATTERY. Ragged; torn. Another meaning was cross; peevish; ill-tempered; ill-natured; disagreeable; unwell. "Old mistress is tedious tatter". P+G (See Scrow, Frail)

TATTY. Testy. + (See Tatter)

TAUF, TOFF. The refuse of peas, beans, after threshing, used as horse-meat. = (See Caving, Gullidge)

TAULEY. A taw or marble. +

TEAM. A litter of pigs or a brood of ducks. +P

TEAMSTER. Name of man who worked with horses. *= (See Waggoner)

TEARFUL. A job or work or task that is very arduous or exacting to bring the person doing it almost to tears. †

TEAR RAG. A rude, boisterous child; a romp; one who is always getting into mischief and tearing his or her clothes, hence the name. +

TED. To make hay, by tossing it about and spreading it in the sun. +

TEDIOUS. Acute; violent; excessive; "tedious bad", "tedious good"; also long, but not necessarily wearisome, as the word is now used. P+

TEE-DANCE. A child's see-saw. = (See Titterney-Tortarney)

TEEN. To make a hedge with raddles. P+ (See Raddles)

TEENER, TENER. A man who makes a hedge with raddles and maintains a raddle-fence. + (See Raddles)

TEES. A part of a cart-horse's harness; the draughts which are fixed to the hemwoods of the collar and to the rods of the cart; the ties. + (See Hemwoods)

TEG. A sheep of the first year. + (See Tag, Tagge)

TELL. To count. Related to the Teller in common use, such as a bank teller an official who counts money paid in. "Here's the money. Will you tell it out on the table?" +

TELL-TALE-TIT. A children's expression, used to a child that runs and tells its parents, teacher, etc., every time other children do something to annoy the child or they do something naughty or wrong. "Go home to your mummy, you tell-tale-tit". =*

TEMPERAMENTS. Changeable; uppish; unsettled; most frequently applied to the weather. "Oh, it's got its temperaments has the weather". =

TENTER-GROUND. Ground where tenterhooks were placed in former times for stretching skins, linen, etc. From this task arose the expression to be "on tenterhooks", i.e. at full stretch, nervous, etc. +

TERRIBLE. Extremely; exceedingly. "Frost took tips terrible, but taint touched roots o' tothers". +

TERRIFY. To annoy; frighten; to disturb; to tease. The flies were said to terrify the cattle. A bad cough was said to be terrifying. "Baby can't wear wool. It terrifies him too much". "Don't de flies terrify today". + (See Toify)

TETAW. A simpleton; a fool; a ninny. P+

THAT. So; to such a degree. "I was that mad with him I could have scratched his eyes out". +

THAYER. Theirs; belonging to them. † (See Thern, Therren)

THEIRN. Theirs. = (See Thern, Therren)

THEM. Contraction from they'm, i.e. they am. "How be all at home?" "Them all well, without mother and she be tedious bad wid de brown titus ".(bronchitis) P+ (See Am)

THERN. Theirs; belonging to them. † (See Therren, Thayer)

THERREN. Theirs; belonging to them. † (See Thern, Thayer)

THICK-THUMBED. Clumsy; awkward; also untidy; sluttish. P+

THILL-HORSE. As Vill Horse. Anglo-Saxon thill means shafts.

THIS-HERE. This in an intensive form. "He was sitting on this-here very chair, when all of a sudden down he goos in one of these 'ere plexicle fits". +*=

THISSER, THISYER. A corruption of This-Here (which see). †

THISTLE-DODGING. Digging up thistles with a Dodger (which see) (See Thistle-Packing). †

THISTLE-PACKER, THISTLE-PECKER. A man who hoes up thistles, it also referring to the tool, a small,

111

sharp hoe, the Thistle-pecker, or cutter, used for the task. A man who spent most of his working life in the past at this job got the nickname of "Pecker" or "Packer". †
THISTLE-PACKING, THISTLE-PECKING. Hoeing up thistles. † (See Thistle Dodging, Dodger)

Thistle Spud

THISTLE-SPUD. A tool with a short narrow blade that was used to get around and lift the thistles out instead of the longer narrow blade of the Pecker that pecked them out; also used for other weeds such as docks and those with long tap roots and then called a Weed Spud. = (See Thistle-Pecker, Pecker)
THOFT. Thought. "Who'd 'ave thoft it!" +
THOVE. Thieved; stole. +
THREDDLE. To thread a needle. P+*=
THRIBLE. Treble; three-fold. +
THRO. From; fro. "To and thro", i.e. to and fro. P+
THROT. Throat. P+
THROWS. A public highway; a thoroughfare. The four throws was the point where four roads met. + (See Went)
THUMBHEADS. Mice, usually Field Mice or Voles. =
THUNDER BUG. A Midge. + (See Bug)
THURROCK. A wooden drain under a gate; a small passage or wooden tunnel through a bank; two fields with a ditch separating them the ditch being piped and filled with earth. In Sheppey if Hares gained the refuge of a thurrock before the hounds could catch them they were considered to have gained sanctuary and were not harmed. + (See Thurrock-way, Pinnock),

THURROCK-WAY. The earth in a ditch dividing two fields, piped to allow water to flow through. Wagons passed over the "thurrock-way" to go from one field to another. = (See Thurrock)
TICKLER. Particular. "I lay he's not so tickler as all that". +
TIDDY. Small; tiny. A tiddy hopper is a flea. =
TIDE. The tithe. This is a remarkable instance of the way in which the th is converted into d in Kent, as wid for with, etc. +
TIDY. Considerable; strong. Used to describe strength of wind. "Its a tidy old blow tonight", i.e. "The wind is strong tonight". "A tidy few" meant a good number. A half-tidy distance is a long distance; a tidy amount is a large amount. Still used. +*=
TIE. A foot race between two competitors; a tie was a pair and also the running itself, according to Pegge, was called a tie, to run once was one tie, to run twice was two ties. "When they run several together in that exercise they have called Stroke-Bias that they term a Running. I suppose tis called a tie from the parties being tied, i.e. paired together; Waldershare tie, Old Wives Lees tie". The foot race of only two as meant by Pegge was probably what we call a heat. According to Hasted, "Kent", Sir Dudley Digges, in 1638, left the yearly sum of £20, "to be paid to two young men and two maids, who on May 19th yearly, should run a tye at Old Wives Lees, in Chilham, and prevail. " The lands from the rent of which prize was paid were called the Running Lands. The expression "Ride and Tie" was interpreted to mean that, when two people have one horse, the first rides a certain distance and then dismounts for the second to get up, so that they always tie, or keep together. P+
TIE-TAILS. The name for Herrings which could not be hung up by their heads because they were gill-broken and thus were tied on the spits by their tails for drying. They fetched less money when sold for this reason, but otherwise were perfect to eat. + (See Herring-Hang, Spit).

TIGHTISH LOT. A good many. + (See Tidy)

TIGHT-UP. Make tidy; tidy up. "My missus has gone to tight up." +

TILL. Tame; gentle. +P

TILLER. An oak sapling or other young timber tree of less than six inches and a quarter in girth. In Sussex it is known as a teller or tillow. + (See Quant)

TILT1. The moveable covering of a cart or wagon; generally made of sailcloth or canvas. +

TILT2, TILTH. Condition of arable land; getting the land in good condition for sowing. "This land is in good tilth". "He has a good tilth". P+

TILTER (OUT OF). Out of order; out of condition. "He's left that farm purty much out o' tilter, I can tell ye". + (See Out of Kilter)

TIMANS. Dregs or grounds poured out of a cask after the liquor is drawn off. Literally "teemings" from the Middle English "temen" and from Anglo-Saxon teem, to pour out. P+

TIMBERSOME. Troublesome; tiresome. In Sussex Timmersome means timid, timorous. + (See Timmy)

TIME-O'-DAY. To pass the time-o'-day was to greet a person who you chanced to meet on the road with a "Good morning", "A fine day", "Looks like rain", etc. "I ain't never had no acquaintance with the man, not no more than just to pass the time-o'-day". +

TIMID. Something fragile or easily damaged or broken was said to be timid or very timid. =

TIMMY. Fretful. Possibly abbreviation of Timbersome (which see). +

TIMNAIL. A vegetable Marrow, for timnail jam. Name used in East Kent. +

TIMNAIL JAM. Marrow jam. Still made. =*

TIMNAIL PIE. A pie made using vegetable Marrow. =*

TIN-TAN. In the balance; "all of a tin-tan". =

TINE1. The tooth or prong of a rake, harrow or digging fork. +P (See Shear, Speen).

TINE2. To shut in; to fence; to enclose. +

TIPPLE. To fall; possibly a variation of tip over. †

TIPPLED. Fell down. † (See Tipple, Tippling)

TIPPLING. Falling down. † (See Tipple, Tippled)

TIPTOE. An extinguisher, so-called in West Kent. P+

TIP-TONGUED. Inarticulate; indistinct in utterance; lisping. "He talks so tip-tongued since he come back from Lunnon we can't make nothin' o' what he says otherwise". +

TIRESOME. Causing bother or trouble but not needing repairs or replacement. A man examining a fence would say "The posties are a little bad (loose) but not tiresome at all". =

TIRYEN. A form of Trinity, thus "Tiryen church" : Trinity Church. +

TISSICK. A tickling cough. +

TISSICKY. Tickling. "A tissicky cough won't let me alone". +

TIT. To gossip; to tell tales. Usually used by children to describe another who carries tales. "Don't have nothing to say to her, she's a tit-tale". =* (See Tell-Tale-Tit)

TITHER. To trifle; to tither about, i.e. to waste time. +

TITTLE-BAT, TICKLEBAT, TIDDLEBAT. A Stickleback, freshwater fish. =* (See Crowfish, Prickybat)

TIVER. The red ochre used for marking sheep; the act of marking sheep; to tiver them. + (See Tivered)

TIVERED. Branded. =*

TO-AND-AGAIN. To and fro; backwards and forwards. +

TO-AND-THRO. To and fro. = (See Thro)

TOAR. Long, coarse, sour grass in fields that were understocked; toare being grass and rubbish on cornland after the corn is reaped. P+

TOBIT. A measure of half a bushel. + (See Tofet, Tofiet, Tovet, Tolvet)

TOE-PEG. Cramp in the toes; stiffness causing cramp. =*

TOFET. As Tobit (which see)

TOFF, TAUF. The pods of peas and the ears of wheat and barley after they have been threshed. Used in East Kent. + (See Caving, Gullidge)

TOFF-SIEVE, TOFT-SIEVE. A sieve or screen for cleaning wheat. +

TOFIET. Half a bushel. G (See Tobit, Tofet, Tovet, Tolvet)

TOFT. A messuage; a dwelling house with the adjacent buildings and curtilage and the adjoining lands appropriate to the use of the household; a piece of ground on which a messuage formerly stood. +

TOIFY. Variant of terrify, but used also as pester, annoy, tease. = (See Terrify, Terrifies.) =

TO IT. Towards it; to do something; tackle a task. Omitting the verb do, which is understood. Remind a Kentish Man or Man of Kent of something he has been told to do, but which you see is still undone and the chances are he will reply "I'm just a going to it", i.e. "I am just going to do it." +

TO WRONGS. Out of order. "There's not much to wrongs with the world at the moment". = (See Rights, Droits)

TOKERS. Toker Beans were Broad Beans. =

TOLL. A clump or row of trees. Sometimes seen in the centre of a field as a wind-break, but becoming less common as they tend to make the land immediately close to them unproductive, so are being felled to bring the piece of land into cultivation. A Rook-Toll is a rookery. + (See Pett, Shaw)

TOLLER. Tallow. =

TOLVET. (See Tovet). =+

TOM. A cock; also applied to a male cat. += (See Tommy)

TOMMY1. A cock; a male cat. = (See Tom)

TOMMY2. The green food, Dandelion, etc, gathered to feed a Rabbit being fattened for Christmas. "I mustn't forget to give the Rabbit his tommy" (See Tommy3)

TOMMY3. A workman's dinner. =* (See Bait, Progger, Nuncheon)

Tommy Hoe

TOMMY HOE. A small tool on a short handle about a foot long, with one or two curved tines or speens about three inches long, drawn through the soil in a circle close to the hop plant to find any runners. = (See Dressing Knife, Kent Hoe, Corn Hoe, Half-Mattock, Clod Hoe, Axe Een Mattock, Weald Hoe, Plate Hoe, Peck, Double-sider Hoe)

TON, TUN. The great vat wherein beer is worked before it is tunned or cleansed. Sometimes used in public house names, an example being "The Three Tuns" at Lower Halstow near Sittingbourne. +=*

TONGUE1. The projecting part of the cowl of an oast, which causes it to turn round when acted on by the wind. + (See Cow)

TONGUE2. To use the tongue in a pert, saucy and rude way; to scold; to abuse; to give back-answer as from a servant to a master or mistress. "Sarcy little hussey! I told her she shouldn't go out no more of evenings and, fancy, she just did turn round and tongue me, she did". +P

TOOAD. A Toad. + (See Paddock)

TOOAT. All; an entirety; the total. "The whole tooat av't". +

TOOK-TO. To take to; to become attached to; to become fond of. "My, how the old dog took-to you surprised me". =*

TORF. Chaff that is raked off the corn, after it is threshed, but before it is cleaned. + (See Toff)

TORTOISE. The Cuttlefish, so-called at Folkestone. + (See Inkspewer, Man-Sucker)

TOT. The root of a plant. =

T'OTHER DAY. The day before yesterday. An accurate expression, because other, in Early English, invariably means second and the day before yesterday is the second day reckoning backwards. It is remarkable that second is the only ordinal number of French derivation. Before the 13th century it was unknown and Other was used instead of it. In more recent times this expression has come to mean any time previously, but recently in the last week or so. "I met Mr Parker t'other day and it was good to see him in health still". +

TOTHER-ME. A field or mead other than the one you are in. =

TOTT. A clump or tuft; a tott of grass. =

TOVET. Half a bushel. G (See Tobit, Tofet, Tofiet, Tolvet)

TOVIL. A measure of capacity. This word appears to be a corruption of two-fill, i.e. two fillings of a given measure. +

TO-YEAR. This year; as today is this day. P+

TRACK. To tread down; mark out the road, such as was the case with a snow-covered road or lane, if there had been much traffic on it. After a heavy fall of snow it was common in the past to hear a person say: "I

114

couldn't get on much, the snow isn't tracked yet". + (See Tread)

TRAIPSE, TRAPES. To tread about; to drag along the ground; to trail something, such as the folds of a long dress. Before it lies down to sleep a cat will traipse round and round making its bed more comfortable. "Don't traipse about in all that wet". =* (See Stotch)

TRAWVES. Another way of saying Troughs. =

TRAY-RING, TRAY-WEDGE. The fastenings by which the Scythe blade is secured to its Bat. + (See Cray Ring, Sneath)

TREAD1. A wheel tread; a rut made by a cartwheel; a track. P+*=

TREAD2. The threads, etc., in a raw egg. "Would you clear the tread in that egg". =

TREDDLES. The droppings of sheep. + (See Sheep's Treddles)

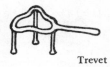

Trevet

TREVET, TRIVETT. A trivet; a three-legged stand on which to place a tea-kettle or saucepan. The expression "as right as a trevet" referred to the fact that unless the trivet was placed up correctly and standing evenly it would tilt over to one side. Originally trivet meant three feet. P+

TRILL. To trundle a hoop. + (See Troll, Trole, Trull)

TRILLY ALLY. Fancy work, such as bits stuck on for ornamentation only. In fretwork the trilly ally bits are the fancy pieces or fiddly bits. =

TROLE. To trundle a hoop or bowl a ball along the ground; to roll something. *+= (See Trill, Trull)

TROLL. As Trole and Trull and Trill, but also meaning "to go on one's way". "Well, I must be trolling off to Sevenoaks". =

TROT. To be "in a trot" was to be perturbed, anxious, unsettled, in a fluster. =

TROUBLED TO GO. Hardly able to get about and do one's or tend to one's daily tasks. "Many a time he's that bad, he's troubled to go". +

TRUCK. Used as dealings with; association with. "I want no truck with a man like that". =*

TRUCKLEBED1. Word used contemptuously of an underling or low breed person. "I won't have nothing to do with that trucklebed". +

TRUCKLEBED.2 A bed that runs on truckles, i.e. low running wheels or castors and was thus easily run in and out under another, higher bed. In the daytime the trucklebed was stowed away under the chief bed in the room and at night was occupied by a servant or a child. Because of its being a meaner bed the word was used in contempt (See Trucklebed1)

TRUG, TRUGG. A kind of light, strong basket, that originated in East Sussex, much used by gardeners and others, for domestic use. Made of thin willow slats or strips arranged on a cleft ash or chestnut frame to form a blunt-ended boat shape, with a fixed sweet chestnut handle in the middle, on the underside there being two pieces of willow as feet to keep it steady when standing. + (See Bodge, Sliver, Stud, Chip, Punnet)

Trug Bodge

TRUG-BODGE. A Trug Basket. = (See Alley Bodge, Bodge)

TRULL. To trundle; to bowl with a cricket ball, but also as Troll meaning to go on one's way. GP+ (See Trill, Trole)

Trush

TRUSH. A hassock for kneeling on in church. +

TRUSSEL. A trestle or tressel; a barrel-stand. +

TRY. To boil down lard. P+ (See Browsells)

TUCK. Took. =

TUG. The body of a wagon, without the hutch; a carriage for conveying timber, etc. + (See Baven Tug, Bobbin-Tug)

TUGS. The hames, rigid frames on a horse's collar. *=

TUKE. The Redshank (Tringa totanus), a common bird on Kentish shores and mudflats. +

TUMBLING-BAY. A small waterfall or cascade. Used in West Kent. +

TUMP. A small hillock, mound or irregular rising on the surface of the pastures and fields, such as an old ant-hill. Now universally applied to a Mole-Hill. +=*

TUN. P (See Ton)

TUNNEL. A funnel for pouring liquids from one vessel into another. P+

TURMUTS. Turnips. =

TURN-WREST-PLOUGH, TURN-WRIST-PLOUGH. (pronounced turn-rees-plou). A Kentish plough with a moveable mould-board. It is said that the flinty ground of Kent proved too much for the wooden ironshod ploughs then used so a plough called the Turn-Wrest was evolved. Fitted to a 10 foot oak beam the plough-share or iron weighed 52 pounds and it needed four strong horses to work it. += (See Reece, Wreest)

TURD, TERD. A cow or horse dropping. = (See Speene, Treddles)

TUSSOME. Hemp or flax. Used in West Kent. P+

TUT. A corruption of teat. P

TUTH. Tooth. †

TWANG. A peculiar flavour; an unusual tang; a strong, rank unpleasant taste; also called a Tack (which see). "This 'ere butter's got a queer twang to it". +*=

TWEAN-WHILES. Between times. +

TWIBIL. A hook for cutting beans. Literally two or double Bill. + (See Pea Hook, Ripping Hook, Wheat Hook)

TWINGE. An Earwig. P+

TWINK. A sharp, shrewish, grasping woman. +

TWITTEN. A narrow way or passage. =

TWITTER[1]. To twist; to tease. +

TWITTER[2]. A state of agitation; a flutter or fluster thus "I'm all in a twitter". +

TWITTER[3]. Pegge states "A fit of laughter; "He's in a mighty twitter". P

TWO. Used in the expression such as "My husband will be two men", i.e. so different from himself; so angry,
that he will not seem the same person; beside himself with rage. P+

TYE, TIE. An extensive common pasture. + (See Tie)

TYVER[1]. (See Tiver)

TYVER[2] A resemblance to a parent. "Oh, he's tyvered right enough." = (See Bly, Bligh)

U

UCK. Pull out; throw up. †

UCK UP. To help up with; to lift up. †

UCKY. If the outer skin of beans or peas were still tough to eat after cooking they were said to be "ucky". Similarly nuts that were not pleasant to eat were "ucky". =* (See Hucky, Stringy)

ULLAGE. In the modern English language this word refers to filling up a cask to the bung or eye, the amount by which the cask or bottle of liquor is short of being full. In Kent dialect it was commonly used in the expression "Useless ullage" applied to a worthless, thoughtless, feckless person. =

UMBLEMENT. Complement; a number or total. "Throw in another dozen to make up the umblement". +

UMBRELLA. A method of training hops in a hop garden. = (See Band, Upright, Butchers)

UNACCOUNTABLE. Excessively; exceedingly; very. "You've been gone an unaccountable long time" +

UNCLE OWL. One of the four species of Skate (Rajidae) but I have been

Uncle Owl

116

unable to trace which one. —A.M. Most likely the Common Skate (Raja batis) as this is found off southern coasts, whereas one of the others is a deepwater fish of northern distribution and another is rare in British waters. +

UNCOUS. Melancholy. + (See Unky, Ellinge)

UNDERNEAD. Underneath. +

UNDERSPINDLED. Undermanned and underhorsed. Used of a man who has not sufficient capital or stock to carry on his business competently. +

UNFORBIDDEN. Uncorrected; spoiled; troublesom; unrestrained. "He's an unforbidden young rascal". +

UNGAIN. Ungainly; awkward; loutish; clumsy. "He's so very ungain". +

UNHANDY. Awkward; clumsy; also inconvenient; difficult of access; not very convenient to plans. "Watch her feet! The old mare's frisky and unhandy today". =*+ (See Strommocks, Unthrum, Buck-fisted, Cack-handed, Fumble-fisted, Ham-fisted)

UNKER. Money paid for work of an obnoxious character; of a confined character. Used in Chatham Dockyard and Medway Towns for work in such conditions in the dockyard and ships † (See Unker Money)

UNKER MONEY. Now known as dirty money, extra money paid for dirty jobs or unhealthy work. Used in Chatham Dockyard and Medway Towns. †

UNKY. Lonely; solitary; melancholy. P+ (See Encous, Ellinge)

UNLEVEL. Uneven; rough. +

UNLUCKY. Mischievous. "That child's terrible unlucky surelye. He's always summ'ers or 'nother and into somethin' ". +

UPRIGHT. A method of training hops. = (See Butchers, Umbrella)

UNTHRUM. Unhandy; awkward. +P (See Ungain, Unhandy, Strommocks)

UPGROWN. Grown up. "He must be as old as that as he has upgrown daughters". Used in East Kent. +

UPSET. To scold; chastise. "I upset her pretty much o' Sunday morning, for she kep' messin' about till she got too late for church." +

UPSETTING. A scolding. + (See Upset)

UPSTAND. To stand up; to be standing. Still used in the sense at meetings when "members shall address the chair and be upstanding when they speak". +*= (See Fore-right, Outstand).

UPSTANDS. Growing trees or bushes cut breast high to serve as marks for boundaries of parishes, estates, etc. +

UPWARD. The wind was said to be Upward when it was in the North and Downward when it was in the South. The North was generally accepted in the past to be the highest part of Britain in terms of travelling upwards, hence to go "up North" or "down South". P+ (See Downward, Out)

URGE. To annoy; aggravate; provoke. "It urges me to see anyone go on so".

URP. A cloud, urpy being cloudy with very large clouds. =

USE 1. To accustom. "Its what you use them to when they be young". +

USE 2. To work or till land; to hire it. A person who uses a farm keeps it in his own hands and farms it himself. To use money is to borrow it. +P

USE-POLE. A pole thicker than a hop pole and strong enough to use for other purposes. +

UTCH-ABOUT. Used in reference to someone who was incapacitated and infirm with a rheumatic ailment and walked with difficulty. "He just manages to utch-about". = (See Hetch, Hotch, Hitch, Itch, Ruggle-About)

UTCHY. Cold. "It's a bit utchy this morning". Also said as Aitchy. =

V

VALE. The Water Vole (Arvicola amphibius). +

VAMPISHNESS. Perverseness; forwardness; disobedience. +

VAST. Very; exceedingly. This word was peculiarly used of small things. "It is vast little". P+

VIGILOUS. Vicious. said of a horse; also to mean a fierce, angry person or animal. P+

VILL-HORSE. The horse that goes in the rods, shafts or thills. The Vill-Horse is the same as the Fill-Horse or Thill-Horse. + (See Rod-Horse)

VINE. A general name given to the climbing bine of several plants, such as the Grape-vine, Hop-vine, etc. + (See Hop-Bind)

W

WACKER1. Active; lively; also angry, wrathful. "He's a wacker little chap". +

WACKER2. Anything or a person beyond normal size or shape, bigger than usual; also meant to be pleased, joyful; grateful; overcome with happiness or excitement. †

WACKER OUT. Lose one's temper. †

WAG. To stir; to move. "The dog wags his tail" is a common phrase still used but in the past it was a local use in Kent to speak of wagging the whole body, the head, the tongue, the hands, etc. Sometimes when an infirm person walked with an awkward gait it was said "There he goes wagging along". "Don't wag your hands about like that". P+

WAGGONER. Man who worked with horses, namely with a horse and wagon. *= (See Teamster)

WAI, WAY. Word of command to a cart-horse, meaning "Come to the near side." + (See Hoot, Whoot, Why)

WAISTCOAT. Although now commonly used for a man's garment it was formerly used for an undercoat, a waist coat, worn by both men and women. + (See Pettycoat)

WAKERELL BELL. The waking bell, a bell rung for rousing or calling people from their beds in the early morning, or rung to tell country folk the hour. At Sandwich one was rung at 5 a.m. Other names were the Wagerell Bell and the Wakerying Bell. +

WALE. A tumour or large swelling. +

WALLER'D. A name for the wind. +

WAN. A wagon; not necessarily a van as generally thought. +

WANDS. Any species of light, bending stick; Willow or other flexible wood. = (See Nut Wands)

WANKLE. Sickly; in poor health; generally applied to a child. +

WAPS, WOPS. Wasp. Similar to haps for hasp, claps for clasp. P+ Used elsewhere.

WAPSIES, WOPSIES, WASPIES. More than one Wasp. "Look out, the wapsies are getting in the jam". *=

WARP. Four things of any kind, such as a warp of Herrings. +P

WARP-UP. To plough land in warps, i.e. with ten, twelve or more ridges, on each side of which a furrow is left to carry off the water. +

WARPS. Distinct pieces of ploughed land separated by the furrows. +

WAR WAPS. Look out; beware. =+

WASH1. A basket used at Whitstable for measuring Whelks and containing about half a prickle or ten strikes of Oysters. A prickle equalled two wash or twenty strikes — a strike is four bushels. + (See Prickle)

WASH2. To mark out with washways, narrow paths cut in the woodland to make the cants in a woodfall. A fall of ten acres would probably be "washed" into six or seven cants. + (See Woodfall)

WASTES. Waste lands; land allowed to become poor and derelict. +

WATER BODGE. A barrel mounted on a four-wheeled trailer platform or truck for transporting water. = (See Alley Bodge)

WATER-BURN. The phosphorescent appearance of the sea caused by marine organisms. The Herring yawlers disliked it because the fish could see the outline of the net and so avoided the latter. +

WATER-GALLS. Jellyfish + (See Galls, Stinger, Sluthers, Miller's Eyes)

WATER TABLE. The little ditch at the side of a road or lane or a small indentation across a road for carrying away the water. + (See Deek)

WATTLE. A hurdle made like a gate, of split wood, used for folding sheep. Now in general use. P+

WATTLE-GATES. See Wattle +

WAUN. Won't; will not. =

WAUR, WAURE. Seaweed. P+ (See Oare)

WAX DOLLS. Fumitory (Fumaria officinalis), growing in neglected fields. So-called from the doll-like appearance of its small flowers. +

WAY GRASS. Knotgrass (Polygonum aviculare), a weed of waste places and fields. +

WEALD. The Weald of Kent. Used in conversation as "the Weald" and to "go into the Weald", as a similar expression was "the Shires". Formerly the Weald was much wooded country but is now cultivated. P+*=

WEALD HOE. A medium shafted hoe with a heavy iron head, but with a single flat blade or plate, about one and a half inches wide where it comes from the head broadening to about four inches wide at the tilling or cutting edge. Similar to a Peck (which see) and a Half-Mattock. Used for general hoeing. † (See Canterbury Hoe, Kent Hoe, Corn Hoe, Tommy Hoe, Clod Hoe, Half-Mattock, Axe Een Mattock, Plate Hoe, Double-sider Hoe)

WEANERS. Pigs 12 weeks or so old. *=

WEASEL-SNOUT. In Kent a dialect name applied to the common Yellow Toadflax (Linaria vulgaris, found in hedges and waste places. The true Weasel-snout or Lesser Snapdragon related to it is a plant of cornfields and sandy stony places. +

WEATHER. Bad, inclement weather. "Tis middlin' fine now, but there's eversomuch weather coming up". +

WEBBING. A piece of tough material slung from the ceiling of the ground floor in the oast, to support the base of the pocket when the hops are being pressed into the latter. *= (See Pocket)

Weed Hook

WEED HOOK, WEEDING HOOK. A tool that uprooted or severed weeds on the pull stroke during use. =

WEED SPUD. (See Thistle Spud). =

WEE-WOEING. Wobbling; loose; unstable; rocking. If the back or leg of a chair or table became loose or was uneven so it did not stand level, but moved about, and tilted it would be said "This chair is wee-woeing about". Alternatively a child rocking a chair would be told "Stop wee-woeing about on that chair". = (See Latchetty, Wocketty)

WEEKERS. The ears. Usually used in "baby talk" when washing a small child. "Mummy will wash in your weekers then you'll be nice and clean again". †*= (See Dandymen, Daddles, Peepers, Wickers)

WELFING. The covering of a drain. +

WELTER. To wither and fade; to wilt. +

WENCE. The centre of a cross-roads. + (See Went)

WENT[1]. A way, from the Middle English went, a way; from the verb, to wend; a path; a country road, a wood path. The plural of wents is pronounced wens (See Wence). A four-went way or four-wents was a cross-roads where four routes met. A four-went post is the Finger or direction post where crossroads meet. +P*= (See Bishop's Finger, Four Wents, Four Went Way, Pointing Post, Throws)

WENT[2]. The middle of a field. =

WENTED. Filling in of an awkward or irregular "cant" at the end of ploughing a field by short caterwise furrows. = (See Cant, Caterways)

WERR. Very; "werrlike" very like. +

WERRY. A weir. The owner of a weir in the sea at Seasalter was the Abbot of Faversham. In the reign of Henry VII it was called Snowt-werry, afterwards Snowt-weir. +

WET. To "wet the tea" is to pour a little boiling water on the tea; this is allowed to stand for a time before the teapot is filled up. Still used among elderly people. To "wet a pudding" is to mix it; the baker is said to "wet" his bread" when he moistens his flour. P+*

WET-FOOT. Having the feet, stockings, boots interior, etc, wet, through rain, or wading in water. "Are you wet-foot?" i.e. "Have you got your feet wet?" Opposite of dryshod. P+=*

WHAT. Used as an introduction to a question. "What, shall we do the fence today?" =

WHAT-FOR. What kind or sort of? Why? "What-for day is't?" i.e. "What kind of day is it?" Also used as why after a question: "Go and help your father in the garden." "What for?" +

WHAT'N. What sort; what kind. Short for what kin, i.e. what kind. "Then you can see what'n a bug he be". +

WHATSAY. Contracted from "What do you say?". Generally used in Kent and Sussex before answering a question, even when the question is perfectly well understood. +

WHEAT HOOK. (See Sickle) =

WHEAT-KIN. A supper for the servants, labourers, harvesters, and other workfolk when the wheat is all cut. The feast also provided at the end of the hop picking season was called a Hop-Kin. +P (See Hop-Kin)

WHEAT-SHEAR. To cut wheat. +

WHER. Whether. "I axed 'im wher he would or not and he sed No." +

WHICKET FOR WHACKET. A phrase meaning the same as "Tit for Tat". GP+ (See Quittee for Quottee)

WHIEWER. A sharp or violent man. From whiew, the noise made in driving hogs. "He is a whiewer", i.e. "He is a shrewd, sharp or violent man". P

WHIFFLE, WIFFLE. To come in gusts; to blow hither and thither; to turn and curl about. "'Tis de wind whiffles all the leaves o' one side". +

WHILK, WHELK, WHITTER. To complain; to mutter. P+ (See Winder, Witter)

WHIPSTICKS. Quickly; directly. +

WHIRTLEBERRIES, WHORTLE-BERRIES. (Vaccinium myrtillus), also called Bilberries, Blueberries, or Blackhearts. P+

WHISPERING THE DEATH OF A PERSON. A very old practice common in many parts of England, but equally in Kent. When the master or mistress of the house died or another member of the family, where a hive of bees were kept it was customary for someone, usually the person who tended the hives, to go to the bees and whisper to them that the person was dead. It was believed the bees would grieve and either decide to stay at the place of a death or swarm and abandon it. Similarly another practice was for a shepherd or herdsman to whisper to each of the cattle and sheep that its old master was dead. +

WHIST. Quiet; silent; "Stand whist! I can hear de old rabbit". +

WHIST-QUIRT. Very quiet. †

WHIST-QUIRT-FELLER. A very quiet, unassuming, perhaps shy, fellow. †

WHITETHROAT. The common summer bird visitor with this name, (Sylvia communis) arriving in Kent usually had the adjective "jolly" prefixed to its name in the past, i.e. "There's a jolly Whitethroat singing." The song, however, is a rapid twittering warble, made usually from the top of a hedge when the bird's white throat is conspicuous. +

WHITTEN. The Wayfaring Tree (Viburnum lantana). +

WHOOT. Word of command to a cart-horse, meaning "Go to the off side". += (See Wai, Way, Why)

WHORLBARROW. Wheelbarrow. +

WHY. Word of command for turning a horse to the left. Probably a variation of Wai. = (See Wai, Way, Whoot, Gee)

WIBBER1. A wheelbarrow; short for wilber, a contraction of wheelbarrow. + (See Whorlbarrow)

WIBBER2. To use a wibber. "I wibber'd out a wibberfull". +

WICKERS. The ears. (See Weekers) =

WID. With; also widout is without. P+

WIDDERSHINS. Going contrary to the course of the sun. Used elsewhere, in particular Sussex. =

WIFF. A with, withy or bond, for binding fagots; a hazel or other pliable stick twisted and used to tie up fagots or pea-boughs. Previously only the large kind of fagot, which went by the name of Kiln-Brush, was bound with two wiffs; other smaller kinds with one. Later all fagots were tied up with two wiffs. P+ (See Kiln-brush, Baven, Fagot)

WIG. To anticipate; over-reach; baulk, cheat. +P

WIK. A week. +P

WILK. A Periwinkle. From Anglo-Saxon wiloc. +

WILLJILL. A hermaphrodite; an animal or plant capable of fertilising and of being fertilised; an animal or human with traces of both male and female characters and sex organs. A Snail is an example of a Willjill. +P

Willow Gull

WILLOW-GULL. The Sallow or Goat Willow (Salix caprea), so-named from the male golden catkins resembling yellow down of a young gosling which was called a Gull in Kent. +P

120

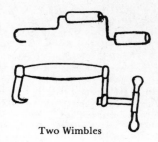
Two Wimbles

WIMBLE, WIMBOL, WYMBYLL. An instrument for boring holes, turned by a handle; used by wattle makers; also a tool operated like a carpenter's brace, made of wood or iron with wood handles, used to twist lengths of straw into rough ropes or bonds to bind corn sheaves and hay trusses. +

WIMMELER. Variant of Wimble; the tool used to twist straw bonds. =

WIND. To twist; to warp; thus a board shrunk or swelled, so as to be warped, was said "to wind" and when it was brought straight again it was said to be "out of winding"; also meant to be restless, as in pain from rheumatism, etc. "I had a terrible poor night surely. I did turn and wind so." +P

WIND-BIBBER. A berry or haw of the Hawthorn. + (See Aazey-Garzeys)

WINDER1. To whimper, as a child does when it is restless and uneasy, but does not cry properly. P+

WINDER2. A Wigeon (Anas penelope), a water bird. +

WINDGE. Wind in an infant's stomach. †

WINDGEY. A baby or infant with wind. †

WINDGINESS. A state of wind or belching in an infant. †

WINDROW. Sheaves of corn set up in a row, one against another, that the wind may blow between them; or a row of grass thrown up lightly for the same purpose in haymaking. P+

WINDY-FIED. A reference to the windy weather; a windy day was "proper windy-fied." †

WINTER-PROUD. Said of corn which is too forward for the season in a mild winter. +

WIPS. Wisp, like waps for wasp. Anything bundled up or carelessly thrown upon a heap, as "The cloaths lie in a wips" i.e. tumbled, in disorder. +P (See Ax, Haps, Wops, Waps)

WIRE. Rooks wire down beside the young shoots of wheat or beans to pull them up and eat the grain or bean at the base. =

WIREWEED. The common Knotgrass (Polygonum aviculare), so-named from its tough, wiry stems and prostrate habit. + (See Way Grass)

WIRING. Name for the two parallel sets of wires which supports the hop bines in the air and are themselves supported by the poles. =

WITTER. To murmur; to complain; to whimper; to make a peevish, fretting noise. P+ (See Whilk, Whelk, Whitter, Winder)

WITTERY. Peevish; fretful. + (See Witter)

WITTY. Well-informed; knowing; cunning; skilful. "He's a very witty man, I can tell ye." +

WIVVER. To quiver; to shake. +

WOADMEL, WODMOLE. A rough material made from coarse wool. +

WOBBLER. Warbler, either referring to a human singer or warbling, singing bird. †

WOCKETTY. Loose, but applied to a chair or moveable object rather than something fixed, such as a door. "I shall have to mend this chair. The legs are getting too wocketty". =

WOIN. Won't; will not. "Goin' 'arvestin' this yer?" No, cos they woin 'av yer." =

WONKLE. (See Wankle)

WONLY. Only. +

WON'T BE SED. An argumentative, obstinate person. =

WOOD-FALL. A tract of underwood marked out to be cut. The underwood for hop poles is felled about every twelve years. +

WOOD LODGE. A wood-shed. *= (See Lodge).

WOOD NOGGIN. A term applied to half-timbered houses. +

WOOD-REEVE. A forester, woodman, woodcutter. A person whose duties concern the care and maintenance of woodlands. In North Kent a variant of this was a man who bought standing timber to fell it and sell for firing, logs, fencing, poles. Elsewhere the latter was called a Wood-Shuck (which see). +

WOOD-SHUCK. A buyer of standing or felled timber. +

WOODEN HILL. The stairs; used with reference to going up the stairs to bed. "Tis time to go up the wooden hill". =

WOPS. Wasps. (See Ax, Haps, Wips)

WORKISH. Bent upon work; industrious. "He's a workish sort of chap". +P

WORKY-DAY. Work day, as distinct from Sunday. P+ (See Sundays and Worky Days)

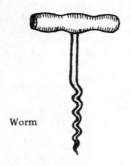

Worm

WORM. A corkscrew. +

WORRIT. Worried; to worry. +

WORST. To defeat; to get the better of; to overthrow. + (See Bested)

WOT SAY. (See What Say)

WOUNDY. Very. + (See Vest, Werr)

WRAXEN, WREXON. To grow out of bounds, as applied to weeds; also to infect, to taint with disease. P+ (See Rexon, Raxen)

WREEST. That part of a Kentish plough which takes on and off and on which it rests against the land ploughed up. + (See Reece)

WRING1. To blister. +

WRING2. To be wet. +

WRIT. Written or wrote to. †

WRONGS (TO). Out of order. "There's not much to wrongs". The antithetical phrase "to rights" is common enough but "to wrongs" was rarely heard outside of Kent. +P (See Rights, Droits)

WRONGTAKE. To misunderstand a person's actions or speech. +P

WROPT. Wrapped. =

WURR. Were as in "they were". †

WUSTUS. Oasthouse. =

WUT. Word of command to a carthorse to halt. = (See Wai, Whoot)

WUTS. Oats. +

Y

YAFFLE1. The Green Woodpecker (Picus viridis virescens). Dialect name now in universal use. +=*

YAFFLE2. To eat greedily, to drink greedily, so as to make a noise. + (See Yoffle, Yuffle, Bolt, Gollop, Scorf, Guzzle)

YAR, YARE. Nimble; swift; spry; brisk. P+

YARD. A rood; a measure of land. In Henry III's reign goods, butter, etc. were also bought and sold by the yard and not weight. P+

YARPING. Whining; grizzling; complaining. Said of a young child or animal. Used elsewhere. =

YANTLET. Variant of Yenlet. There is a South Yantlet Creek between Nor Marsh and Bishops Ness Island off Gillingham in the lower reaches of the Medway. *=

YAWL, YAWLING. In the past when the Herrings arrived in shoals off Folkestone the yawls went out with their fleet of nets yawling, i.e. the nets were placed in the water and allowed to drift along with the tide. P+

YAUGH. Dirty; nasty; filthy. P+

YAWNUP. A lazy and uncouth fellow. =

YAX. The axle-tree. = (See Ax)

YE. You. "What did ye do with it?"

YELD. To yield. P+

Yellow Bottle

YELLOW BOTTLE. The Corn Marigold (Chrysanthemum sefetum). Similar are Red Bottle (which see) and Blue Bottle (which see). +

YENLADE, YENLET. Names for the north and south mouths of the estuary of the Wantsum, when it made Thanet an island. Now non-existent. From the Anglo-Saxon gen-lad, meaning a discharging of a river into the sea or of a smaller river into a larger one. + (See Yantlet)

YEOMAN. A person who farmed his own estate; a small landowner. Owner of free land to the value of forty shillings yearly and entitled to certain rights. Of sufficient rank to be commemorated on a number of gravestones seen in country church-yards of Kent by the author. "Here lies Joseph Norton, Yeoman, etc." (See the jingle: A Knight of Cales, etc" in the Terms, Sayings, etc. chapter). +P

YER. Here. "Yer un be is": "Here it is". =

YET. Even. Used as an intensifier, as "neither this nor yet that". +P

YET-NA. Yet; as "He is not come home yet-na". Here the suffix na is due to the preceding not. +P

YEXLE. An axle. P+

YOFFLE (See Yaffle2)

YOG. A fire, usually used for cooking a kettle or to have a warm up at lunch or Bait time. =

YOKE1. A farm or tract of land of an uncertain quantity. Presumably such a measure of land as one yoke of oxen could plough and till. P+

YOKE2. In East Kent the term for the time of eight hours for a team to work. When the horses went out in the early morning and worked all day until about two or three o'clock, then went back to the stable they made what was called "One Yoke". Sometimes when there was great pressure of work they made "Two Yokes", going out as before and returning home for "bait" at 10 o'clock, then going out again for further work at 1 o'clock and coming home finally at 6 o'clock. There was a slightly varied procedure in West Kent. + (See Bait, One Yoke)

YOKELET. An old name in Kent for a little farm or manor. + (See Joclet)

YORKS. The straps, strings or bands just below the knees worn to keep bottoms of breeches out of the mud. Also to form a loose pocket over the knee to save wear and probably split-ting. Also called Redgers. *=

YONKS. Years ago. =

YOUR'N. Yours. = (See Hern, Hisn, Ourn, Theirn, Yowun)

YOW. A ewe. =

YOWL. To howl. +

YOWUN. Yours. = (See Hern, Hisn, Ourn, Theirn, Your'n)

YUFFLE. (See Yaffle2)

PROVERBS RELATING TO THE COUNTY OF KENT
Compiled by Dr Samuel Pegge
Edited by the Rev. Walter W. Skeate

The following Collection of Proverbs was added by Dr Pegge to his Collection of Kenticisms, to render his account of the provincialisms more complete. It is here printed from the autograph MS., with a few corrections, etc., as noted, and with a few additions by myself, which are distinguished by being placed within brackets. I have also included seven more, from Mr Hazlitt's "English Proverbs and Proverbial Phrases", London, 1869. These are the ones numbered 6, 23, 28, 33, 50, 53, and 58.

As the Proverbs are jotted down in the MS. without any proper arrangement, I have arranged them in what seemed to me to be the best order. Thus, Proverbs 1-13 all contain the word Kent, and are in alphabetical order; Proverbs 14-20 contain the word Kentish, the substantives to which that adjective belongs being in alphabetical order; Proverbs 21-59 relate to place in Kent, also alphabetically arranged; whilst Proverbs 60-73 are of more general application. The reader who observes this may easily find any Proverb at once. — W.W.S.

1. A Knight of Cales,
   A Gentleman of Wales,
      And a Laird of the North Countree;
   A Yeoman of Kent
   With his yearly Rent
      Will buy 'em out all three.

"Cales knights were made in that voyage (i.e. in the expedition to Cadiz, formerly called Cales) by Robert, earl of Essex, to the number of sixty; whereof (though many of great birth) some were of low fortunes; and therefore Qu. Elizabeth was half offended with the earl, for making knighthood so common. Of the numerousness of *Welch gentlemen* nothing need be said, the Welch generally pretending to gentility. *Northern Lairds* are such, who in Scotland hold lands in chief of the king, whereof some have no great revenue. So that a *Kentish Yeoman,* by the help of an hyperbole, may countervail, etc. Yeoman, contracted for *gemein*-men from *gemein,* signifying 'common' in Old Dutch, so that a *yeoman* is a *commoner,* one undignified with any title of gentility; a condition of people almost peculiar to England and which is in effect the basis of all the nation" — Ray; Proverbs (Kent). (The etymology of *yeoman* is disputed. I refer the first syllable to the A.S. gá, a district, and I find Mr Wedgwood is of the same opinion; in fact the Old Frisian *gaman,* a villager, is the same word. Cf. Germ *gau.)*

"Better be the head of the yeomanry than the tail of the gentry" — Ray. The Scotch proverb "A good yeoman makes a good woman" and "the yeoman of the guard", which shews that, though this word be now in great measure confined to the limits of Kent, one seldom hearing of any other than the yeoman of Kent, yet it was once of more general use; and it is notorious that there are in no parts such wealthy farmers, cultivating either their own estates or very large takes from other people, as there are in this county; some having, in tillage, not much less than £1000 a year, and others the like quantity in grazing.

"All blessed with health, and as for wealth,
  By Fortune's kind embraces,
A Yeoman grey shall oft outweigh
  A Knight in other places." — Durfey's Song.

Hazlitt, in his English Proverbs, gives this in the form following:
"A Gentleman of Wales,
  with a Knight of Cales,
    and a Lord of the North Countrie,
a Yeoman of Kent
upon a rack's Rent
  will buy them out all three."

He refers to Osborn's "Traditional Memoirs of Q. Elizabeth", circa 1650. The last three lines are given in the form — "a yeoman of Kent, sitting on a penny rent, is able to buy all three.

2. A Man of Kent, and a Kentish Man

(Left unexplained as it may well be. The most probable solution of the matter is that the two expressions are synonymous. Yet the current idea is that "a man of Kent" is a term of high honour, whilst "a Kentish man" denotes but an ordinary person in comparison with the former. See "Notes & Queries", 3rd S. viii, where Mr G. Pryce affirms that the men of West Kent are undoubtedly "Men of Kent", while those of East Kent are only "Kentish Men". Again, in "Notes & Queries", 3rd S. vii, J.F.S. claims that the phrase "Men of Kent" should be restricted to natives of the *Weald* of Kent. Disputants should note that "Men of Kent" are said, in the A.S. Chronicle, AD. 853, to have fought in Thanet; whilst in the ballad of "William the Conquerour", in vol. iii of the Percy Folio MS, the men who came from Dover and Canterbury are thrice called "Kentish-men". Whence it appears that the men of East Kent have borne both titles and no doubt the same may be said of the men of other parts of the county. The phrases merely involve "a distinction without a difference"). (See my listing "Kentish Men" in the Dictionary giving yet another variation also my item "A Man of Kent" in following chapter — A.M.)

3. As great as the devil and the Earl of Kent.

(The reference is to Hawkesworth's edition of Swift's Works, the passage occurring in Dialogue iii of his "Polite Conversation" and runs thus:

"Lady Stuart. Miss, I hear that you and lady Coupler are as great as cup and can."

"Lady Answerall. Ay, Miss, as great as the devil and the Earl of Kent".

It is clear that great here means thick or intimate; for a few pages previously, in Dialogue i, we have the phrase — "as great as two inkle-weavers", i.e. weavers of tape. It is stated "The villanous character given by history to the celebrated Goodwin, Earl of Kent, in the time of Edward the Confessor, occasioned this proverb".

4. Fair Maid of Kent

(I.e. Johanna, the wife of Edward the Black Prince). She was commended for her goodness as well as beauty. She was a patroness of Wicliffe.

5. Holy Maid of Kent

(Elizabeth Barton, executed April 21, 1534, by order of Henry VIII, for exciting an opposition to his marriage with Anne Boleyn.)

6. Kent and Keer

Have parted many a good man and his meer. Higson's MS Coll.

(Perhaps keer only means care here, as meer means mare. Cf. Proverb 62 — Bad for the rider, etc.).

7. Kent; red Veal and white Bacon.

White bacon is their pickled pork; and they are apt to neglect the well ordering of their calves, whereby the veal is ordinary enough; especially compared with that on the other side of the river, in Essex.

8. Kentshire
   Hot as fyre.

This county is remarkably hot on account of its chalk hills and chalky as well as gravelly roads.

9. Lythe as Lass of Kent.

I.e., gentle, lithsom, etc. See Percy's "Songs". (Spenser has it, too, in the Sheph. Kal (Februarie), where he says of a bull — "His dewelap as lythe as lasse of Kent". The passage in Percy's Songs is in the poem of Dowsabell, by Michael Drayton, where, in stanza 5, Dowsabell is said to be "Lyth as lasse of Kent".)

10. Neither in Kent nor Christendom.

(Nor in all Kent, nor in Christendome); Spenser's Shepherds' Kalendar (September). "That is," saith Dr Fuller "our English Christendom, of which Kent was first converted to the Christian faith; as much as to say as "Rome and all Italy" or "the first cut and all the loaf besides"; not by way of opposition, as if Kent were no part of Christendom, as some have understood it". "I rather think that it is to be understood by way of opposition and that it had its original upon occasion of Kent being given by the ancient Britons to the Saxons, who were then pagans. So that Kent might well be opposed to all the rest of England in this respect, it being pagan when all the rest was Christian" — Ray. Pursuant to this interpretation, Mr Ray explains the Cheshire proverb — "Neither in Cheshire nor Chawbent" that is, he says, "Neither in Kent nor Christendome", Chawbent being a town in Lancashire, — Ray. Dr Fuller and Mr Ray agree as to the sense but they differ as to the figure of this proverb. I incline to Dr Fuller's opinion and I am willing to account it a climax, rather than an antithesis, it being probaby occasion'd, as a multitude of proverbs are, by the jingle of the K and C; you have above — "Neither in Cheshire nor Chawbent". If this saying took its rise in Kent, as is most probable, every county being given to specifie and take notice of themselves it puts the figure beyond dispute; but if it was taken up in London, or in any other of these southern parts, yet Kent, being the nearest county with a C, and the only county in England that begins with a C (sic) and is a monosyllable, we shall find no reason to depart from this interpretation. To support this antithesis Mr Ray thinks it had its origin from Kent's being given, by the Britons, who were Christians, to the pagan Saxons, but surely it can never be so old. It must have been, according to that supposition, a British proverb, which is scarce credible. Dr Fuller brings it something lower in time, but not much, supposing that it was taken up after the kingdom of Kent was converted to Christianity by Augustine and his fellow-labourers, but before the rest of the island had received the faith; in this case, it might be an Anglo-Saxon proverb. But there being no proof nor no probability of its being so very ancient 'tis more natural to imagine that it came into use in later times, two or three centuries ago or so, and that it was owing to nothing else but the gingle. A proverb of much the same sort as this, is that of *spick-and-span-new* (here Pegge goes into the etymology of the phrase) (There are also several instances of the use of the phrase, one being "The best wheat in all Kent or Christendome").

(Ray is certainly all wrong here (Pegge was right to support Fuller) and Fuller right. Kent is obviously singled out as containing the metropolis (Canterbury) of all English Christendom, and being famous throughout all Christendom for the shrine of Saint Thomas — W.W.S.) (There is also another possible origin. It possibly means "neither here nor there; not one thing or the other; or lost in some

127

pagan place". It may be a corruption of Sir Thomas Wyatt the Elder's lines in the 16th century: "But I am here in Kent and Christendom, among the muses where I read and rhyme". But Wyatt himself may have got the gist from the Kentish saying and adjusted it — A.M.)

11. St Michels Mount who does not know
    That wardes the Westerne coste?
  And of St Brigets Bowre, I trow,
    All Kent can rightly boaste" — Spenser's Sheph. Kal. (Julye).

St Michael's Mount; 'tis near Abergavenny in Wales. But as to St Bridget's Bower, I have enquired of the aged Dr Brett and Mr Bull and cannot learn that there is any one remarkable hill in this county so called; and I incline to believe that the large and long ridge of hills that passes east and west the whole length of the county, above Boxley, Holingbourne, etc., is meant by this expression. (St Michael's Mount is near Marazion in Cornwall and gives its name to Mount's Bay. The whereabouts of St Bridget's Bower is more difficult to determine.)

12. St Tyburn of Kent

In an Old Dialogue printed by Wynkyn de Word, part whereof is inserted for blank pages at the end of a copy of Bp. Fox's book "De vera differentia Regiae Potestatis et Ecclesiasticae", belonging to the Rev. Dr Thomas Brett "Imaginacion", one of the Interlocutors, says to Perseveraunce, "Than sholde ye have many a sory mele; I wyll never gyve you mete ne drynke" — (and confirms this by swearing) "By saynt Tyburne of Kent". In the parish of St Thomas-a-Waterings, which is in Kent (as I think) there was a place of execution. The counterfeit Earl of Warwick was hanged at St Thomas Waterings, 15 Hen. VII. Thomas-a-Waterings was the place of execution for the prisoners of the King's Bench; but then that prison being in Surrey, the place of execution must have been in Surrey. Quaere therefore how this matter was yet (sic). . . . Stanley, Bishop of Sodor and Man, wishes untrue writers "would offer themselves unto St Thomas Waterson" a corruption probably of Waterings: "Memoirs of Stanley". According to Drake's "Eboracum" Tyburn was a general name for places of execution. (The Watering of St Thomas, i.e. of the Hospital of St Thomas the Martyr, Southwark" — Morley's "English Writers").

13. Strong Man of Kent

"In this parish (St Laurence) was born (William) Joy, who in King William IIIrd's reign, had such a reputation for very extraordinary strength of body, that he was called the *English Sampson*, and the *Strong Man of Kent* and had the honour done him of being taken notice of by the king and royal family, and nobility of the realm, before whom he performed his feats, tho' some attributed them to craft and slight. In 1699, his picture was engraved, and round it several representations of his performances, as pulling against an extraordinary strong horse, jumping, sitting on a stool without touching the ground, breaking of a rope which would bear 35 hundred weight, lifting a weight of 2240 pounds. He afterwards followed the infamous practice of smugling (sic) and was drowned 1734" — Lewis, "History of Tenet". Dr Pegge also gives the reference — Wm. Joy, Tom Brown, i., page 248. (William Joy is buried at St Peter's church, St Peter's near Broadstairs, close by the path just inside the main churchyard entrance, the grave marked by a headstone — A.M.) "The Strong Men of Kent" is a proverb that referred to the numerous times when men from the county served, often as archers, in wars either for or against the king in civil wars, or in the nation's wars overseas.

14. A Kentish Ague

Take this county in general and it is, I believe, as healthy as most counties in England; 'tis preferable to many of them in this respect. Dr Harvey used to call Folkstone the Montpellier of England, and the scituation (sic) of that place, beyond all dispute, is so good, that there is no room to suspect that great man of partiality to the place of his nativity. But this hinders not, but there are some parts notorious for bad air, as Rumney Marsh for instance, which, as we shall see, is the place pointed out by the old saw, for having "Wealth and no Health". However, it was not this tract that gave occasion for this brand of infamy and made the Kentish ague so renowned, but rather the more northern parts, which, bordering upon the Medway and the Thames, are flat and marshy, very low and very unhealthfull. And whereas the road from London to Canterbury lies chiefly through this tract, having one river or the other almost constantly in view, this sickly race of people are in the way of all passengers, who cannot fail sometimes of seeing them in the paroxysm. This is now one of the most beaten publick roads in England, being the great inlet into the kingdom from foreign parts. But there was a time, viz., when in the times of the popish ignorance and superstition the shrine of St Thomas at Canterbury was in such repute and pilgrimages thither were so meritorious that, as we are credibly informed, there were 100,000 strangers present at his jubilee in 1420. See Somner's Antiq. of Kent. Now people in their travels beyound seas, and in their visits to St Thomas, saw no other part of Kent but this, where they beheld agues and aguish countenances every mile, and therefore might well return with the impression of an ague strong upon their minds, and might well annex it to the idea of Kent. But this is likewise become a metaphorical expression for the French disease, which seems is also called the Covent-garden ague and the Barnwell ague.

15. Kentish Cherries

SEE Proverb 19. The triangular cherry in Kent, Dr Plott in his letter to Bp Fell, looks upon as a singularity. Camden says Kent abounds with cherries beyond measure "which were brought out of Pontus into Italy 680 years after the building of Rome and 120 years afterwards into Britain". In the margin — "Plin., 1, 15, cherries brought into Britain about the year of Christ 48" (see also proverb 63).

16. Kentish Cousins

The sense of this is much the same with that which you have in Mr Ray — "cousins germans quite remov'd". This county being two-thirds of it bounded by the sea and the river, the inhabitants thereof are kept at home more than they are in inland counties. This confinement naturally produces intermarriages amongst themselves, and a relation once begun is kept alive and diffused from generation to generation. In humane and generous minds, which have always been the characteristic of this people, friendships and familiarities once commenced, are not easily dropt; and one needs not wonder that amongst, such, affinity may be sometimes challenged where the lines may be worn out, or that the pleasantry of less considerate aliens shou'd make a byword of an instance of such simplicity of manners. It is observable that antiently our forefathers mostly made matches within their several counties, which was certainly the case in this province, as is evident from the genealogies. (We might also include here the expression "Kentish Fire", which sometimes means, I believe, a kind of sustained and continuous applause. Haydn, in his Dictionary of Dates, has the following article: "Kentish Fire, a term given to the continuous cheering common at the Protestant meetings held in Kent in 1828 and 1829, with the view of preventing the passing of the Catholic Relief Bill").

17. Kentish Longtails

"Those are mistaken who found this proverb on a miracle of Austin the Monk, who preaching in an English village, and being himself and his associates beat and abused by pagans there, who opprobriously tied fishtails to their backsides — in revenge thereof such appendants grew to the hind parts of all that generation. For the scene of this lying wonder was not laid in any part of Kent, but pretended many miles off, nigh Cerne in Dorsetshire. I conceive it first of outlandish extraction and cast by foreigners as a note of disgrace on all Englishmen, though it chanceth to stick only on the Kentish at this day. What the original or occasion of it at first was, is hard to say; whether from wearing a pouch or bag to carry their baggage in behind their back, whilst probably the proud monsieurs had lacquies for that purpose; or whether from the mentioned story of Austin. I am sure there are some at this day in foreign parts, who can hardly be perwaded but that Englishmen have tails." Ray — "Why this nickname (cut off from the rest of England) continues still entailed on Kent, the reason may be — as the doctour (i.e. Fuller) conjectures — because that county lies nearest to France and the French are beheld as the first founders of this aspersion". Dr Fuller has rightly rejected the miracle of St Augustin, for the groundwork of this reflection; that fact happening in Dorsetshire, though Jo. Major the Scot brings it into Kent. Lambarde, Peramb. But surely the Doctor is hardly consisting with himself, when afterwards he assigns this story concerning Austin as a possible occasion of it. It seems he was very doubtfull of its origin and knew not upon what to fix it, unless (upon) that story, or a remote conjecture concerning I know not what pouches which the English might weare behind their backs; he supposes that at first this was a general term of reproach upon the whole English nation, though afterwards it adhered to the Kentish men only, they being the next neighbours to France, "which is beheld as the first founder of this aspersion". But conjectures apart, Polydore Virgil (Anglicae Historie) expressly lays the scene of a story wherein Thomas a Becket was concern'd at Stroud (Strood) in Kent, that is brother-german to that which Alexander Essebiensis tells of Austin in Dorsetshire. I shall give you Mr Lambarde's version of that passage of Polydore, in the Peramb. "When as it happened him (ie Becket) upon a time to come to Stroud, the inhabitants thereabouts, being desirous to spite that good father, sticked not to cut the taile from the horse on which he rode, binding themselves thereby with a perpetual reproach: for afterward, by the will of God, it so happened, that every one which came of that kinred of men which had plaied that naughty prank, were borne with tailes, even as brutes bee". Here's foundation enough in reason for a proverbial sarcasm; and Polydore, a tax gatherer of the popes, and not our neighbours the French, as is suggested, was the founder of the assertion; and it appears from Dr Fuller's testimony, that it was once currently believed and plentifully used by foreigners. But a full confutation of this ridiculous fable you may read at large in Mr Lambarde. See . . . A general reproach on Englishmen, Matthew Paris.

(The reference in Matthew Paris shews that the saying is far older than the time of Polydore; I must add that, in the old Romance of Richard Coeur de Lion is a remarkable passage in which the Emperor of Cyprus dismisses some messengers of Richard with the contemptuous words: "Out, taylards, of my paleys! Now go and say your tayled king that I owe him no thing!" A taylard is a man with a tail; the tailed king is Richard I himself.) (Kentish Longtails was also a nickname for native-born inhabitants of Kent, and the name for wild oats — See Long tails in the Dictionary — A.M.)

18. Essex stiles, Kentish miles, Norfolk wiles, many men beguiles.

"For stiles Essex may well vie with any county in England, it being wholly divided into small closes, and not one common field that I know in the whole county. Length of miles I know not what reason Kent hath to pretend to; for, generally speaking, the farther from London the longer the miles; but for cunning in the law and wrangling, Norfolk men are justly noted" — Ray. (Dr Pegge suggests that the miles in Kent were once much longer than they are now, adding —) Stow reckons it but 55 miles from London to Dover and now it is not less than 75. Leland calls Wye but seven miles from Canterbury and now they esteem it full ten. From Betshanger to Canterbury, about 100 years ago, 'twas 8, in the next generation it was 10, and now it is gotten to be 11 miles . . . (Mr Hazlitt (English Proverbs) says — "An Essex stile is a ditch; a Kentish mile is, I believe, like the Yorkshire way-bit and the Scottish mile and a bittock, a mile and a fraction, the fraction not being clearly defined. As to Norfolk wiles, I should say that this expression is to be understood satirically, as Norfolk has never been remarkable for the astuteness of its inhabitants, but quite the contrary". Perhaps, however, there is reference here to the litigious spirit which some have attributed to the people of Norfolk. At any rate, we must not forget that the phrase occurs in Tusser, who, in his verses on his own life, thus alludes to his marriage with his second wife, who was from Norfolk — "For Norfolk wiles, so full of guiles, Have caught my toe, by wiving so. That out to thee I see for me No way to creep —" where "thee" means Suffolk). (See Kentish Miles, Further Terms, etc. — A.M.)

19. Kentish Pippins

Mr Lambarde, in the Peram., edit. 1656 says "but as for orchards of apples, and gardens of cherries and those of the most delicious and exquisite kindes that can be, no part of the realm (that I know) hath them either in such quantity and number, or with such art and industry, set and planted. So that the Kentish man must surely of all other may say with him in Virgil — "Sunt nobis mitia poma, Castaneae molles". And again, in his account of Tenham — "this Tenham with thirty other parishes (lying on each side this portway and extending from Raynham to Blean Wood) be the Cherrie Garden and Apple Orchard of Kent . . . Our honest patriote Richard Harrys (fruiterer to King Henrie the 8) planted by his great cost and rare industrie, the sweet Cherrie, the temperate Pipyn and the golden Renate . . . about the year of our Lord Christe 1533", etc. Camden says Kent "abounds with apples beyond compare".

20. A Kentish stomack

I remember a gentleman of this county, who took his batchelor of Arts degree at Cambridge, being a student in St John's College there; and when he was askt the question, according to statute, "quid est abyssus?" answered "Stomachus Cantianus". The first I presume that chiefly contributed to raise this reproach on the Kentish men, was Nich. Wood, concerning whom see Sir John Hawkins' Life of Dr Sam. Johnson. Otherwise, as to my own observation, I never could perceive that the people of this county were at all remarkable for gluttony. Taylor, the Water Poet, was himself a great eater, and was very near engaging with the above-mentioned Wood "to eat at one time as much black pudding as would reach across the Thames at any place to be fixed on by Taylor himself between London and Richmond" — ibid. (A Kentish stomach meant a strong stomach. — A.M.)

21. Naughty Ashford, surly Wye, Poor Kennington hard by.

We have in Mr Ray several of the like short descriptions in verse, concerning places in other counties; but this, which relates to this province, he has omitted. It is very pithy and significant, but for the exposition of the particulars at large, I must refer you to the "History of the College of Wye." (There is a variation of this verse concerning these places in "Further Terms, etc." — A.M.)

131

22. If you'll live a little while, Go to Bapchild; If you'd live long, Go to Tenham or Tong.

These last two lines contradict No. 54 wherefore I suppose 'tis banter. Bapchild is indeed a bad and unhealthy situation. (It is adjacent to Tong, which adjoins Teynham) (See similar verses in "Further Terms, etc." — A.M.)

23. As old as Cale-hill (Kent) — Clarke's Paraemiologia, 1639.

Cale-hill is also the name of a hundred, which contains Pluckley, Charing, etc.

24. A Canter

A small easy gallop, which I presume (is) so called from the city of Canterbury, as some here in Kent will often call it; as if it were a pace much us'd by those who in former times went in pilgrimage to the famous saint there, Thomas a Becket. (Mr Hazlitt in his English Proverbs has — "A Canterbury Gallop. In horsemanship, the hard gallop of an ambling horse; probably described from the monks riding to Canterbury upon ambling horses". (This is the true etymology of canter).

25. Canterbury Bells, Canterbury brochis

The former are mentioned by John Fox, in Martyr. i., and mean small bells worn by pilgrims (rather, fastened to the trappings of pilgrims' horses) in their way to Canterbury. For the latter, see Chaucer. A broche is properly a bodkin but means more generally a trinket or anything valuable. (The expression of "Canterbury brochis" is not in Chaucer, but in the anonymous continuation of the Canterbury Tales; see Chamber's Book of Days, i.)

26. A Canterbury Tale

(Hazlitt, English Proverbs, has "A Canterbury Story, i.e. a long yarn; supposed to be derived from Chaucer's famous series of Tales." In Fuller's Worthies, ed; 1662, we find — "Canterbury Tales. So Chaucer called his Book . . . But since that time, Canterbury Tales are parallel to Fabulae Milesiae, which are charactered nec verae nec verisimiles, meerly made to marre precious time, and please fanciful people. Such as the many miracles of Thomas Becket, etc.)

27. Canterbury is the higher Rack, but Winchester is the better Manger.

"W. Edington (Mr Hazlitt has Dr Langton for W. Edington, a curious misprint), Bp of Winchester, was the author of this expression, rendring this the reason of his refusal to be removed to Canterbury, though chosen thereunto. Indeed, though Canterbury be graced with an higher honour, the revenues of Winchester are greater. It is appliable to such, who preferre a wealthy privacy before a less profitable dignity" — Ray. Wm. Edington, bp of Winchester, died October 7, 1366. Simon Islip, a bp of Canterbury, died April 26, 1366, and Simon Langham succeeded him in the metropolitical chair; and thus it seems this sorded prelate did not enjoy the manger he was so attacht to long after this.

28. Canterbury is in decay, God help May.

Lottery of 1567 (Kempe's Losely MSS).

29. Cantuaria Pisce (redundans)

In Somner's Antiquities we have this account. "Certain old verses made in commendation of some cities of this kingdom singular in affording some one commodity or other, commend of Canterbury for her fish; wherewith indeed, by reason of the sea's vicinity, as Malmsbury hath long since observed, her market is so well supplied, as none that know the place will think the poet flattered her. The verses are in the margin"; and there they run thus —

"Testis est London ratibus, Wintonia Baccho,
Herefordeque grege, Worcestria fruge redundans,
Batha lacu, Sarumque feris, Cantuaria pisce".

A great part of the fish was wont to come from Whitstaple and the present fish market was more antiently call'd the Whitstaple market. (The Latin verses may be found at length in Henry of Huntingdon.)

30. For company, as Kit went to Canterbury.

When a person goes any whither for no reason at all, and it is asked "What did he go for?" the fleering answer is — "for company, as Kit went to Canterbury"; alluding to more particular person of that name, I suppose, who was always ready at every turn to go everywhere and with every body that ask'd him. (Mr Hazlitt in his English Proverbs has — "For want of company, Welcome trumpery" which is doubtless to the same effect.)

31. Smoky Charing.

(Charing is near Ashford.) (See "Dirty Charing" in "Further Terms, Expressions, etc." — A.M.)

32. If you would goe to a church mis-went, You must go to Cuckstone in Kent.

— "Or very unusual in proportion, as Cuckstone church in Kent, of which it is said, "If you would goe etc" — Dr Plot's Letter to Bp Fell, in Leland, Itin. ii. (Mr Hazlitt, citing Halliwell, says — "So said, because the church is "very unusual in proportion". It refers to Cuxton, near Rochester.)

33. Deal, Dover and Harwich,
   The devil gave his daughter in marriage;
  And, by a codicil of his will,
   He added Helveot and the Brill.
(This satirical squib is equally applicable to many other seaports. — Ray.)

34. Deal Savages, Canterbury Parrots,
   Dover Sharks, and Sandwich Carrots.
Gardening first used as a trade at Sandwich; Harris. (Mr Hazlitt in his English Proverbs, has "A Dover shark and a Deal savage.)

35. A Dover House.

(I.e. a necessary house, as Dr Pegge says in the Glossary.)

36. As sure as there's a dog in Dover.

That is, as another adage has it, "as sure as a gun". The two d's in dog and Dover, have created this trite saying. (This presumably means that something is really certain and as definite as the fact that large numbers of dogfish ("dogs") were landed at Dover.

37. Dover, a Den of Thieves.

Dr Smollett, Trav. ("Dover is commonly called a den of thieves", Smollett's Travels through France and Italy; Works, vol. viii).

38. A Jack of Dover.

"I find the first mention of this proverb in our English Ennius, Chaucer, in his Proeme to the Cook — "And many a Jack of Dover he had sold, Which had been two times hot, and two times cold." "This he (Dr Fuller) makes parallel to crambe bis cocta; and appliable to such as grate the eares of their auditours with ungrateful tautologies of what is worthless in itself; tolerable as once uttered in the notion of novelty, but abominable if repeated" — Ray. (Mr Hazlitt says in his English Proverbs — "A Jack of Dover, i.e. a sole; for which Dover is still celebrated. There was an old jest-book with this (no doubt then popular) title, printed in 1604 and 1615. Whether Chaucer meant by Jack of Dover a sole or a dish warmed up (rechauffe) it is rather difficult to say").

39. From Barwick to Dover, three hundred miles over.

"That is, from one end of the land to the other. Parallel to that Scripture expression "from Dan to Beersheba" — Ray. (A similar saying is "From Dover to Dunbar" which Dr Pegge has noted. The poet Dunbar uses the expression "all Yngland, from Berwick to Kalice (Calais)", see Specimens of English, 1394-1579, ed Skeat).

40. From Dover to Dunbar.
Antiqu. Repertory, vol.i.

41. When its dark in Dover,
'Tis dark all the world over.

42. A North-east Wind in May
Makes the Shotver-men a Prey.

Shotver men are the mackerel fishers and a north-east wind is reckon'd at Dover a good wind for them. Their nets are called shot-nets.

43. Feversham (or Milton) Oysters.

These are both places in Kent and not very far distant. The oysters dredged at one or the other are equally good, and they are now esteem'd the best the country affords. Oisters, like other things, have taken their turn. In Juvenal's time the oisters of Richborow shore were famous. Mr Lambarde commends the north and south yenlet (Yenlet or Yenlade, i.e. estuary) for producing the largest oysters. (See Yenlet and Yenlade in the Dialect Dictionary — A.M.)

44. To be married at Finglesham church.

There is no church at Finglesham; but a chalkpit celebrated for casual amours; of which kind of encounters the saying is us'd. Quaere, in what parish Finglesham is? (Finglesham is one of the four boroughs in the parish of Northbourne, or Norbourne, which lies to the west of Deal. See Hasted's History of Kent, iv.) (As there was no church in this small hamlet the expression also referred to couples living together as man and wife but not married — i.e. "married in Finglesham church — A.M.)

45. Folkestone Washerwomen.

These are the white clouds which commonly bring rain.

46. Rumbald Whiting.

Harris. For this see Glossary. (It is placed here, as referring to Folkstone). (See in Dialect Dictionary — A.M.)

47. Fordwich Trouts.

This Portus Trutulensis was a station for the (Roman) fleet; Beatus Rhenanus suggests that it was the same with Portus Rutupinus, and Sir Henry Savil tells us, that some read Rhutupensis for Trutulensis, which yet I suppose is only a gloss, receiv'd, in some copies, into the text. It is thought to have been called Trutulensis from the trouts, trutae, which then might probably be very eminent in this road, as they are at this day in the stream or river that runs into it; Harris. The excellency of the trouts in the Stour, especially that part which runs by Fordwich, is celebrated both by Camden and Somner; and I suppose they continue to be as good as ever; for a noble lord has of late caus'd himself to be made mayor of Fordwich for the privilege, as is suppos'd, of having now and then one. Somner.

48. Frindsbury Clubs.
Lambarde, ed. 1596.

(The story in Lambard is to the effect that a skirmish once arose between the monks of Rochester and the brethren of Stroud, wherein the latter, who had hired some men from Frindsbury armed with clubs to help them, gave the monks of Rochester a severe beating. "And thus out of this tragicall historie arose the byword of Frendsbury clubs, a tearm not yet clean forgotten. For they of Frendsbury used to come yearly after that upon Whitson-Monday to Rochester in procession with their clubs, for penance of their fault, which (belike) was never to be pardoned whilest the monks remained". Ireland's Views of the Medway, states to the effect that "a singular custom used to be annually observed on May-day by the boys of Frindsbury and the neighbouring town of Stroud. They met on Rochester bridge, where a skirmish ensued between them. This combat probably derived its origin from a drubbing received by the monks of Rochester in the reign of Edward I" etc.) (See Item 29 in "Further Terms, Expressions, etc." chapter).

49. Let him set up shop on Goodwin Sands.

"This is a piece of country wit; there being an aequivoque in the word Goodwin, which is a surname and also signifies *gaining wealth* " — Ray. (Dr Pegge adds some passages which help but little, chiefly from Somner, Ports & Forts, who combats the current opinion that the sands were caused by an inundation in the year 1097 and proposes a later date. See Proverb 59. Mr Hazlitt explains the phrase of *being shipwrecked.)* (This proverb was also used as an expression for someone planning to do something foolish — A.M.)

50. Greenwich Geese.

I.e. Greenwich pensioners. See Brady's Varieties of Literature.

51. The Vale of Holmsdale
    Was never won, ne ever shall.

"This proverbial rhythme hath one part of history, the other of prophecy. As the first is certainly untrue, so the second is frivolous and not to be heeded by sober persons, as neither any other of the like nature" — Ray, who places this saying to Surrey. Mr Lambarde, in the Peramb. of Kent, writes this old saying thus — "The Vale of Holmesdale, Neuer wonne, nor neuer shale", and gives us the meaning of Holmesdale in the following words: "This (viz the castle of Holmsdale in Surrey) tooke the name of the dale wherin it standeth, which is large in quantity, extending itselfe a great length into Surrey and Kent also; and was, as I conjecture, at the first called Homesdale, by reason that it is for the most part, conuallis, a plaine valley, running between two hills, that be replenished with stoare of wood: for so much the very word, Holmesdale, itself importeth. And so in the title of that chapter, "Holmesdale, that is to say, the dale between the wooddie hills". It must be confessed that this interpretation agrees perfectly with that part of this vale which lies in Kent, being that valley wherein Westerham, Brasted, Sundrich, Chevening, Otford, etc. are situate; but I am in some doubt whether holme signifies a wood; for holm, according to the Remains (i.e. Camden's) denotes "plaine grassie ground upon water-sides or in the water". In the North of England the word holm is very common in this sense, both by itself and in composition. "And this Kentish vale, besides the river Derwent running through the midst of it, has a multitude of springs and bournes issuing out at the foot of those two ridges of hills, on each side of it; and by means of them and the river, it is in sundry places very wet and marshy; and such moist places overgrown with alders, they call moors" — Note by Dr Pegge. Mr Ray disputes the truth of the historical part of this proverb but we read enough in Mr Lambarde to shew that there are grounds enough for it, and that however fond and idle it may be as a prophecy, yet it wants not a foundation in history. "In this dale, a part of which we now crosse in our way to Sennocke, the people of Kent, being encouraged by the prosperous successe of Edwarde the king (the

135

sonne of Alfrede, and commonly surnamed Edwarde the Elder) assembled themselves and gave to the Danes, that had many yeeres before afflicted them, a most
sharpe and fierce encounter, in which, after long fight, the prevailed, and the
Danes were overthrowne and vanquished. This victorie, and the like event in
another battaile (given to the Danes at Otforde, which standeth in the same
valley also) begate, as I gesse, the common byword, as amongst the inhabitants
of this vale, even till this present day in whuch they vaunt after this manner —
"The Vale of Holmesdale, Neuer wonne, nor neuer shale" — Lambarde. (This
proverb no doubt refers also to the old story about the success of the Kentishmen
in resisting William the Conqueror, and preserving their old customs. But this
story, however commonly believed by the people of Kent, rests on insufficient
proof. For the story of the Kentishmen's resistance see the ballad of "William
the Conqueror" in the Percy Folio MS. iii.)

52. He that rideth into the Hundred of Hoo,
    Besides pilfering Seamen, shall find Dirt enow.
    "Hollinshed the historian (who was a Kentish man) saith that Hoo in his time
was nearly an island; and of the hundred of Hoo, he saith the people had this
rime or proverb", etc. Harris. (This pensinular lies between the Medway and the
Thames).

53. Long, lazy, lousy Lewisham.
    This proverb has been preserved rather by the alliteration, than its being
founded in truth — Ray. (I believe there is a local tradition that the epithet was
conferred on this place by King James I.) (See "Further Terms, Expressions,
etc." regarding a variant of this proverb — A.M.)

54. He that wil not live long,
    Let him dwell at Muston, Tenham or Tong.
    We are indebted to Mr Lambarde for this, who concludes his chapter of
Tenham with saying — "Touching the sickly situation of this town, and the
region thereabout, you may be admonished by the common rythme of the
countrie, singing thus", etc. (Muston is Murston — A.M.)

55. Northdown Ale.
    Mr Ray mentioning some places famous for good ale, amongst the rest has
"Northdown in the Isle of Thanet", vide Lewis, Hist, of Tenet.

56. A Rochester portion.
    I.e. two torn smocks and what Nature gave. Grose's Classical Dict. of the
Vulgar Tongue.

57. Conscience is drowned in Sandwich Bay (or Haven)
    A story they have there of a woman's wanting a groat's worth of mackarel.
The fisherman took her groat and bade her take as many as she would for it.
She took such an unconscionable many, that, provok'd with her unreasonable-
ness, he cry'd — "Is that your conscience? then I will throw it into the sea". So
he threw the pence into the water and took the fish from her. Hence came it to
be commonly said — "Conscience is drowned in Sandwich haven".

58. Starv'em, Rob'm, and Cheat'm — Kent.
    Stroud (Strood), Rochester and Chatham — Ray. (This is believed to have
originally began with soldiers and seamen stationed locally, referring to the
impositions that shopkeepers, innkeepers, etc., in these three places practised
on them — A.M.)

59. Tenterden steeple the cause of Goodwin Sands.

"This proverb is used when an absurd and ridiculous reason is given of any-thing in question: an account of the original whereof I find in one of Bp Latimer's Sermons in these words. (Then follows the well-known quotation (printed at length in Hazlitt's English Proverbs) about the old man who remembered that) 'before Tenterden steeple was in building there was no manner of talking of any flat, or sands that stop't up the haven; and therefore, I think that Tenterton steeple is the cause of the decay and destroying of Sandwich haven'. Thus far the bishop" — Ray. The vulgar notion of this proverb is, that Tenterden steeple, being built by an Archbishop of Canterbury (whose property those sands were when they were terra firma, or at least, upon whom it was incumbent to maintain the dykes and walls for the defence of them) at that instant, when that tract of dry ground was in danger of being overwhelm'd by the sea, the good man went on with that building, to the prejudice of those low grounds; which, through that neglect, were entirely and irrecoverably lost. You have here now a mechani-cal account how the steeple was the cause of the sands, if you will believe it, and are got a step further than the old man's information carried you. However, we have from this old man's account the precise time of the beginning of this saying, viz. in Henry VIIIth's time, that great man, Sir Thos. Moore, being the person who is (in Latimer's sermon) called Mr Moore; and also the precise time of the emergence of these sands; whereby you may resolve Mr Somner's doubts and set Mr Twyne, Mr Lambarde and others right in the matter. (Here follows a long and dull quotation from Somner's Ports & Forts, which refers to the formation of the sands to a supposed inundation in the time of Henry I. Mr Hazlitt quotes the proverb in the form following:

"Of many people it hath been said
  That Tenterden steeple Sandwich haven hath decayed".
    Lottery of 1567 (Kempe's Losely Papers, 1836)

See Lewis's History of Tenet; Sir Edward Dering's Works. "The petrifying waters . . . of Tenterden steeple in Kent, for which it is no less famous than for being the cause of Godwin Sands" — Dr Plot's letter to Bp Fell; Leland, Itin. ii. (A variation is "Tenterden steeple made the Goodwin Sands" and that they were either part of the Kent mainland or an island owned by Godwin, Saxon Earl of Kent, called Lomea. The archbishop of that time devoted money intended for sea defences for the area to building Tenterden steeple and so the sea burst through, inundating valuable land and there has been the dangerous shoal ever since. There might be a grain of truth to the "legend" which began it at a time when the nuns of Minster, Isle of Sheppey, owned land and property at Tenter-den — A.M.)

60. As a Thorn produces a Rose, so Godwin begat Editha.

Harris. (Saxon Earl Godwin of Kent was considered a thorn in the side of pro-Norman Edward the Confessor and thus disliked by the king's favourites who were mainly Norman. The powerful Godwin nevertheless had managed to place Edward on England's throne and married his own daughter, Editha, to Edward. During the period of Godwin's banishment Edward put his own wife, "the fair Editha", into a nunnery.

61. At Betshanger a Gentleman, at Fredvile a Squire,
    At Bonington a Noble Knight, at . . . a Lawyer.

Lawyer is to be pronounced Lyer, as is common now in some counties. This relates to the worshipful family of the Bois's, of which four several branches were flourishing at once at those seats here mentioned. (In a complete version the missing place is London — A.M.)

62. Bad for the Rider, Good for the Abider.

Pehaps this is not appropriate to Kent only, but the badness of the roads in the Weald of Kent and Rumney Marsh, together with the richness of the soil in both tracts, has made it very common in the Kentish man's mouth. It seems they have a saying of this sort in French "bon pais, mauvais chemin" — Ray, who writes the proverb above in an uncouth, unmusical manner — "The worse for the Rider, the better for the Bider".

63. Cherries: If they blow in April,
       You'll have your fill;
       But if in May,
       They'll all go away.

But, tho' this may be so in general, yet in the year 1742 it was otherwise. For, tho' it was a backward spring, and the trees were not in bloom till late in May, I had a great quantity of White and Black Hearts. (See Proverb 15).

64. Fogge's Feast.

This is an antient saying, when any accident happens at an entertainment. For it seems, at a dinner made by one of the family of Fogge, the servant threw down the venison pasty in coming over a high threshold. He bade his guests not to be concerned, for there was a piece of boil'd beef, and a dish of pease, but the dogs fell upon the beef and the maid buttering the pease flung them all down.

65. Health and no Wealth;
       Wealth and no Health;
       Health and Wealth.

Thus Mr Ray — "Some part of Kent hath health and no wealth, viz, East Kent; some Wealth and no Health, viz., the Weald of Kent; some both Health and Wealth, viz. the middle of the country and parts near London". Mr Lambarde, taking occasion to quote this observation, in his chapter of Romney (Peramb.), expounds it differently from Mr Ray. "The place (i.e. Romney marsh) hath in it sundry villages, although not thicke set, nor much inhabited, bicause it is hyeme malus, aestate molestus, nunquam bonus; evill in winter, grievous in sommer, and never good, as Hesiodus (the olde poet) sometime said e of the countrie where his father dwelt. And therefore very reasonable is their conceite, which doe imagine that Kent hath three steps or degrees, of which the first (say they) offereth Wealth Without Health; the second giveth both Wealth and Health; and the thirde affoordeth Health onely, and little or no Wealth. For if a man, minding to passe through Kent toward London, should arrive and make his first step on land in Rumney marshe, he shall rather finde good grasse under foote than wholesome aire above the head; againe, if he step over the hilles and come into the Weald, hee shall have at once the commodities of both caeli and soli, of the aire, and of the earth: but if he passe that, and climbe the next step of hilles that are betweene him and London, hee shall have wood, conies, and corn for his wealth, and (toward the increase of his health) if he seeke, he shall finde famem in agro lapidoso, a good stomacke in the stonie fielde". According to this account, the matter stands thus, Health and no Wealth, the N.W. parts of Kent; Wealth and no Health, Rumney marsh; Health and Wealth, the Weald; which seems to me the most rational, and the truest in fact; especially if it be remembered, that such general observations as these are not to be taken universally or understood in a rigorous strictness. Mr Ray is certainly wide of the mark and it may be observed that, as Mr Lambarde puts it, it should seem that this old saying originally regarded and took its rise from a progress or passage through the county in a direct road from Rumney marsh to London and not from the several parts of it as they may be pickt out here and there. Mr Camden expounds differently from all. "The inhabitants, according to its scituation, from the Thames

138

southeward, distinguish it (Kent) into three plots or portions (they call them deegrees — So Lambarde above — Note by Dr Pegge); the upper, lying upon the Thames, they look upon to be healthy, but not altogether so rich; the middle part to be both healthy and rich; the lower, to be rich, but withal unhealthy (Rumney marsh) because of the wet marshy soil in most parts of it: it is however very fruitful in grass". (See Item 6 "Further Expressions, Terms", chapter.)

66. Justice Nine-holes.

Referring to Smarden, in the deanery of Charing, Harris says, in his History of Kent, "In this church, as Fox takes notice in his Acts and Monuments and in the year 1558, which was the last year of Queen Mary, one Drayner, a Justice of the Peace, made use of the Rood-loft, which then was standing here, to place spies and informers in, in order to take an account who did not duly perform the Popish Ceremonies; and that they might discover this the better, he made for them nine peeping holes in the loft; and because he was so severe, and punished such as did not conform, the people hated him, and gave him the name of Justice Nine-Holes; and that expression is still retained as a mark of contempt in this county".

67. Neghe sythe selde,
    and neghe syth gelde;
    and fif pond for the were,
    er he become healder.

(In Lambarde's Peramb. of Kent, in an Old French Charter of Gavelkind, temp. Edw. I., it is explained how a tenant who has forfeited his tenancy may regain it by paying a fine, "sicome il est auncienement dist: Neghe sythe selde, and neghe syth gelde; and fif pond for the were, er he bicome healder"; i.e. (if I rightly make it out) — he gave nine times and let him pay nine times, and five pounds for his "wer", ere he becomes tenant. The "wer" is the man's own value or price, as explained in Bosworth's A.S. Dictionary, etc.)

68. Se that hir wende,
    Se hir lende.

(In Lambard's Peramb. of Kent, in an Old French Charter of Gavelkind, temp. Edw. I it is explained that a widow is entitled to half her husband's lands and tenements, but forfeits these at once if she ceases to be chaste; in which case she must be maintained by her betrayer; "dont il est dist en Kenteis: se that hir wende, se hir lende"; i.e. he that turneth her about, let him lend to (or maintain) her. See Proverb 69. Mr Scott Robertson kindly sends me a proverb from "Consuetudines Kanciae" in the Queenborough Statute-book, about A.D. 1345, relating to the above-mentioned privilege of a widow. It runs thus — "Si that is wedewe, si is leuedi"; i.e. she that is a widow, she is a lady. Si for she is an old Kentish form.)

69. (The) Father to the Bough,
    And the son to the Plough.

"This saying I look upon as too narrow to be placed in the family of proverbs; it is rather to be deemed a rule or maxime in the tenure of Gavil-kind, where though the father had judgment to be hang'd yet there followed no forfeiture of his estate; but his son might — a happy man according to Horace's description — paterna rura bobus exercere suis. Though there be that expound this proverb thus — "the Father to the bough, i.e. to his sports of hawking and hunting, and the Son to the plow, i.e. to the poor man's condition" — Ray. This last must be looked upon as but a secondary and borrowed sense of the old rhyme; for originally it respected only that privilege of Gavel-kind (which) Mr Ray mentions, and accordingly it took its rise from thence. See Lambarde's Perambulation. (Ray's second suggestion is wrong. The sense is put beyond all doubt by the charter in Old French which Lambarde prints, where it is explained that if the father be attainted of felony and suffer death, the estate (in gavelkind) does not escheat, but goes to the heir, who "les tiendra per mesmes les seruices et customes sicome ses auncestres les tyndront: dont est dist en Kenteis: the fader to the boughe and the son to the plogh".) (The father to the bough (gibbet), the son to the plough, refers to one of the privileges of gavelkind enjoyed in Kent, in which the son inherited his father's property even though the parent was executed for high treason; or, in many felonies, only the goods and chattels, but not the lands were forfeited to the Crown, on the execution of the criminal. Gavelkind was an ancient Saxon custom distributing an equal division of the lands of the parent among his sons or children. From the Anglo-Saxon gafol, tribute, although it has been suggested gavelkind is a corruption of the German gieb alle kind, "give to all the children" — A.M.)

70. To cast water into the Thames.
    "That is, to give to them who had plenty before; which notwithstanding, is the dole general of the world" — Ray. (Dr Pegge claims this for Kent, as bounding the Thames. The proverb is alluded to in Piers the Plowman.)

71. The ducks fare well in the Thames;
    This Mr Ray has. (Claimed for Kent, as in the case of No. 70.)

72. To come out of the Shires.
    This is a proverbial saying relative to any person who comes from a distance. And the ground of it is that the word shire is not annexed to any one of the counties bordering upon Kent, which are Sussex, Surrey, Middlesex and Essex; so that to come out of a shire a man must necessarily come from beyond any of these neighbouring provinces. (See Sheeres in the Dialect Dictionary — A.M.)

73. Yellow as a Peigle.
    The Peigle is a cowslip, verbasculum. I never heard this simile or Proverb but in Kent. See Gerard's Herbal, who writes paigle. ("Yellow as a paigle" is common in Essex and Cambs. Ray gives "as blake (i.e. bleak, pale) as a paigle" as a Northern proverb.)

Besides the above, I find in Dr Pegge's MS. the following notes, etc.

"To sit in Jack Straw's place". (Unexplained)

"An Eastry flower". A double crown on an horse's head; meaning, I suppose, a recommendation to an horse at Eastry fair. A corruption for an ostrich feather, which the country people call ostrey or eastry. (One at least of these explanations must be wrong.)

"All-fours". "A game very much played in Kent, and very well it may, since from thence it drew its first original. (All Fours is a game played by up to four people, with a complete pack of cards, six cards each player, the name being derived from the four chances High, Low, Jack and Game, each making a point — A.M.)

FURTHER TERMS, EXPRESSIONS, SAYINGS AND PROVERBS

During the time I spent making my own collection of examples of the Kentish Dialect I also heard or received other terms, expressions, sayings and proverbs in addition to those quoted by Dr Pegge in the previous Chapter.

Many of these originated in Kent, concerning Kentish subjects, and have remained in the county. Others began here but spread to neighbouring counties and elsewhere for universal use, as did some of the Kentish dialect. Yet other examples originated elsewhere but were brought into the county by "furriners" and became established. Another variation is that some of the sayings, as were some of the dialect words, were the personal concoction of the user and passed into a wider use by those people living or associating with the user who learnt and themselves used the saying, etc. These then tended to be handed down from generation to generation. Other expressions are no longer used, being replaced by a modern expression but are still remembered by elderly people. Taking the view that dialect and these expressions are closely bound together in Kent's history I have thought it worthwhile to include those I have collected, whether known to a wide public or unknown to them. Where known I have also stated their explanation or origin.

Alan Major

1. Kent is famed for hops, fair maids and civility.

2. In addition to Proverb 2 in the previous Chapter: "A Man of Kent and a Kentish Man". Formerly "A Man of Kent" was a man born between the Kentish Stour and the sea, all others being "Kentish Men". Another version said that a "Kentish Man" was one born in Kent, but not of Kentish parents, while a "Man of Kent" was one whose parents and ancestors were Kentish. A more common version is that a "Man of Kent" is one born east of the river Medway, while a "Kentish Man" is one born west of the Medway. "By dis, dat, den, Yew can tell the Kentish Men". This is a parody of the Cornish couplet "By Tre, Pol and Pen, You can tell the Cornish men".

3. Kentish Miles (See Proverb 18, "Essex Stiles, Kentish Miles, etc." previous Chapter). This was used as an allusion that the Kentish labourer's mile was about one and a half. In reality Kentish miles were no longer than in other counties, but it is supposed that before the introduction of turnpikes many of the Kentish roads, especially those in the Weald, were in a bad condition and almost impassable in wet weather, so that a carriage could not travel except slowly, perhaps a few miles an hour, and so the miles seemed of extraordinary length to the travellers.

4. Kentish. This word was frequently applied to something special to the county. Kentish Ague (See Proverb 14 previous Chapter), was the shivery, malaria-type fever once commonly prevalent on Romney Marsh and in other stagnant, marshy, low-lying areas. (See Ague in Dialect Dictionary.) Kentish longtails were wild

Oats (See Proverb 17 previous Chapter, also Longtails in Dialect Dictionary) Kentish cousins had a similar meaning to "Scotch cousins" (See Proverb 16 previous Chapter) (See also Kentish stomach, proverb 20, meaning a strong stomach, Kentish cherries, proverb 15, and Kentish pippins, proverb 19, in previous Chapter).

5. Native-born people of Kent used to speak disdainfully of other persons from different counties and if the latter did not come from Surrey, Sussex, or Essex, they came from "out of the Shires". (See Shires, Sheeres, in Dialect Dictionary.) Sussex was known to Kent people as "Silly", while Surrey was known as "the county of fools". This is difficult to understand, since the two counties are adjacent, and thus Kentish people near the boundary had much trade with Surrey.

6. Health without Wealth; Wealth without Health; Both Health and Wealth. These refer to the three parts of Kent. The first was considered to be East Kent, the part adjoining to the sea which was extremely pleasant and healthy, but had much poor land. The second was considered to be the Weald and Romney Marsh, famous for its fine pasture and rich graziers, but trying for the health and particularly subject to the ague (which see in Dialect Dictionary). The third part was the area of Kent in the neighbourhood of London, where the situation was healthy, the soil good and the inhabitants thus rich. Alternatively there was a slight variation. "Wealth without Health" was applied to the cold and dreary marsh areas of the coast and around the mouths of the Medway and Thames, that produced good pasture but very bad for the health. "Health without Wealth" referred to the areas of the chalkhills and Downs, where the soil was not good but had bracing clean air. "Both Health and Wealth" applied to the sandstone ranges and the Weald, with luxurious valleys, fertile fields and tree-clad hills, where the inhabitants were thus healthy and wealthy. (See Proverb 65 previous Chapter.)

7. There are many Proverbs and Quatrains that refer to local areas and parishes in Kent, sometimes describing their peculiarities, in addition to those stated by Dr Pegge. For a large number of them there is no known explanation for them and why they were composed. Possibly many of the more sarcastic were written by local rhymesters elsewhere, because there was much rivalry between villages, to taunt inhabitants of such places and warn visitors going there of what to expect. Some of the Proverbs, Quatrains, etc., may also have or had a grain of truth in them and arose accordingly. They are:—

8. Long, lazy Lewisham, Little Lee,
Dirty Deptford, and Greenwich free. (See 53 previous Chapter.)

9. Sutton for mutton, Kirby for beef,
South Darent for gingerbread and Dartford for a thief.
The latter almost certainly refers to the Fair at Dartford where the unsuspecting might become a victim of a pickpocket. The reference to South Darent as an area for "gingerbread" may mean it was a pleasant place of fertile meadows and good land along the river Darent.

10. If you'd live long, Go to Teynham or Tong. Strangely this verse contradicts another used in Kent: He that would not live long, Let him dwell in Murston, Teynham or Tong. (See Proverbs 22 and 54 in previous Chapter.) This contradiction most likely means that many of the place names were used not so much to state facts, but to make a derisive quatrain that rhymed.

11. Kill 'em, Cart 'em and Bury 'em, i.e. a saying for referring to Chilham, Chartham and Canterbury.

12. Rye, Romney and Hythe, for wealth without health;
    The Downs for health with poverty;
    But you shall find both health and wealth
    From Foreland Head to Knole and Lee.
See Item 6 and Proverb 65 previous Chapter. The Lee stated may be either Leigh near Tonbridge or near Blackheath.

13. Dirty Charing lies in a hole.
    It had but one bell and that was stole.
This reference to "dirty" is difficult to understand when Charing's past religious history is remembered. Item 8 refers to "dirty Deptford". It is possible that, when the jingle was composed, "dirty", referring to either place, did not mean what it does today. A more likely explanation is "smoky Charing" and "smoky Deptford".

14. Hucking glass breeches where rats run on tiptoe". Explanation unknown.

15. "You've got no calves to your legs like the Pluckley girls and are obliged to wear straight stockings."

16. Go to Monk's Horton,
    Where pigs play on the organ.

17. Proud Town Malling, poor people,
    They built a church to their steeple.

18. Poor Lenham. Possibly an agricultural reference to the once poor and barren soil there and the low financial state of its inhabitants.

19. Surly Ashford, Proud Wye,
    And lousy Kennington lieth hard by.
(See Proverb 21 in previous Chapter.)

20. Proud Wingham, Wicked Ash and Lazy Sandwich.

21. Ramsgate capons (herrings), Peter's lings,
    Broadstairs scrubs and Margate kings.
Various products from these parts of Thanet. Capons were red herrings; ling is a type of fish in the Cod family. There were also several others: Faversham, Milton and Rainham oysters, Deal crabs, Fordwich trout, Medway shrimps and smelts, all thus named for their superiority.

22. When England wrings, the island sings. A reference to the dry nature and the chalky soil of Thanet, so that a wet summer is good for the crops.

23. Earl Godwin and his Court are hungry. An expression used by Deal fishermen when a storm was imminent and referring to the stranding and destruction of ships by the Goodwin Sands, which were supposed to be his property. According to legend Godwin was believed to still keep court under the Sands. (See Proverb 59 previous Chapter.)

24. In days past Folkestone was referred to in various expressions, one being "Silly Folkestone". There were also "Folkestone Girls" and "Folkestone Washerwomen", referring to cloud formations (See in Dialect Dictionary).

25. Greenwich Geese was a nickname for the pensioners at the Greenwich Naval Hospital.

26. Why, you've only two sticks and a piece of paper, like a Rainham fire.

27. Get on anyhow, as they do at Rainham, referring to anyone muddling along, making do with what they have, in similar vein to Item 26.

To go on like they do at Rainham, to behave in a disorderly manner. Another deprecating reference was to "Rainham Fair", indicating it was a badly run affair.

28. Cowden Play meant any silly way of acting or playing.

29. Frindsbury Clubs is a term that refers to the men of Frindsbury having to go to Rochester every Whit Monday with their clubs and staves as a penance. (See Proverb 48 previous Chapter.) This dates back to an occasion during a severe drought in the area when the monks of St Andrews, Rochester, decided to go to Frindsbury Heights on a pilgrimage to pray for rain. The day was very windy and so as to seek some shelter from its bluster upsetting the singers in the procession they sought permission to pass through an orchard owned by Strood Hospital. Unfortunately, although the Master agreed to let them do this he did not inform other people concerning the monks' procession crossing the orchard and while they were doing so men and lads from nearby Frindsbury village fell upon the monks to drive them away. The monks gave as good as they received, hitting out with crosses, banner poles and staves. After order was restored and the monks returned to Rochester the penance was imposed on the Frindsbury men. But the object of the monks' pilgrimage was supposedly achieved as it rained and broke the drought the same day.

30. Men of Swanscombe fear neither man nor devil, alluding to their resistance to the Norman invasion.

31. Born down Ryarsh Sandpits, meant that the person referred to was illegitimate.

32. It won't happen till the moon comes down in Calverley Road, local in the Tunbridge Wells area, to mean something that is almost impossible.

33. Ickham, pickham,
   Penny Wickham,
   Cockalorium jay,
   Eggs, butter, cheese, bread,
   Hick, stick, stone dead!"
This was an old rhyme used for counting out objects, mostly by school children, that may possibly have originated in the Ickham and Wickhambreaux area near Canterbury.

34. On Shrove Tuesday, if they were able to obtain small garlands of wild flowers young children would call at cottages and houses to say:
   "Flowers, flowers, high-do,
   Sheeny, greeny, rino,
   Sheeny, greeny, sheeny, greeny,
   Rum, tum, fra."

35. Michaelmas Day, October 11th, was the day when labourers, servants, etc., were hired for the year (See Shining Stick in the Dialect Dictionary). Two farm hands met that day. One asked the other; "Stop agen (again) or how?" which meant are you hoping to stay with your present employer or are you looking for another job.

36. It is a fault in man or woman To steal a goose from off a common — But it admits of less excuse To steal a common from a goose.

This old verse was almost certainly composed to refer to the fact that once many areas had commons on which livestock could be grazed free, until the vast Enclosures of common land put an end to this.

37. A whistling woman and a crowing hen,
    Are neither good for God nor men.
A possible explanation for this is that a woman who whistled acted like a man, above her station and un-feminine, and therefore would dominate her husband.

38. An old Kent song:
    "The hop that swings so lightly
    The hop that shines so brightly
    Shall still be cherished rightly
    By all good men and true.
    Thus spake the jovial man of Kent
    As through his golden hops he went
    With sturdy limb and brow unbent
    When autumn skies were blue."

39. An old Kent rhyme about thunder and lightning:
    If it sinks from the north,
    It will double its wrath;
    If it sinks from the south,
    It will open its mouth;
    If it sinks from the west,
    It is never at rest;
    If it sinks from the east,
    It will leave us in peace.

40. There are several Kentish sayings concerning the weather as follows: A drip in June keeps things in tune; The frost has captured Mrs Scrace's taturs", meaning the frost has damaged the foliage or spoilt the crop; Half the wood stack and half the hay and half the winter has passed away.

41. Christmas and a little before, the apple goes and not the core, Christmas and a little later, the apple goes and the core comes after. This presumably meant that before Christmas apples were plentiful so only the flesh pulp and not the core was eaten. After Christmas when fruit was scarce people were glad to eat all the apple, core included.

42. A Kent saying refers to St. Vincent's Day, 22nd January:
    Remember on St Vincent's Day,
    If the sun his beams display,
    Be sure to mark the transient beam,
    While through the casement sheds a gleam.
    For tis a token right clear
    Of prosperous weather all the year.

The following sayings and expressions, etc., have been used in Kent, some for centuries and can be assumed to be Kentish in origin. Several are referred to in the dialect dictionary, such as prick up ears, won't be said, whistle and ride, etc., but included here again for those referring to such items collected in one chapter rather than scattered through the Dictionary:

42. When the sage blooms there will be mischief.

43. He wants that as much as a toad wants a side pocket.

44. Don't go groping about like a blind hen looking for a worm in a hedge.

45. You prick up your ears like an old sow in beans. (See in Dialect Dictionary)

46. That would make a donkey run away from his beans.

47. Go and pour water into the Thames. (See Proverb 70 previous Chapter).

48. Parsley goes nine times to the Devil before it comes up, referring to the long time the seed takes to germinate. Used elsewhere.

49. Potatoes should be planted when the moon is full.

50. People standing in the centre of West Malling would say that "if you can hear a train its going to rain".

51. Out Will's Mother's Way, meaning somewhere else; in the distance, on the horizon. "It's coming up black for a storm and looks as if it's already raining Out Will's Mother's Way." Origin and who "Will's Mother" was are unknown, but there are several similar expressions, with slight word variations, used in other counties, one being Gloucestershire, where the expression emerges, e.g. as "It's dark over Our Bill's Mum's Mind".

52. Now den git an olt on it, i.e. Now then get and claw hold of it, grasp it.

53. He wont be said today, i.e. He is obstinate today. Also Won't be druv, i.e. Won't be driven.

54. Went like a shot out of a shovel, i.e. quickly. May not be especially Kentish although formerly commonly used.

55. All in a tremor and a trot, in a state of jitters and nerves.

56. I wonder what's up now? i.e. I wonder what is wrong now?

57. Here comes old Scratchit, i.e. to describe someone coming with a message, even if the surname of the hearer is known. (See Scratchit in Dialect Dictionary).

58. Road or shape. This was used in conversation to mean that something or someone would arrive by some means or other, somehow, eventually. "I suppose she'll get here by some road or shape."

59. To feel like going up to Heaven in a flag basket, is to feel exasperated.

60. Jumping up in the air and hanging by nothing, is also to feel irate and annoyed. A similar expression is "Enough to make anyone jump into the middle of next week". A variant of the latter has a different meaning. When someone is suddenly startled or frightened it is said "Enough to make me jump into the middle of next week".

61. You dont know your mistakes till you're half across the water, i.e. elderly, infirm and nearly dead.

62. There's always ways and means, i.e. a solution, a way out.

63. A pocketfull of dead hopes", i.e. a pocket in which something sought cannot be found; a hopeless task or desire.

64. They're proper brother and bob, i.e. friendly, united.

65. Much as hardly, not quite; nearly; almost.

66. Not force put, i.e. under no pressure, not obliged to.

67. Got me comic struck, i.e. made me laugh, amused me, had me full of mirth.

68. If children asked what was for dinner they would be told either "Air Pie and a run round the table" or "Bread and Pull-it" (which see in Dialect Dictionary, also Larloes and Medlars).

69. A street call (See Mouth Almighty in Dialect Dictionary):
Mouth Almighty
Chops all greasy
A little bit of fat goes down easy.

70. Shoot the cat, i.e. vomit. Used elsewhere.

There are numerous sayings, etc., either used in agriculture and farming or associated with it:

71. A query asked of anyone showing signs of affluence, spending freely, was "What! Sold your hops?"

72. That's near enough for hog shearing, i.e. that will do, it will serve; be passed; pass in a crowd.

73. To whistle and ride meant to talk and joke (whistle) as much as you like but get on with your work or the job (ride) at the same time. It was used in the East Kent Yeomanry and by those who worked with horses. To two men standing and talking it would be said: "Come on, whistle and ride".

74. Goin' 'arvestin' this year?: "Going harvesting this year?"
No, coz they woin 'av yer: "No, because they won't have you".

75. All to work, all to play,
Pick up your hops and run away.
A hop garden jingle, including two calls: the first starts the picking in the morning and again after dinner, i.e. "All to work". The second call ends the picking for the day, i.e. "All to play", although this in my lifetime was largely replaced by "Hops up". The latter has also replaced "Get your hops ready" in many gardens when pickers put the hops they have in their baskets, etc., into the bins ready to be measured by the measurer (which see in the Dialect Dictionary). "All to dinner" is self explanatory.

76. Good rye grows high.

77. When a sheep baas it loses a bite.

78. Where clads (clods of earth) prevail the turnips fail.

79. Up horn, down corn; this meant that while cattle (meat) were dear, corn (for bread) was generally cheap.

80. As yellow as a corpse candle.
A saying dating to pre-reformation times.
The following was sent to me by Mr Ray Baldock of Lamberhurst:

"When horses were being teamed, steered by a wagoner's mate using a whip, different words were used as commands. At the end of a field, to turn back, the words were: Mether or Mother gee Whit. To turn or move to the right the word was: Hoot. To turn or move to the left the word was: Igh (eye). When working in a garden, field, etc., to go from one end to the other you have done one End. To go from one to the other and back again you have done a Went. When working down ground or harrowing in corn, etc., to go over the ground twice is to "Went it"."

Some sayings:

A lame animal is "As lame as a cat". Any animal with fleas or lice is "As lousy as a Cuckoo". Anything sleeping soundly is "As fast asleep as a church". Anything crooked is "Straight as a donkey's hind leg". To talk a lot is "To jaw the hind leg off a donkey". Another way of saying large numbers are concerned is "There are Forty Leven Thousand and One".